Floating Worlds

The Letters of Edward Gorey
& Peter F. Neumeyer

Edited by Peter F. Neumeyer

Pomegranate

SAN FRANCISCO

Published by Pomegranate Communications, Inc.
Box 808022, Petaluma CA 94975
800 227 1428 • www.pomegranate.com

Pomegranate Europe Ltd.
Unit 1, Heathcote Business Centre, Hurlbutt Road
Warwick, Warwickshire CV34 6TD, UK
[+44] 0 1926 430111 • sales@pomeurope.co.uk

An **Edward Gorey**® licensed product. © 2011 The Edward Gorey Charitable Trust
Text and letters written by Peter F. Neumeyer © 2011 Peter F. Neumeyer
All imagery courtesy of Peter F. Neumeyer and The Edward Gorey Charitable Trust

Page 4 (portrait from life, signed by Don Bachardy and Edward Gorey, commissioned by Gotham Book Mart):
Don Bachardy (American, b. 1934)
Edward St. John Gorey, 1974
Graphite on paper, 73.9 x 58.7 cm (29⅛ x 23⅛ in.)
National Portrait Gallery, Smithsonian Institution, Washington, DC, NPG.2000.102
© Don Bachardy
Photograph courtesy National Portrait Gallery, Smithsonian Institution / Art Resource, NY

Page 130: Gerard ter Borch (Dutch, 1617–1681)
Man on Horseback, 1634
Oil on panel, 54.9 x 41 cm (21⅝ x 16⅛ in.)
Museum of Fine Arts, Boston
Juliana Cheney Edwards Collection, 61.660
Photograph © 2011 Museum of Fine Arts, Boston

Library of Congress Cataloging-in-Publication Data

Gorey, Edward, 1925–2000.
 Floating worlds : the letters of Edward Gorey and Peter F. Neumeyer /
edited by Peter F. Neumeyer.
   p. cm.
 ISBN 978-0-7649-5947-9 (hardcover)
1. Gorey, Edward, 1925–2000—Correspondence. 2. Neumeyer, Peter F., 1929–
—Correspondence. 3. Artists—United States—Correspondence. 4. Authors,
American—20th century—Correspondence. I. Neumeyer, Peter F., 1929–
II. Title.

 NC139.G63A3 2011
 700.92—dc22
                    2011009842

Pomegranate Catalog No. A197

Designed by Patrice Morris

Printed in China

20 19 18 17 16 15 14 13 12 11   10 9 8 7 6 5 4 3 2 1

Contents

Reverend Grey
April 12, 1974

Bachardy

Acknowledgments

My sincere thanks, first, to Connie Vinita Dowell, dean of libraries, Vanderbilt University, who seven years ago mounted an impressive Edward Gorey exhibition at the Love Library at San Diego State University. Dowell's taste and foresight and administrative virtuosity quite literally have set in motion all that follows here. It was at this exhibition that I first met Andreas Brown, co-trustee of the Edward Gorey Charitable Trust, who heard me read a few brief excerpts from Edward Gorey's letters and urged me to publish them. Andreas has continued to surprise me with his own insights into the iconography of Edward Gorey, and I remain grateful to him for his advice and for his friendship. The Love Library staff at SDSU, especially Lyn Olsson, Cristina Favretto, and Mark Lester, generously assisted at the time of the exhibition.

At Pomegranate Communications, I'm beholden to the publisher, Katie Burke. At the outset of our cheerful collaboration, she performed the difficult task of imposing a plausible temporal sequence on Edward's and my letters. And at every subsequent step, with her selective eye and with her probing questions, she has been a generous co-editor. For the layout of this book, I thank Pomegranate's Patrice Morris, who has surprised and delighted me by creating our design, elegantly and coherently deploying Edward Gorey's many envelopes and sketches throughout the book, and assembling our telling book jacket. Pat Harris has been a scrupulous editor, patient, precise, and blessed with insight. The index she has composed, itself, aspires to the condition of art. I also owe sincere thanks to Stephanie King, associate publisher. Never have I worked with colleagues as warm and kind as these at Pomegranate, and with some there, too, who played a role and whose names I will never know.

My agent, George Nicholson, of Sterling Lord Litristic, Inc., has guided me through unfamiliar pathways and continues to be a friend and a wise counselor.

I am grateful to R. Andrew Boose, co-trustee of the Gorey Charitable Trust at the law firm of Davis Wright Tremaine, LLP, for granting all needed permissions while at the same time responsibly attending the interests of the Trust. I've had commendable and continuing support from all who are even remotely involved in this enterprise.

Harry Stanton's role is recounted and refracted through two sensibilities throughout these letters. I thank him fondly, and I'm grateful to his daughter, Elizabeth, for permission to reproduce her father's letter.

Helen, my wife, has been my co-conspirator, it seems forever, so—heartfelt—this is absolutely her book, too.

Peter F. Neumeyer
Kensington, CA 94707

PHOTOGRAPH PROBABLY BY HARRY STANTON

"It all comes of having found you to talk to."

—Edward Gorey, October 21, 1968

Introduction

Dreams, symbols, and images pierce the day; a disorder of imaginary worlds flows incessantly into this world . . .

—Jorge Luis Borges

When Edward Gorey died, on April 15, 2000, at the age of seventy-five, he had dedicated his estate for the benefit of "a charitable trust which he established for the welfare of all living creatures . . . not only cats, dogs, whales, and birds, but also bats, insects, and invertebrates."[1]

Long before that, he wrote to me that he had misgivings while setting out poison bait for ants—"I am really more and more tolerant to all insect life, as life goes on"— and commented that he was always having to save earwigs when his family brought them in on flowers or foliage for bouquets.[2]

The year before that, I had created a short bedtime picture story about a housefly. I had long been aware of the ruminations of one of my favorite writers, the eighteenth-century John Clare, who had an affinity for all things small and who had written of those buzzing insects, "These little indoor dwellers, in cottages and halls . . . dancing in the window all day . . . [T]hey are the small or dwarfish portion of our own family, and so many fairy familiars that we know and treat as one of ourselves." Very much on my mind, too, as I often reminded Edward, was Laurence Sterne's benevolent character Uncle Toby (from *Tristram Shandy*), who addresses a fly he's about to release out the window: "Go, poor devil, get thee gone, why should I hurt thee?—This world surely is wide enough to hold both thee and me."[3]

My watercolor housefly for that bedtime story, and perhaps a kindred sympathy for all creatures alive, spiritedly and loquaciously informed the friendship of Edward Gorey and me so long ago, when we created our first book about just such a creature.

"You know far more about me than anyone else in the world," Edward Gorey wrote to me in November 1968. In fact, much of what I know of Ted (as his friends called him) I learned from the letters collected here. However, to suggest that Gorey "revealed" his inner self in these letters would be an overstatement. Just who Edward Gorey's inner self might have been remains highly conjectural. Quotidian "reality" was problematic for Ted, and so he was not entirely joking when he signed one letter "Ted (I think)" and wrote in another, "There is a strong streak in me that wishes not to exist and really does not believe that I do."

---

1. Andreas Brown, *Edward Gorey: A Brief Biography* (Edward Gorey Charitable Trust, 2009–2011).
2. See page 210, his letter of April 8, 1969 ("8.iv.69," in Gorey's customary way of expressing dates).
3. Quoted in Peter F. Neumeyer, *Homage to John Clare: A Poetical and Critical Correspondence* (Peregrine Smith, 1980), 19.

Most of my correspondence with Edward Gorey took place during a thirteen-month period from September 1968 to October 1969. The ostensible reason for this exchange was to collaborate on three children's books for which I had written the text and Ted was doing the illustrations. In fact, for this short time letters flew back and forth between us at a fast rate, and their topics ranged far beyond our three books. The letters gave occasion for Ted to articulate his views on authors and artists. They gave insight into what Ted thought he was doing as he created his own work. And they chronicled the rapid growth of a deep and mutual friendship. After little more than a year, the correspondence dwindled as abruptly as it had begun.

I have of course kept most of Ted's letters, as well as the gloriously illustrated envelopes with which he graced them. In light of his body of work, and because of the interest that his private person has aroused, I feel strongly that these letters should not be lost to posterity. I still read in them Ted's wisdom, charm, and affection and a profound personal integrity that deserves to be in the record. As for my own letters to Ted, I had no idea that he had kept them until one day a couple of years ago when a co-trustee of his estate, Andreas Brown, sent me a package of photocopies of my half of the correspondence. I am very grateful for that.

The majority of our letters, postcards, and notes are represented in this volume. Others have been lost; some have been omitted because their content is inconsequential or addresses personal issues that should remain private. My letters, in their sometimes sketchy haste, reflect the busy and at times scattered nature of my own life at that time.

PHOTOGRAPH BY HELEN NEUMEYER

In 1963, we—my wife, Helen, our three little boys, and I—moved east from Berkeley, California, to Medford, Massachusetts, and I started my first full-time postdoctoral job as an assistant professor at the Harvard Graduate School of Education. I was teaching two or three courses that were new to me, conducting tutorials for the English department (as best I recall now, one on Mark Twain and Freud, the other on poetry), and living, intensely and exploratively, for the first time in beautiful New England. I had also involved myself in some measure in anti–Vietnam War causes and was serving actively as president of Medford's new Education Council—a sort of district-wide PTA. At the same time, I was publishing academic articles on Thomas Mann, Shakespeare, Jonathan Swift, and Thomas Hardy and editing a book of essays on Franz Kafka.

In the fall of 1968, I began looking for a new position in an English or literature department, and the following spring we moved to Stony Brook, New York—a new environment and a new set of courses. Our boys, Dan, Chris, and Zack, revved up the quieter moments, and we had a rich and full home life—taking trips to seashore and mountains, skating, swimming, reading, climbing ropes, enduring reluctant music lessons, and, most memorably, boiling down and correctly reassembling chicken bones.

By the end of 1969, Edward Gorey and I had essentially created three books together. Ted would come to our house in Medford, and we would walk and talk and plan intensely. Ted adapted to our domestic arrangements gracefully. He'd even draw pictures and play Monopoly on the floor with the children. Occasionally, too, we'd meet at the house he shared with his relatives on Cape Cod, and once he and I got together at his apartment on East 38th Street in Manhattan, where books were aligned two deep on his shelves. Much of what we had to say to each other, and much that Ted seemingly just wanted to get on paper, was written during that period. Throughout this time, we also kept each other supplied with our favorite books.

But how in the world did Edward Gorey and Peter Neumeyer ever actually meet in the first place? It's one of those stories—both implausible and memorable.

When our boys were very young, I'd occasionally write and paint a storybook for them on one of those small, spiral-bound watercolor tablets. When they were four, six, and eight, one of these books was called *Donald and the . . .* and featured the housefly, with its beautiful luminous wings. At the same time as I painted this

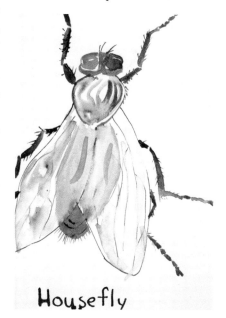

little book, I was also writing a textbook for college freshman English classes. One day, Harry Stanton, an editor and vice president with the textbook publisher Addison-Wesley, came to my house to talk about our textbook. While I was in the kitchen getting glasses of bourbon for us, Harry was rummaging on my desk—which, of course, he should not have done. "Peter," he called out, holding up the "Donald" he had discovered, "forget about the textbook. Let's do children's books."

The rest of that afternoon, Harry and I talked "Donald" books.

But I'm certainly not an artist. My watercolors, as evidenced by the fly you see here, are elementary. Harry, however, thought they'd do fine. He even had me revise the setting in which Donald lived, changing it from suburbia to an urban cityscape, for that, Harry thought, would make the book more marketable.

Housefly

friday, august eleventh

peter

i thought i would write to say

hi

nice day for racoons and people

let's keep the children's book and the lit program separate

deal with uncle me on the former, with our school division
on the latter

nice and clear cut?

i've had the benefit of some very reputable advice on the
children's stories (and poems)

there is no need to strain for an anthology of stories

i would like to start off with one story - the housefly

it's not too small to be a book

it's very nice

it needs some work

but not too much

i can give you some articulate suggestions on what (we think)
needs to be done

possibly before labor day, but not later than the week after

lunch

if you can rework the story and want to, we can sign a contract
and proceed to publish without delay

ur lead and be faithful

:ceptable to both of us

, conflicts about your

lecide to work together

:ories or poems to make
:ythmic way, as it grows

and then you will be famous

and will be identified with flies in the public mind

always

ok?

harry the hat

Meanwhile, back at Addison-Wesley, cooler heads prevailed. Someone recalled that a few years back there had been a fine young artist named Edward Gorey at Doubleday who had done the covers for a line of elegant Anchor paperbacks. Why wouldn't he do for illustrating *Donald*?

Quickly contracts were signed and Ted began his drawings.

And soon Harry thought Gorey and I should meet. So in the late summer of 1968, he took us sailing in his little boat off the beach at Barnstable, in Cape Cod.

For the most part, Ted and I sat stone-cold silent, bow and stern, stumped for easy banter.

Blessedly, time passed. The sail ended, and we rowed the dinghy back to the dock. Harry stepped onto the dock, but as Ted stretched one leg onto the pier, the dinghy scooted out from under him and skittered away, and Ted fell in between. I grabbed his arm, hooked him fast somehow, and took off after the dinghy, which was floating out with the tide.

When I returned, Ted was standing totally still, silhouetted against the dusky sky, his left shoulder protruding from his back like the broken wing of a bird.

Minutes later, in the emergency room of the Hyannis hospital, the three of us waited. And we sat and we waited, and waited, until Ted whispered to me, "I think it's popped back into place."

We attempted to leave. But once checked into the Hyannis hospital, you don't up and leave. You stay until you're discharged.

So again we sat. To while away the time, we fetched the *Donald* illustrations from the car. Ted was as he has often been described—a striking, tall Viking of a man weighted with a heavy metal pendant, his fingers laden with substantial rings—but now wet and bedraggled. Incongruous in the claustrophobic waiting room, we startled the emergent citizens of Hyannis.

Even after what seemed hours, we weren't let out. And it was then that Ted made for the bathroom, reappearing a moment later cradling a blanket in his arms.

"Nurse," he said, "nurse, I had it all by myself. Now can we go?"

Still no escape. We reacquainted ourselves with every drawing for the book. We heeded especially Donald's beautiful mother, the peregrinating shoe under Donald's bed, and the umbrella-stand dragon slayer (Donald's seafaring father?) for the book's back cover. And we admired the looming housefly. In his

letter accompanying the final drawing of the fly (pages 32–33), Gorey wrote that it had been drawn from life. At the top of the letter he glued a one-and-a-half-inch scrap of paper with a dot, a little bump (you can *still* feel it!), and the designation "Model's head."

The saga of Edward Gorey and our editor, Harry Stanton, is well documented in these letters. Ted was implacable about not conceding an inch to him in matters editorial. In retrospect, I had an easier relationship. At times, I was perfectly willing to concede when publication was at issue; at others, in Harry's thinking, I appeared unmovable. Still, it's important to note that Stanton was in a way responsible not only for the Neumeyer-Gorey publication sequence but also, in a way, for the epistolary friendship that followed. And although Stanton's editorial views were often reasonable, by 1968 Ted had good cause to be confident of his own fictional universe, much more than I did of mine.

Although Ted wrote to me, "I've never had anything to do with the author of a book I was illustrating before," we both were sparked into spurts of vivifying and shared creativity by our friendship. In 1968, I wrote a whole series of "Donalds" in record time and another series featuring a boy named Lionel, who, unlike Donald, has a father who is very much present (although no evident mother) and consequently inhabits a very different psychic world. We worked closely together, quickly producing *Donald and the . . .* (1969), *Donald Has a Difficulty* (1970), and *Why We Have Day and Night* (1970).

Gorey also made storyboards and preliminary drawings for two other stories. In *Donald Goes Away,* Donald is featured on a "heath," looking bored. He digs a hole to the center of the earth, where he finds . . . ah, how exhaustively we discussed that! On the back cover, Gorey planned to display a "furze cutter," according to my Hardyesque text. In the other book, Donald, airborne and hanging on to an umbrella (shown on one of Gorey's envelopes—page 123), comes down in a land of people of color. The precise color was a matter for discussion between us (pages 119–123).

The "Donald" stories were projected to go on forever. Gorey wrote to me in October 1968, "I have just purchased lots of pristine new file folders. They await such things as . . . revised Donalds, new Donalds, new Lionels, what else?" Soon after, he wrote, "My mind's eye sees a shelf of Neumeyer/Gorey works. Will Harvard have a room devoted to our memorabilia? It had better." For the second book, *Donald Has a Difficulty,* Gorey's idea was for a first edition of 500 copies with one of his imprints, Fantod Press, and after that, we'd burst out with what he called our "allegorical epic"—a "Tolstoian" panorama I had proposed (page 68).

Gorey himself overflowed with ideas for the projected series. His *Donald Makes a List* was to be a beautifully worked out and somewhat autobiographical story in which Donald carefully wipes his pen and goes to work drawing "all sorts of wild, poetic baroque things, . . . to have no point except [their] own existence" (page 45). This

Donald was inspired by Jorge Luis Borges's curious tale "The Analytical Language of John Wilkins," which divides all animals into categories such as "(a) those that belong to the emperor, (b) embalmed ones, (c) those that are trained . . . etc." Gorey also suggested a "night-piece for Donald done in absolutely simple unshaded line," a *Donald's Alphabet,* a *Donald's Dream,* and "a Donald . . . done in silhouette like some of the 19th century German things" (page 45).

In talking about Donald, Ted and I would hearken back to some of our favorite authors—often Borges, or the seventeenth-century English physician and writer Sir Thomas Browne. We both had a special fondness for Browne's *Hydriotaphia, or Urn-Burial,* a treatise on buried Roman urns, as well as for his odd *Garden of Cyrus,* a long essay on quincunxes (which are configurations of five), with its glorious concluding paragraph. Basil Bunting and Ralph Hodgson were a couple of our more esoteric points of reference. In conversation, Ted often cited Cyril Connolly's *The Unquiet Grave* and *The Rock Pool,* Flann O'Brien's *The Best of Myles,* and L. H. Myers's *The Near and the Far.* Ted had been a French major at Harvard, so at times his reading, as well as his two-deep-shelved books, gave off distinctly Gallic emanations. He introduced me to Raymond Queneau's *The Blue Flowers* and *Exercises in Style* and *The Journal of Jules Renard.*

Always and forever, though, his mind would circle back to Japanese art and writing, and to Zen expressions in particular. He sent me a postcard bearing a photograph of a stone garden at Ryōan-ji, a Zen temple in Kyoto, with a note that this was the one place he would most want to see in all the world. I have in front of me the four hardcover volumes of Japanese poetry he gave me, introduced and translated by R. H. Blyth, to whom he referred frequently. He was infatuated with the eleventh-century Lady Murasaki and her *Tale of Genji,* with *The Pillow Book* of Sei Shōnagon of the same period, and with the art and craft of *tenkoku,* or engraved seals. He also sent me the Penguin Classics collection of Matsuo Bashō's verse as well as Blyth's engaging and humane *Zen in English Literature and Oriental Classics.* Yoshida Kenkō's fourteenth-century *Essays in Idleness,* translated by Donald Keene, was another favorite for Ted; I still keep it close at hand, well underlined, and send photocopies of section 131 to friends I deem in need.

As I browse my shelves now, my eye falls on *Gracián's Manual* (or *The Art of Worldly Wisdom*), a sort of Machiavellian vade mecum, in which vein we also both admired and traded volumes of Heraclitus and Marcus Aurelius. My edition of *The Greek Anthology* was a gift from Ted. Among his other top favorites was Pierre Choderlos de Laclos's *Les Liaisons dangereuses,* which I had not read before he sent me a copy. He introduced me as well to Rayner Heppenstall, J. Meade Falkner, six volumes of Jacob Abbott (which he sent me), and E. V. Lucas and George Morrow's *What a Life!*[4]

---

4. E. V. Lucas and George Morrow, *What a Life!* (Methuen, 1911), reprinted in 1975 by Dover Publications with an introduction by Gorey's Harvard friend John Ashbery.

龍安寺の石庭（京都）
"Seki-Tei", Garden with natural stones arranged
(Kyoto)

NEW YORK N.Y.
PM
1965

ALWAYS US
ZIP CO

UNITED STATES WASHINGTON 5¢

This is the one thing in the
world I would rather see
than any other, though I
hardly imagine the photo-
graph gives much of an
inkling why.
    Still, now you know....

Mr Peter Neumeyer,
12 Powder House Road Ext.,
Medford, Mass. 02155.

Ted also had a fondness for the "Paddington" books, which I never followed up on. And probably it was Gorey who first introduced me to the enthralling children's poetry anthologies by James Reeves. Generously, Ted also sent me catalogues from art exhibitions, to which he had better access in Manhattan than did I. But above all it was the paintings of Max Ernst, and Albert York, as well as those of René Magritte, that excited him, and we certainly had a shared admiration for Francis Bacon, Balthus, and the eloquent silences of jars and bottles painted so movingly by Giorgio Morandi. I was already familiar with these painters (except York), but to receive them in concentrated doses in one-man catalogues, along with Ted's epistolary commentary, was very special.

These book exchanges were not all one-sided. If there was any area in which Ted had not read as much as I had, it was German literature. Thus, either I would tout something sufficiently often in our exchanges to interest him or I would send him English translations of Rainer Maria Rilke's poems, Heinrich von Kleist's *Michael Kohlhaas,* or works by E. T. A. Hoffmann, with whom he was familiar. Thomas Mann would come up in our conversations—and I made no headway there. Ted did somewhat more happily take to Adelbert von Chamisso's *Peter Schlemihl,* the story of a man who loses his shadow—a lovely Goreyesque notion. Also, some years before, I had translated Hermann Hesse's novella *Knulp,* just because I wanted my monolingual friends to be able to read it. I sent my translation to Ted, who responded satisfactorily. I have since learned, from Brad Gooch's biography of Frank O'Hara, that when O'Hara and Gorey were roommates at Harvard, O'Hara translated that book.[5] So Ted may well have known it. But he never told me that.

I also alerted Ted to the strange stories of William Sansom, Antonia White's *The Lost Traveller,* and the Victorian poet William Morris, a man who had been as engrossed in designing wallpaper as was Ted himself. (The letter on page 86 reveals how drawing wallpaper sometimes got the better of Ted.) It surprises me now to be reminded that I introduced Ted to Herman Melville's *Bartleby, the Scrivener* and that I revived Ted's interest in Henry David Thoreau. I had read Thoreau virtually anew after going for an enthusiastic swim in Walden Pond almost as soon as we arrived in New England.

Another world of writing I introduced to Ted was almost as new to me as it was to him. I marvel still at his tolerance of my new and temporary enthusiasm. For a number of years, while I was finishing my PhD, I had been immersed, immured, in the library at the University of California, Berkeley, among all books literary. Then, with my new job at the Graduate School of Education, I was suddenly removed to a place where the majority of my colleagues thought of themselves as social scientists. Eventually this focus became a frustration for me, but when it was new I dived in, wanting to discover what there was to be learned. In one instance, I was teamed up with a former superintendent of schools from Louisiana to teach a course

---

5. Brad Gooch, *City Poet: The Life and Times of Frank O'Hara* (Alfred A. Knopf, 1993), 118.

for school administrators. Our subject was philosophical: what sort of education, and for whom. I enjoyed it greatly; I liked that sort of inquiry. At the same time, for other courses, I had to familiarize myself with basic linguistics, which also was new to me but certainly a pleasure. So I was reading Noam Chomsky, for me the new Galileo, blazing across my horizon with a modest-appearing, groundbreaking pamphlet titled *Syntactic Structures* (Mouton, 1957). And there were others—some of whom glittered for only a moment—whom I was reading assiduously and who shaped my thinking profoundly at that time; they straddled philosophy, sociology, and education and pedagogy and were far from the field of literature. Among these were Abraham Maslow, Liam Hudson (particularly his intriguing book *Contrary Imaginations,* which Ted commented on with skeptical virtuosity), Basil Bernstein on language, the timely and ingenious Erving Goffman, Michael Polanyi with his powerful concept of "tacit knowledge," A. S. Neill (*Summerhill*), and, for practical glimpses into contemporary schools, Herbert Kohl and the writings of our new friend Jonathan Kozol.

I sent books and articles by these folks to Ted. And I know now that, perhaps because the concepts of which they wrote were enticing to me, I overdid it, deluging him with material that in retrospect looks distant from his interests and was sometimes, as he noted, infested with jargon. The remarkable thing is that he did read them, and he responded with wit and insight and every appearance of interest.

Indeed, wit and insight were deeply ingrained in Ted, as were good common sense and a profound generosity of spirit. The good common sense could come as a surprise to those who didn't know him well, given the dramatic first impression Ted made with his jewelry and the fur coats he wore in the winter, before he put them aside sometime in the 1980s. But in conversation, unless you hit the hot buttons of film, ballet, or literature, he'd be low-key, thoughtful, sometimes diffident, even unremarkable. He was a fine listener. His responses to chance encounters would be kindly—as illustrated when he wrote to me about a Gorey fan, a girl who phoned out of the blue to ask to visit him (page 206). His view on celebrities could be more complex; witness the disdain he expresses for Leonard Bernstein, and then his reconsideration, and after that his musings about the mentality revealed by having oneself photographed or memorialized on film in the first place (page 71). Ted's responses to people were certainly not simple, and his assessments were eminently shrewd.

All in all, notwithstanding occasional explosive expressions of exasperation—or "*Anyhooo,*" sputtered with finality, indicating that he had come to the end of *that* line of conversation—Ted took life in stride and with good cheer. And he managed to do more things in one day than seems possible.

The number of films he saw is legendary. In March 1969, things became "fraught," as he says, as "two of the five films I most want to see in all the world are going to be shown at the Museum of Modern Art on Thursday, April 3rd and Thursday, April 17th, . . . serials by Louis Feuillade, *Tih Minh* which lasts seven hours and *Barrabas* which lasts eight, and since it is entirely possible I shall never have another chance to see them, despite the fact I have never before driven two hundred and fifty miles each way to see a movie there is nothing for it but to do so." After that, he would see Feuillade's "*Judex* and its sequel" and Clouzot's *Les Espions* and the new *La Prisonnière.* And so it goes: *Barbarella, Hot Millions, Lady in Cement, The Boston Strangler, Illusion of Blood,* and on and on.

And then the ballet. In January 1969, Ted is at a loss for "where this week went. Apart from the usual eight ballet performances, nothing seems to have happened or been accomplished" (page 174). And three months after that, there was the "especial problem" of four ballets to attend on the coming weekend (page 228).

And then the reading. Ted once expressed surprise at what all he imagined I had read (page 83), but it was obviously no contest—none at all. In French or in English, Ted had become an enthusiast of Pierre Choderlos de Laclos, Isadora Duncan, Isabelle Eberhardt, Ono no Komachi, Mrs. (Elizabeth) Inchbald, Yasunari Kawabata, Jacob Abbott, Dorothy Wordsworth, Lady Murasaki, Daisy Ashford, Amanda Ross (of British publishing distinction), and "Violent Pageant" (i.e., Violet Lee Paget). At the same time, he responded thoughtfully to the books and articles I sent. Add to all this the letters he wrote in 1968–1969, the exhibitions he saw, the work he produced, and the jigsaws he worked on (page 77)—most likely a family pastime—and you have the picture of a man with sixty-hour days.[6]

And "family pastime" leads to the observation that it would be a mistake to think of Ted working uninterrupted, in isolation and in solitary splendor. Often, Ted worked amid family members and fond relatives who owned the house in the early years, who came and went with their children and animals, and for whom Ted quite frequently cooked—with some pride and with considerable pleasure—not least David Eyre's pancakes (pages 61–62), tested and attested by your present author. Among these relatives was his aunt Isabel, who "got a sinister infection while in Zurich"—a Gorey plot right there—who Ted rescued from the bus station in Hyannis and of whom he wrote both novelistically and with unfeigned affection (page 211).

After enough family interaction, Ted would again retreat "from the sounds of the vacuum cleaner and three small children to my somewhat chilly attic until it's time for, I hope, a drink and for me to cook dinner" (page 56), and there he'd work, crosshatching and devising the endless and infernal wallpaper that sometimes drove him to distraction. It was not only the wallpaper, of course, but also his inundation with new projects, which seems a plausible cause for the sudden falling off of our

---

6. It is customary to note that Ted addictively watched television. I have no firsthand knowledge of this.

Yet the human heart is an invisible
and dreadful being.

Lady Murasaki

There is no truth; if there were, it
could not be known; if known, it could
not be communicated.

Gorgias

Dreams, symbols, and images
pierce the day; a disorder of
imaginary worlds flows
incessantly into this world;
our own childhood is as
undecipherable as Persepolis
or Uxmal.

J. P.

Printed in Sweden

Post Card

Mr Peter Neumeyer,
12 Powder House Road East,

Oh, that silver and ebony inkstand with
a deer, a fawn and the inkstands formed
with stumps of trees all in chased silver—
it did not look like what it was, it
was lovely.

Ouida

correspondence. In his ever shorter notes near the end, Ted's mood ranged from exasperation with the demands of his work to melancholy: "I am working like mad, which has put me into a sort of continuing stupor, so that I keep myself half-thinking of work whatever else I am doing . . . and if I don't faint dead away from exhaustion . . . I may actually sooner or later finish up" (page 229); "I'm so far behind on my work that there seems no reasonable expectation of ever catching up . . . No doubt things will change, or vanish, or something . . . Drawing going no worse than usual, but I find myself uncertain and doing the wrong sort . . . and the only way I can cope is to keep myself in a semi-trance state about everything else" (page 191); "I have been overcome by the utter tedium of it all (mostly the stupid book I am doing stupid drawings for)" (page 237). Later, playfully but hardly encouragingly, he would send messages such as the label from an anchovy can and an odd piece of string taped to a card.[7]

The lightly stated notion that if he never catches up, "things will change, or vanish" is profoundly Goreyesque. I've already stressed Ted's fascination with mutability and his cheery skepticism, as when he signed a letter "Ted (I think)." Actually, half of the numerous literary selections that Gorey sent in letters or on cards touched on this theme of the evanescence or deceptiveness of appearance, the illusoriness of the world, and—finally—the unfathomableness of existence itself. In postcard after postcard Ted repeated the idea, citing, for example, Jorge Luis Borges, to the point that "there are poems written by believers whose nominal subject is the sea or twilight; somehow they are symbols of the secret . . ." (December 1968), or, paraphrasing from an anthology of Japanese court poetry, "There must be a something which is above and beyond . . . what the poem says and the words that say it if the poem is to be a good one" (page 201). And these quotations go to the heart of what he himself jokingly termed "E. Gorey's Great Simple Theory About Art" (page 39):

> This is the theory . . . that anything that is art . . . is presumably about some certain thing, but is really always about something else, and it's no good having one without the other, because if you just have the something it is boring and if you just have the something else it's irritating.

---

7. In 1968 Gorey "was working on and published three of his own books, and completed six illustrated books by other authors—including *The Jumblies,* one of his Edward Lear masterpieces. At this time, too, he completed several book and periodical contributions [and] a small illustrated cookbook, and he assisted with a one-man exhibition [of] his own work. In 1969 he worked on and published four of his own books [and] illustrated three books by other authors, including his second Edward Lear masterpiece, and a second small, illustrated cookbook. In 1970 he completed several projects begun in 1969, including three of his own books [and] five books illustrated for other authors, and assisted with a New York City exhibition of his own work." Andreas Brown, personal communication, April 7, 2011.

Later, Ted elaborated, extending the theory to experience in general (page 201):

Then there is the vaguely Zen thing about before Zen trees are trees . . . and then . . . as you get into Zen trees are no longer trees, etc. but then when you have got satori or whatever, trees are again trees, etc. but somehow differently.

    . . . perhaps these two ideas are the same thing, that the extra something in a good work that you find you cannot pin down to any part of it, is what indicates that the thing has passed from being merely it is through it is not (but something else understood) and finally reaching it is again.

Although the syntax is a bit twisty, here Ted says that, beyond the representation in a work of art, you pass to a secondary evolution or stage that is essentially indescribable, until—in the end—you come back again to a transfigured and truer meaning. The passage through the secondary stage is wordless, which is also the reason (Ted says) he does not use metaphor: "because it leaves the thing in the second stage."

Ted thought of our phantasmagorical world as being one in which the appearance is deceptive. At times he seemed to wonder whether, again in the words of Borges, art itself might be merely "a disorder of imaginary worlds." In fact, later on, Ted sent a postcard (page 18) quoting Plato's *Gorgias:* "There is no truth; if there were, it could not be known; if known, it could not be communicated."

That's in keeping with his telling confession that "I tend to become unnerved [when someone] has responded to something I have said or done just as if I were an actual person the same as you (especially) or anyone else" (page 66).

Well, I never doubted Ted's presence. He even now still is an "actual person" for me. These letters vividly bring back his generosity, his humor, and—yes—his genius. But as the pace of this correspondence may eventually have become unmanageable, we may each have reflected on the second sentence in section 131 of Kenkō's *Essays in Idleness:* "True wisdom consists in knowing your own capacity and stopping at once when something is too much for you."

Editorial Notes

In transcribing these letters, which were originally created using manual typewriters, we retained their original syntax and punctuation except in rare circumstances where we felt a slight modification was needed—for instance, where the addition of a comma would help the reader.

Edward Gorey often preferred British spellings; we kept them where he used them. But we corrected misspellings and obvious typos, unless they made sense in the context of the letters.

Short omissions from the letters are marked by ellipses inside square brackets; omissions of a paragraph or more are marked by three asterisks. Ellipses without brackets are the authors' own.

Where words were underlined for emphasis, we kept the underlining. Titles of books, plays, artworks, and the like were often cited using initial capital letters or, sometimes, all capitals; we changed these to italic type or to roman type with quotation marks.

Aside from its use in titles, italic type indicates handwritten notations in the original letters.

Sept. 15 [1968]

Dear Ted (does one <u>write</u> "Ted" to an Edward?)
  After I wrote the enclosed letter to Harry Stanton, I thought 'Why be so circuitous?' Therefore, at risk of being one of those difficult authors who always seem to think they know what it all should look like, let me simply put the matter to you. And if you answer that you consider yourself finished with the matter and don't want to fuss with it again at this point—ok, and I'll understand. Or—and I don't know the protocol in such matters—if the illustration is your exclusive reservation, ok too.[8]
  But if you think the point worth considering, I'd be very pleased.

See you soon, we hope
Peter

[enclosed letter]

Sept. 15, 1968

Dear Harry,

* * *

  re *Donald and the . . . ,* as much as Gorey has done for that story, I've finally come around to feeling that (perhaps too late) I ought to say what has become clearer and clearer to me—that the last picture ("Housefly") leaves something to be desired. The rest are all marvelous—just great. But that one—well, by making the fly just one item in that over-furnished room which we've seen before and about which we've laughed before, a lot is taken away from the fly. The room, and the great bust, have had their innings; now it's time for the unveiling. And the way I'd always seen it—there, in all its stark horror (but can one beat the drawing of the mouth?) is that sizzing, germ-carrying bluebottle! He should carry the day, honing his sticky forelegs, all in solitary splendor. (Then the new superduper P.S. page with the barefoot, dragon carrying daddy is fine.)[9]
  What do you think? [. . .]

yours,

---

8. These first letters in our correspondence discuss whether the fly in EG's illustration for *Donald and the . . .* should be pictured with people and items in the room or all alone—a solitary fly.
9. This became the illustration on the back of the book jacket.

Sept. 16, 1968

Dear Ted

First, and above all, thank you for the splendid bit from Wordsworth. It has affinities to much underestimated minor 18th century people who are very good if read slowly enough—like Mark Akenside, or "The Seasons"' James Thomson. The measured calm of Thomas Gray, with intimations of Wordsworth's "Intimations." I didn't know the lines, but am very fond of them now.

As for the Goosefish that choked to death on a large Codfish—marvelous too. And not even the name of the artist on it. Reminds me a bit of the brothers Albright, two weird painters who haunted my dreams when I was quite young.

* * *

I have finished *Do Not Fear a Visit to the Dentist,* and another slightly disagreeable Donald story, but the first needs an alternative ending, and the second needs ageing. Both, however, should come to you in the next two weeks.

It dawned on me in the night, after you left, that of course you had done the haunting cover for Franz Kafka's *Amerika.* All those covers are quite an exhibit to look at lined up in a row. The Perry Miller ones become all the more peculiar in their lack of human beings.[10]

These are just miscellaneous thoughts piled up at the end of the day. Let me say again, don't take my letter regarding the end of *Donald and the . . .* as burdensome if you just don't see it that way.

We do hope to see you soon. Of course any time you're up here, you are welcome. And we should be down, camping in a friend's winter-empty house, by mid-October, and will call on you then if you have time.

yours,
Peter

---

10. During EG's first visit to our house, I suddenly realized that he was the artist who had done the covers for a number of paperbacks on my shelf. Not yet being particularly acquainted with EG, I hadn't made the connection. When I did, I laid out a number of those books on our living room floor, including those on American literary history edited by Perry Miller.

16.ix.68

Dear Peter,

I hope you didn't really write those letters on the 15th, because mine was postmarked the 14th.

Of course I'll do a new final drawing. It's your book, and you're the one who should be pleased (to my mind at least), so if this was only the largest reservation of others about the drawings, do for God's sake say so.

I expect I have been somewhat insufferable about it, as I've never had anything to do with the author of a book I was illustrating before, and usually a bare minimum even with the editor. I'm given a manuscript, I do some crumby drawings, and that's that. Life conducted in this remote manner is satisfactorily simple but not very edifying. Obviously it doesn't always work. Had I fifty yarrow stalks I might consult the *I Ching* . . .

Anyhow, do you see the last drawing as nothing but the fly, no Donald, no mother, no decor? Galloping Harry [Stanton] never turned up this weekend, and whoever has the drawings at the moment, I don't, so this is an interim communication.

Ted

Original last picture for *Donald and the* . . . . In this draft the fly was drawn separately and taped to the bust.

middle September

Dear Ted,

Today your kind letter of the 16th arrived. I think I should not really explain the letter of the 15th arriving on the 14th.

As for that fly—yes indeed that's the only reservation. You've made a context for his appearance in the pictures that came before that is a fully created world in itself with the delicate balance of which one should not meddle. In fact Helen thought of keeping it in the grand solo fly picture too by having it (perhaps distorted or fragmented or upside down) reflected in his huge eye. And though, to answer your question specifically, I do in my own mind see the fly quite alone and big and un-detracted from, Helen's alternative appeals equally. But I consider the book very much your and my joint adventure, and hope that you will feel what you are doing is what ought to be. I'd ask, therefore—what looks more right to you? A big, page-covering fly—plunk. Or a similar fly, with mother, Donald, room, mirrored somehow? Or something I haven't thought of?

I'm delighted that you're willing, but equally I hope you're in agreement. You haven't been insufferable at all, and I only hope this will be just the beginning.

Yours
Peter

19.ix.68

Dear Peter,

This Morning, as I was at my Drawing Board, the Twittering that has sounded close to the House the past few Days sounded Even Louder Than Usual, so I went to the Window, and there were Hundreds and Hundreds of Starlings covering our Side Yard; for Several Minutes They were engaged in Some Mysterious Activity of an Agitated Nature, and then They Suddenly Rose in a Peculiar Manner, like a Cloth being snatched up by a Large but Invisible Hand . . .

Here is one version of the poem I was mangling the other night:

A man of words and not of deeds,
Is like a garden full of weeds;
And when the weeds begin to grow,
It's like a garden full of snow;
And when the snow begins to fall,
It's like a bird upon the wall;
And when the bird away does fly,
It's like an eagle in the sky;
And when the sky begins to roar,
It's like a lion at the door;
And when the door begins to crack,
It's like a stick across your back;
And when your back begins to smart,
It's like a penknife in your heart;
And when your heart begins to bleed,
You're dead, and dead, and dead, indeed.

This one is from Walter de la Mare's anthology, *Tom Tiddler's Ground,* but there are others with slight variations.

Enclosed, a (very) rough sketch for the last drawing in two versions: one the fly superbly alone and one with Donald and his mother at the sides. Two variations of this last also occur to me: one with Donald and his mother on the same side, huddled together for protection

One of EG's early sketches. The final drawing—the solitary fly—appears on page 32.

as it were, and the other with their two figures very minute in the distance; the only drawback to this is that they have been exactly the same size throughout the book. In case it isn't clear, the fly is standing on the tablecloth, hence the slight curve.

God will hear and answer prayer,
    This the Scriptures plainly show.
Often he will answer, Yes.
    Sometimes he will answer, No.

                (R. F. Palmer, S.S.J.E.)

I went and looked at the Chinese Bug book at the bookshop in Hyannis. It is very large, very modish illustration-wise, all splashy gold and red and putty-colour and woodcutty-looking, and the text is the sort that goes with that sort of illustration, flat and sentimental.

* * *

'Literature!' said Lady Adela. 'I'd like to know what good literature is to anybody. Give <u>me</u> something to <u>read</u>.'

                (*Lady Adela,* Gerald Gould)

I've been thinking off and on about your hiding something book.[11] It has a Donaldish air about it to me. Does this make any sense?
If you were agreeable, I'd like to show whatever of yours you wanted to, to my agent, Candida Donadio. It wouldn't interfere with any commitment to Harry.

Anathema, glorious, Napoleon, and war,
Embodiment, arsenic, atrocity, car,
The Hellespont, Hades, hobgoblin, and scourge,
Unpractical, thesis, New Carthage, and dirge,
Pyrosis, synthetic, policeman, and love,
Handmaiden, troubadour, sea-fight, and dove,
Perdition, vainglorious, unsatisfied ever,
Remorseful, undying, and happiness never.

I'll let you rack your brains as to what the above is in aid of.
Your MSS have made me thoroughly, though I hope not bitterly, envious.

---

11. Another spiral-bound watercolor book I did for my children.

Why can't my stuff come out this way? I ask myself, and Echo answers something unintelligible. So I tell myself that if only I could draw better, I could illustrate them better than anyone else. Ha!

> It appears that [Jan Baptist] Van Helmont having asserted that it was possible for a man to extinguish the life of an animal by the eye alone (oculis intentis), [Jean-Jacques] Rousseau, the naturalist, repeated the experiment when in the East, and in this manner killed several toads; but on a subsequent occasion, whilst trying the same experiment at Lyons, the animal, on finding it could not escape, fixed its eyes immovably on him, so that he fell into a fainting fit, and was thought to be dead.

> (*The Night Side of Nature,* Mrs Catherine Crowe)

Now that the rest of my family has disappeared in the general direction of Philadelphia, I am, despite the perfection of the weather—Mr A. E. Housman's 'Beautiful and death-struck year' if ever there was one—buckling down to all sorts of nasty little jobs of the sort that support me, and the last half of a book of my own that was supposed to have been out months ago. So when you see me in October, I may be in a somewhat distracted state, either that or a somewhat loopy euphoria which may result from simply having the book done, all of which is not to say that I won't be very pleased to see you all (I seem to have got mildly tiddly on vermouth cassis so my always shaky syntax is about to fall into discrete bits) so also please feel free to take advantage of my hospitality as much or little as you please (I told you) as I have a fairly recent but violent passion for cooking, and besides, there was a recipe for a sort of perpetual sauce in the *NY Times* this morning, in which you keep cooking everything except fish, and I'm planning to start using it tomorrow . . .

Patriotism.—Advance the right foot; elevate the form to its full height; extend the right arm so that the hand is just raised to a level with the eyes; extend the left hand so that the wrist is on a level with the waist; let the hands be open with palms horizontal with the body.

Yours too,
Ted

Saturday [September 21, 1968]

Dear Ted,

Your good letter was very welcome today. I cannot hope to match your intermezzos, but send you nonetheless greetings from Christopher Smart, who had the habit of falling on his knees in the street and praying, but of whom Dr. Johnson said when told this, "I had as soon pray with Kit Smart as with anyone."[12]

* * *

Thank you for the de la Mare, which is truly chilling. I will memorize it while doing innocent things. And thank you for the books, of which more below—and for the rough sketch of the fly. What do I think . . . I suppose superbly alone might be even better than with even a diminished Donald and mother, since alone like a statue you have no measure, no orientation—he looks huge on the page—but there is no way you can tell; you can't be sure, and in that disorientation (like the inability to judge distances if you cover one eye) there is a degree of terror too, which might be made the very slightest bit trivial by the additional prompts of Donald and mother. I think that's what I think—but I'm not sure. What do you think? Or can you perhaps think of something I haven't even dreamed of? Offhand, yes—at the moment, of those possibilities we have talked of, the fly alone seems best. But don't let me dictate your work if you disagree or if you can think of something better.

As for the books of Mr. Blutig, Mrs. Dowdy, and Mr. Gorey—thank you so very much.[13] What a busy year 1966 was! The surreal *Inanimate Tragedy* is cold and steely—quite chilling I think—in its suggestion of a depopulated world—Lewis Carroll, early still life surrealists with pots and pans, or Fernand Léger cogs and wheels. The graceful horizon or top-of-landscape line, the nice back cover, the puzzling cover design which is warmer than the contents. *The Evil Garden* and *The Pious Infant* are great, great fun—and *The Evil Garden*'s plants are very beautiful, and suggest other things, like matching Euell Gibbons survival books with a book of natural hazards—sumac, deadly nightshade, amanita, etc.—done just the slightest ambiguous shade off key. Wonderful tendrils, and the most graceful back cover on *The Evil Garden*. The moth and the hairy bugs will have wrought a change forever in

12. I must have included with this letter sections of Christopher Smart's long, enigmatic eighteenth-century poem *Jubilate Agno,* at that time one of my favorites.

13. Blutig (Ger. "bloody"), Dowdy, and Müde (Ger. "tired") were among many pen names EG used for his books. Fanny Eliza and Henry Clump (see page 30) are both featured in EG's *The Pious Infant;* the story's last illustration depicts a cemetery with one stone engraved "E.G." Even this early in our friendship, Ted was beginning to send me copies of all his books to date.

our family. The one-dimensionality of the figures in white against the full plants at the end—O. Müde should be alive today!

Henry Clump and Fanny Eliza will stand with Oliver Goldsmith's *Vicar of Wakefield,* True Sensibility, Pathos, Instruction. And the EG tombstone brings a tear to the eye.

* * *

You are very kind, both about the hiding something book, and about the manuscripts in general—and with the offer to show your agent what I have. That would be tremendously nice of you, and I accept with pleasure. Most things now are typed in very rough form only, handwritten between the lines—so Helen and I will type a few things this week and send them to you with the hiding book. One trouble. I find myself incapable of judging my own things with any confidence; I just don't see them clearly. May I ask of you that if anything I send you is embarrassingly subliterate, you return it to me without showing someone else. You'd be doing me a favor—really.

* * *

Please remember that we have room, lots of room, and that you're welcome to stay with us anytime, letting domestic events rattle around you.

yours,
Peter

P.S. Helen just came home. She agrees on the fly. With little people—there's too much hint he is an unusual fly, a fairy-tale fly bigger than people (even though you can argue simply perspective). So the fly alone, to do its strange work unaided. The people come back nicely at end and on endpaper.

[undated; probably September 24, 1968]

Tuesday afternoon

Dear Peter,

I've spent most of the day drawing sordidly conceived and erratically hung wallpaper, which is meant to be a particularly subtle objective correlative for anguish and alienation in the mind of the protagonist of the book I'm working on, which I wonder if I am <u>ever</u> going to get finished. A terrible mistake got itself made when the text was bought before I had done the drawings. Anyway, I have paused to recruit my brain, spine, fingers, etc. with a large mug of tea.

<u>I'm</u> certainly not going to think up anything better than the fly all by itself in awesome splendour, so I think I'll go ahead and do it. The text is all lettered, and I've started on the border as it were for the drawings on the jacket and binding; this is wallpapery too, but elegant and asymmetrical with various patterns in a vaguely Japanese manner. As a word picture I feel this leaves something to be desired; however, you'll see it when it's done.

When I ran into Harry on Sunday buying the papers, he said he was coming by tomorrow. Whether he does or not remains to be seen; he appears more furiously busy than ever. I murmured when asked that I had heard from you and that we were in correspondence about the final drawing, at which point he began making editorial noises of a generalized nature. I smiled pensively and made some small remark indicating modest acquiescence. If you do not take my line of thought, I shouldn't wonder.

More on this anon, should he turn up.

Whenever this gets stuck in the mail, you will find enclosed three more efforts by Herr Blutig, translated by Mrs Dowdy (who else could bring him without injury—aesthetic—into English?) though as yet Müde's drawings have not been found (read done). Also, on recollection, a fourth, for which they have.

Apart from hoping to impress you with how talented I am, so that you will want me to illustrate many, many of your books (there's a really brilliant non sequitur here), I also have a favour to ask in respect to the three without drawings. (The one with is entitled *The Tuning Fork* and I cannot decide which German title to use: *Der Zeitirrthum* or *Der Stiefelknecht*. I'm not at all certain the articles are correct, since I know no German whatever, or for that matter even whether the words exist in that form; my only German dictionary is an ancient Tauchnitz which even I can tell is extremely bizarre. It <u>says</u> the first word means 'chronological mistake' and the second 'boot jack'. I am incompetent, I fear, to explain why I have selected these titles. End of extended parenthesis.) To return.

← *Model's head*

Thursday morning

    Time for another mug of tea. The fly drawing
is done, and I think it looks right, despite my
somewhat twitchy state, as I spent a thwarting
afternoon yesterday drawing it several times and
making a hash of it, which is neither here nor
there. No Harry Stanton turned up, which was probably just as well. So you will not wonder perhaps,
I add that it was a corpse before I began using it
(actually I recognized him when I found him on the
floor as one I had seen several days ago on a window because he only had five legs), and that eventually the above came off in my hand. When I have
had tea, I shall whiz off to Hyannis in an attempt
to get a photostat or at least a xerox of the drawing to enclose.

    Last night I ensconced myself in the only drive-
in left open hereabouts and sat through two little
works entitled Blood Fiend and Brides of Blood. I
must admit that even my passion for horror movies
and the ability to sit through practically anything
thrown on the silver screen barely got me through
them. The latter, however, did have a somewhat
over-ripe leading lady named Beverley Hills and a
band of Filipino dwarves whose presence was never
commented upon, which was particularly odd since
the picture was about instant mutations of various
nasty varieties as a result of atom bomb tests. It
is things like this that keep one functioning sometimes. Me at least.

hree things on
ly, I have been
the past twenty
, which is
nstantly writing
he tedium of
educes me to
. Which is why
at the moment.

In short, do you think you could think up what the German titles of these works might be; if they worked out literally that would be okay of course, but I suspect there would be better ones which weren't, perhaps from the point of view of both sound and sense. Which I doubt if I am making. Worse and worse. I don't like *The Stupid Joke* in English, but have been unable to think up anything better, as it gives too much away to do the obvious and put 'bed' in the title. I think perhaps I'd better stop and do something else, such as look for my cats, all of whom seem to have disappeared.

Thursday morning
[Taped to the top left-hand corner of this page of the letter is the actual head of a fly. At time of this writing, it is a bit crusty, although still there.]

Time for another mug of tea. The fly drawing is done, and I <u>think</u> it looks right, despite my somewhat twitchy state, as I spent a thwarting afternoon yesterday drawing it several times and making a hash of it, which is neither here nor there. No Harry Stanton turned up, which was probably just as well. So you will not wonder perhaps, I add that it was a corpse before I began using it (actually I recognized him when I found him on the floor as one I had seen several days ago on a window because he only had five legs), and that eventually the above came off in my hand. When I have had tea, I shall whiz off to Hyannis in an attempt to get a photostat or at least a xerox of the drawing to enclose.

Last night I ensconced myself in the only drive-in left open hereabouts and sat through two little works entitled *Blood Fiend* and *Brides of Blood*. I must admit that even my passion for horror movies and the ability to sit through practically anything thrown on the silver screen barely got me through them. The latter, however, <u>did</u> have a somewhat over-ripe leading lady named Beverley [Beverly] Hills and a band of Filipino dwarves whose presence was never commented upon, which was particularly odd since the picture was about instant mutations of various nasty varieties as a result of atom bomb tests. It is things like this that keep one functioning sometimes. Me at least.

At one point I had about eighty-three things on my mind to put in this. Unfortunately, I have been the world's worst letter-writer for the past twenty years, though you might not think it, which is partly accounted for because I am constantly writing them to people in my head and then the tedium of putting it all down badly on paper reduces me to paralysis in front of the typewriter. Which is why I can't think what any of them were at the moment.

I could only get a Xerox, which has a certain ghostly charm lacking in the original, but it will give you an idea I hope. Feeling very politic, or the reverse, I'm not sure which, I popped another Xerox of it into the mail to Harry. (At this point

Paranoia whispers 'They are going to instantly call each other up on receipt of them and say "Ugh".') Oh well, I hope not.

* * *

Needless to remark, I'm looking forward to getting as many MSS as you care to send, and any new thoughts on the ones I already have. I'll give you what useless thoughts I have on the subject before sending them off to Candida. It would be nice if Harry would commit himself to another Donald book before too long so that I could add it to my list of commitments before other things come along, which they better well had if I'm going to go on surviving.

Thank you muchly for the invitation to stay with you; I rather think I'll want to take you up on it sometime before I go back to New York the middle of November. I suspect that the way life sometimes has of working itself out with a total lack of consideration for one's wishes is going to make the one weekend I have a houseful of people on my hands the weekend you and family will be here on the Cape. We shall no doubt see . . . In any case, I hope we'll have various projects to talk over before too long, and so forth. [. . .]

Ted

September 30, 1968

Dear Ted,

Thank you so much for your last letter, for the elegant sump-lizard bearing its enveloping banner. I think I shall replace my bureaucratic name card on my office door and substitute your beast. As for the ghostly fly—GOOD. It has a pensive look. Brave new world it has just entered, perhaps. By the way, yesterday we all braved the evil smelling mob at the Globe book festival at Suffolk Downs, and one interesting thing there I did see, which you might look at should the Barnstable library have it—Curt Stern wrote for Harvard U. Press a book on genetics, and in it is a very excellent drawing of a fly, no better than yours by any means, nor as contemplative, but having two attractive features: 1) its legs are segmented (jointed) several places below the knee, and 2) it has some gloriously repulsive, germ-carrying hairs—sort of nasal hairs—coming out here and there on its back. Our fly doesn't need that— but I thought it would interest you. Your fly, by the way, is indulging in a rather typical gesture for one of your Victorian gentlemen—such, for instance, as Theoda's [character in EG's book *The Tuning Fork*] uncle might make.

Your letter is filled with so many specific points that, since it's not yet 9 AM, and my thoughts are not yet with me, I will go through your letter trying to answer them seriatim. So this letter will be ugly but inclusive.

1) I was always pleased with what you have done for Donald, and so I look forward very much to seeing the jacket. I hope and think we are off to a grand start and that we can take Donald through a long and sordid life.

2) Ahhh—Harry. Who knows? Will he turn up? How? Whence? Why is he going to California (Helen's question)? Do you think he will publish Donald? Is Harry a mirage?

3) [. . .] As for titles: let me think—

[. . .] *The Tuning Fork*—yes, your proposed articles are correct. [. . .] *The Abandoned Sock* literally, sock is Strumpf (pron. shtrumpf), which, to an English-American ear, must sound pretty funny, and prototypically Teutonic. [. . .] *The Stupid Joke*—there's a German idiomatic expression, "der faule Witz" which means "the stupid joke" but has the added advantage of "faul(e)" meaning "lazy", which is rather pertinent here—no? [. . .]

(Note, on the last couple, I resorted to my *New Cassell's German Dictionary* (Funk and Wagnalls) which, it seems to me, would be a marvelous source of inspiration to you. It makes me aware too what a paltry and childish German I've retained in my active vocabulary, for just thumbing through it I find so much that is hilarious, and that I wouldn't have thought of on my own. Much of it sounds about on your dominant key.) [. . .]

4) I am—I enjoy repeating—absolutely delighted, more than delighted, that you may enjoy illustrating some of my stories. It's hard . . . to put the matter properly, and it may be presumptuous, but I know you will take it as warmly as I mean it if I say that I feel I have found in some measure my artistic counterpart. One wants to resort to trite, but pertinent, clichés about wavelengths etc., but one resists. Anyway, you must know. And I hope Donald, or Lionel,[14] or who knows what misfit monsters, may cause us many happily enigmatic days. (Which reminds me, I'm sure you must know Jorge Luis Borges' work well. If you do not, buy immediately any-all books of his on which you can lay your hands. He was lecturing at Harvard last year by the way, and I'm only sorry we could not have you here for that.)

* * *

5) The model's head is wonderful. I shall keep it. Someday when we are all famous it will be exhibited in the Firestone Library at Princeton, along with the speeches of Thomas Mann (who said the thing about faith and doubt, unfortunately). Famous models' heads: St. John the Baptist, . . . ; Hagbard's uncle; the American flier decapitated by the Japanese in the old photo; Charles I,—what a collection!

6 and 7) I'll mail MSS to you end of this week. A couple are real square, straight shooters, kid stories. Publishable? I don't know. One is rather flamboyant and kaleidoscopic, conceived with illustrations in mind by a friend of mine who is a tapestry designer and studied with Lurçat, but who may not do illustrations—I don't know. Donalds ought to come slowly. There is the temptation to "turn them out" which would not be to their benefit—nor benefit either your soul or mine, I think. Again, I'm delighted at your generous offer to pass these things along to someone who can judge and act objectively.

As for your coming up—great! That invitation remains open. Any time, but if you let us know in advance then there's minimal chance of something like a PTA meeting in our living room at the same time—an event which, come to think of it, you might someday want to expose yourself to just so that you can say you have experienced everything. Perhaps we should PLAN a PTA meeting, discussing hot lunches, just for your inspiration.

* * *

yours
Peter

P.S. Just found your *Hölderlin to Rilke* poems cover![15]

---

14. Lionel was another character about whom I wrote stories. He was of a different nature from Donald, and he had a different family.
15. EG illustrated the cover for *An Anthology of German Poetry from Hölderlin to Rilke in English Translation*, edited by Angel Flores (Doubleday, 1960).

Wednesday evening, 2.x.68

Dear Peter,

For whatever reasons, I find any direct expression of my feelings not difficult, but impossible, so you will have to know without one what they are about our having met and our working together now and in the future. I guess you do anyway. What a revolting way to begin a letter, but I had to say something, however strangulated.

Perhaps Harry is a mirage, which means he did not appear on the horizon here today. If he ever does turn up again, I think I shall be tempted to hurl a cast iron frying pan at his head, if only to see if he is real. What is this about his going to California? When? For how long? (The mind boggles.)

When I do see him, provided I decide that he has nothing new on his mind and that things are where they were, wherever that may be, I think now I shall act as follows. (A bit of preliminary explanation: Harry has for several months had a story by Alphonse Allais[16] that I translated and did drawings for, which at the beginning of the summer he said he would see my agent about the contract when he was next in New York, though nothing has as yet been done about it.) I'll tell him that if the prospect of having three books illustrated by me on his list daunts him, which it very well might, to forget about the Allais—genteel blackmail, this—because I would much rather do another Donald with you instead. With which I should hope to lead up to the fact that as collaborators we are more Grimly Determined than perhaps he is aware. If I were Harry, not being very nice (me, not Harry) this would probably annoy me considerably, but I should think it might make Harry feel Maxwell-Perkinsy.[17] Then perhaps a few specifics about Donald. My thoughts on that further on. And a delicate hint that as I shall be back in New York the middle of November, and not back here until sometime in the spring, it would be advantageous for us all to hash a new book over before I left. And then see what reactions I get, if any. Does this sound about right to you?

I expect we are finding this all a bit more inexplicable or whatever than it is. After all, we are at a high peak of enthusiasm and whatnot, and our first effort isn't even finished yet, and I suppose Harry is reluctant to commit himself too far until he sees how his first list goes;[18] on the other hand, I suppose he really meant it when he said that it was his favourite book of any he'd published, or however it was he put it, or why say it? Ah well.

One other thing. I shall explain to Candida how things stand with us and that I very much hope she will want to handle our joint efforts; I feel I can legitimately ask

---

16. Alphonse Allais, *Story for Sara: What Happened to a Little Girl* (Albondocani, 1971).
17. Maxwell Perkins (1884–1947), editor for Hemingway, Fitzgerald, and Thomas Wolfe, was renowned for being deeply implicated in his authors' editing processes.
18. Stanton was just getting Addison-Wesley's children's list under way.

her as much when I give her your things, and then we find out what she thinks. If all goes well, she could probably pin Harry down to a definite decision. Agents seem to be very good at that.

I can't thank you enough for the titles. I think they are one and all superb, just what I had in mind, and made me howl with glee. Much as I like the chronological error word, whatever it was, I think I'd better treasure it up for something else, and use the other for *The Tuning Fork. Die Reise eines Strumpfes* [*The Journey of a Stocking*] sounds terribly authentic somehow to me. You are much more literate than I, which means in this case I don't get the Hamlet bit, and don't even have a Shakespeare I can look it up in.[19] I take it you couldn't offhand think of a German pun equivalent to 'abandoned', not that pun is exactly what it is. Surely one of the seven types of ambiguity though?[20]

Der faule Witz [*The Stupid Joke*] is perfect, but then I am infatuated with all the other titles, especially *Haushalt Sorgen* [*Domestic Cares*]. (In parenthesis, I've always refused to have things published together, but the Blutig group, of which there are possibly several others, does rather hang together, and HS would make the perfect over-all title.) Of course I can use at least two titles on each one, with the something; or, something else gambit, or do German works do this? You have given me such a surfeit of goodies with *The Unknown Vegetable* that I can't begin to make up my mind. I shall acquire the Cassell's dictionary as soon as possible.

I didn't discover Borges until last spring, but I rested not until I had everything in English, which proved so thwarting because they kept reprinting the same things, and then I managed to get a few more things by resorting to French, and finally, despite three years of high school Spanish twenty-five years ago, the collected works in Spanish and a Spanish dictionary, which await a period of settled calm to be deciphered in. In *Other Inquisitions,* 'The Analytical Language of John Wilkins' contains a list of animals which I am determined to illustrate someday; it may well be the best list of anything ever made, and I suppose Borges himself made it up, but then maybe not, as I have seen things in Chinese dictionaries as mad and unlikely.

Along with your letter today, I got one from my editor at Meredith who has patiently been waiting for several months for me to finish the drawings for a book of mine on opera [*The Blue Aspic*]. It read in toto 'Dear Ted:' The rest of the page was utterly blank. At present I am on a sort of tightrope trying to get it finished as soon as possible; on one side, reality, like emptying the garbage, feeding myself and the cats, etc. and on the other, the drawings, what to put in them, and how. A bit too much either way and everything goes wrong. If I sound bit distrait, that's why.

---

19. I had proposed as a title "through the guts of a beggar," from *Hamlet* IV, 3.
20. EG was referring to William Empson's *Seven Types of Ambiguity* (Chatto and Windus, 1930).

Anyway, my thoughts on Donald. I reread everything[21] a couple of times in the course of the day. I do think if at all possible we should do a second Donald before turning our attention to anything else, just to get him established as it were. Not that I see Donald as a conventional series at all; I mean I don't think either one of us wants to do *Donald at the Seashore, Donald Visits the State House,* etc. I would even go so far, or at least toy with the idea seriously, of no two Donald books being done in the same style, or even the same format. I don't see how you have managed it at all, but I think unquestionably you have, that Donald can be involved in almost anything, from the most trivial incident to the most profound, and that he suits any tone, any style. I'm not putting this very well, but for instance I think the illustrations for *Donald Goes Away* should be much more grey and dark and cross-hatched and three-dimensional, perhaps larger, than in the . . . [*Donald and the . . .*] and Heaven knows how I'm going to get one-tenth of what is in *Donald Helps* into the drawings. Perhaps Donald could even appear in full colour sometime. It's a kind of thing I don't think anyone has ever done before. The five so far are all really very different from each other, which is somewhat disconcerting to the conventional way of thinking, but rather grand, if you ask me. As to which one first, I think *Donald Helps* should be treasured up for a while, it is so rich in all sorts of ways—get me slightly tight sometime and I will go on and on in a metaphysical manner—and would be inclined to do *Donald Goes Away* next. As I believe I said, I have it vaguely planned out in my head, subject to our hashing it over, picture by picture. On the other hand, I think we (Harry and I at least) have underestimated *Donald Has a Difficulty* and *Donald's Surprise,* both of which I think have scratchy places, but are Fundamentally Sound. Now there's condescension for you. *Donald's Surprise* would be out as the second one, if only because it involves being sick again. I mean, after all we don't want the youth of America to suspect Donald of being Neurasthenic. But *Donald Has a Difficulty* attracts me more, the oftener I read it. Both *Surprise* and *Difficulty* are tricky I think because like *Donald and the . . . ,* they take off from cliché situations. Cliché is <u>not</u> the word really, but you see what I mean.

The thing is, and here we come to E. Gorey's Great Simple Theory About Art[22] (which he has never tried to communicate to anybody else until now, so prepare for Severe Bafflement), that on the surface they are so obviously those situations that it is very difficult to see that they really are about something else entirely. This is the theory, incidentally, that anything that is art, and it's the way I tell, is presumably about some certain thing, but is really always about something else, and it's no

---

21. "Everything" being five different manuscripts featuring our original hero, Donald.
22. What Ted here self-deprecatingly refers to as "E. Gorey's Great Simple Theory About Art" is a clear and important statement of his thesis, which—in one way or another—he restates from the beginning to the end of this collection. Heed it well here.

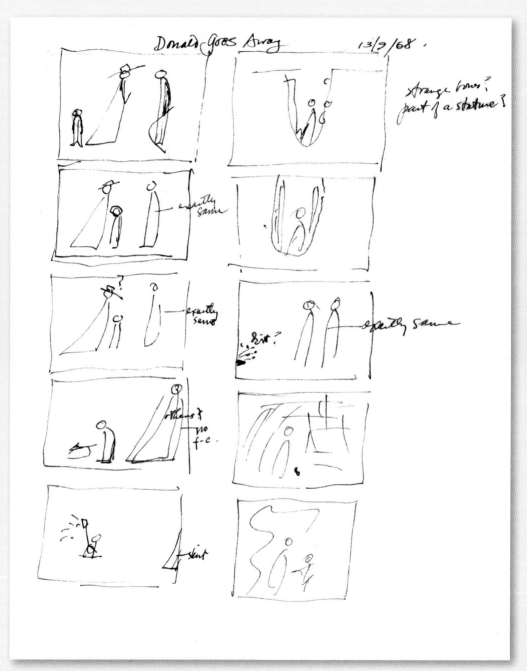

Original rough storyboards for *Donald Goes Away*.

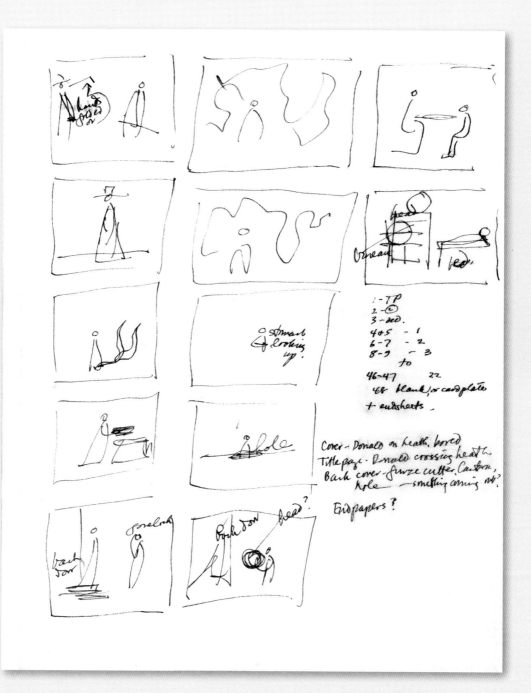

1 - TP
2 - ©
3 - ded
4+5 - 1
6-7 - 2
8-9 - 3
        to
46-47   22
48 blank, or cardplate
+ endsheets

Cover - Donald on heath, bored
Title page - Donald crossing heath
Back cover - furze cutter, Canton,
hole   — something coming out?

Endpapers ?

good having one without the other, because if you just have the something it is boring and if you just have the something else it's irritating. I'm sure there are dozens of reassuring little books that *Donald Has a Difficulty* appears to resemble, but the real point (to me) lies in its pointing out, which no one I know of has ever pointed out, even just to be clever, before, that it is not the first, but the second step which costs.[23] This is a vulgar simplification, but then. Just as *Do Not Fear* (one of the most endearing stories in the English language) is really (I am following ending II) about Inspiration. There's for you. (I am getting somewhat sloshed on Dubonnet, and besides Having Someone to Talk To is going to my head.) Lionel presents hideous illustration problems, I think. (What a lot of parentheses I seem to get myself into, but why is Lionel not Donald? He isn't, but I'll be damned if I can figure out quite why.)[24]

Why We Have D & N[25] is a Challenge; perhaps we can thrash over it page by page one of these days.

Even if I won't be able to bear to look at the finished product, *Donald and the . . .* will, I think, be a help to us in getting people to take other things. Or so I hope. You realize, of course, that <u>nothing</u> I have ever had to do with has ever sold any extraordinary number of copies. However, if you will forgive me, your work has a warmth which may make us rich and famous.

* * *

I'm sending you my latest project (I'm up to volume eight in my head) and something I just illustrated, for why I don't exactly know.[26] The drawings are elaborate out of desperation, but apart from that I don't know; perhaps because I am curious about what you think of the text. I loathed it, but Mrs Spark liked the drawings enough to want me to autograph a copy for her, which is all very dispiriting, as no other author has ever made a similar request and I liked some of her things very much but gave up reading her a couple of years ago, and it all shows how remote we are from each other and how misunderstood everything is, all of which is a rather oblique way of saying how incredibly lucky I feel I have been to run across you and have something come of it.

---

23. In *Donald Has a Difficulty,* Donald's splinter is removed painlessly, but the second step, having alcohol applied to the wound, is the one that hurts.
24. The manuscript for *Do Not Fear a Visit to the Dentist,* one of my Lionel stories. This one may have been Gorey's favorite. Perhaps some of Lionel's difference from Donald can be attributed to the fact that he had a present father—whereas with Donald, that's debatable.
25. *Why We Have Day and Night,* the third book EG and I produced.
26. *The Very Fine Clock* by Muriel Spark.

Thursday morning, 7:30ish

Various bits I think I never got to last night which occurred to me as I was pulling my seemingly scattered limbs together in an attempt to get up.

I thought I would tell Harry that I was going to show your things to Candida and get his blessing so to speak. This also might do a bit about galvanizing him.

Re *Donald Goes Away,* I don't think it ever really did get explained what <u>you</u> felt was the crux of it all so to speak. If nothing absolutely definite, what sort of thing does he run into down there, what sort of thing does happen, does China really enter into it somehow. I expect you made this all quite clear really, and I wasn't listening.

* * *

As long as I am putting a couple of books into the mail, I'll include a Jacob Abbott[27] for you to dip into when you feel inclined.

My walk up town every morning for the mail and the paper is a very Donald-like one these days as it is woolly-bear time (that is what you call those furry brown and black caterpillars is it not?) and there are always several to be dissuaded from crossing the road in the sunshine—by flinging them, gently one hopes, into remote shrubbery.

What is the flaw in my character that makes me dislike Thomas Mann and Goethe so much? What I read of Mann years ago, not that I ever read the long ones except for *The Magic Mountain,* I recall being impressed by, and *Elective Affinities,* even in the obviously awful 19th century translation I have, is one of my favourite books.

And who do you suppose said 'Art is a strange and dubious occupation.'?

Perhaps if I run this up to the postbox fairly soon, the perversity of things will produce Galloping Harry with all sorts of mad commitments for the common good.

'The world is disgracefully managed, one hardly knows to whom to complain.'

In verifying the exact wording of the above from Ronald Firbank's *Vainglory,* I came across this strange and untypically Firbankian bit: 'Although there were moments even still in the grey glint of morning when the room had the agitated, stricken appearance of a person who had changed his creed a thousand times, sighed, stretched himself, turned a complete somersault, sat up, smiled, lay down, turned up his toes and died of doubts.'

---

27. Jacob Abbott was a prolific nineteenth-century author of histories, biographies, and serial children's books designed for personal improvement. Many featured a boy named Rollo, and these were among Gorey's favorites.

Another thought for the day:

A moral character is attached to autumnal scenes; the leaves falling like our years, the flowers fading like our hours, the clouds fleeting like our illusions, the light diminishing like our intelligence, the sun growing colder like our affections, the rivers becoming frozen like our lives—all bear secret relations to our destinies.

(Chateaubriand)

* * *

Apart from my descending on you all sometime or other, I trust you are still coming to the Cape ditto?

* * *

If I reread this effort, it will never get mailed, so I'll just have to wonder what I said.

Yrs,

MR. PETER NEUMEYER
12 POWDER HOUSE ROAD EXT.
MEDFORD MASS 02155

Friday morning [October 4, 1968]

[EG to PN]

You will be relieved to discover this consists of one sheet.

I begin to believe I may actually finish the drawings for the opera book before being claimed by the grave; my mind fizzes somewhat in consequence.

Hesitantly proffered thoughts:

Donald's Dream. It goes no further than the title, but I somehow see <u>that</u> somewhere, sometime in the canon.

Donald Makes a List (obviously inspired by mentioning the Borges one,[28] but then I am always one for filching technical inspiration, as the result never bears any relation whatever to the original). Donald makes careful Donald-like preparations: cleans his pen, receives several sheets of beautiful thick paper from his mother, plants both feet firmly under his chair, and writes out a list, all sorts of wild, poetic baroque things, not necessarily objects, with each item a drawing, and the list to serve no purpose or to have no point except its own existence. When it is finished in Donald's best calligraphy, he puts it away in a drawer, and goes off to the kitchen where his mother gives him an apricot turnover and a glass of milk. End.

A night-piece for Donald done in absolutely simple unshaded line and pale almost no-colours like the envelope I sent you yesterday.

A Donald (the splinter comes to mind) done in silhouette like some of the 19th century German things I've seen. Or is this too confining?

Well, one sheet and a bit over, but I cannot resist passing on for further use the fact that a friend of mine was recently lent a house by a friend where the resident cat had to be given a glass of water before it retired for the night.

A galloping consumption (rather than a pox) to Galloping Harry, or have you heard from him? You may wonder why I simply don't call him up on the phone here, and say I want to talk to him, but when I do things like that for some reason everything immediately works out wrong, so it is far better I wait for him to turn up . . .

I feel I ought to add I hope I am not making you angry.

---

28. Jorge Luis Borges, "The Analytical Language of John Wilkins," in *Other Inquisitions, 1937–1952* (University of Texas Press, 1964).

Friday morning, 4.x.68

Dear Peter,

I feel limp, mudd;ed (muddled, not muddied), and up in the air. It is back to the resources of the kettle and the tea bag for the second time this morning. My typing is obviously not going to be of the best.

Now that I know Harry is in California and not lurking about Barnstable, I can safely forget about him for the nonce. I think your note to him was a much better idea than anything I might have said to him, as when I care about something, I get carried away. You know what my thoughts are, provided you could figure them out, by now on which Donald next, etc, and of course if Harry does want to go on with us, we can have endless (knowing Harry) hashing sessions about them, not my thoughts, but Donald books. (I feel my syntax going, like the funnels of a steamer disappearing below the horizon.)

I know just how you feel about fidgeting over something unless it is actually going to be used; on the other hand I should hope you wouldn't mind talking them over somewhat with me. I have all sorts of fairly complicated thoughts on this general subject, which I don't feel up to trying to go into in a letter at the moment, but they are fairly strong, as you might as well know that I feel our joint efforts are as important to me as my own unaided ditto, and since the latter are whatever life I have so a lot more goes into it, or do I mean them? I do. And what is that last 'so' doing in there? than perhaps it (they) all deserve—I have now begun to get the giggles—I think it's all this tea—so on the one hand I am prepared to do it without any immediate prospect of publication, and on the other to refuse to change it around on the off-chance of same.

This does mean something, which I'll try and explain next week.

There has been a hiatus, explainable shortly.

Dear God, Dear Dorothy Dix, as someone said somewhere. Will Winslow[29] just called, and Harry is not going to California until Sunday or Monday and he is coming down this weekend, so I asked Will to tell him I wanted to talk to him for five minutes eyeball to eyeball, though I did not use that particular expression. It is now noonish. I was obviously rapidly passing into complete incoherence at the foot of page one, so I thought I'd better go off to the supermarket and pull my wits together. All that tea was a mistake. Cooking sherry would have been much less agonizingly diuretic as I waited at the checkout counter . . .

Anyway, Harry is bringing me the Library of Congress Catalog Card Number for the book and the flap copy, which were the last bits I was missing, so hopefully,

---

29. Will Winslow was an associate of Stanton's.

unless I am felled by migraine which I feel lurking around the corner with all this excitement, but then again perhaps not, I'll finish up everything this weekend and send it off to Will the first of the week. I'd bring it up myself—I was about to say I couldn't because my cousin, her infant, a friend of hers and her two infants are arriving, unless I hear to the contrary, Tuesday evening, but further thought reveals there is really no reason why I have to be here, even Tuesday evening, as I can always leave something for them to warm up to eat—provided you had a couple of hours of free time next week. A day or two cannot make all that much difference to A-W's schedule, and I made no definite promise as to day, and you could take a final look at everything before I hand it over. At least it seems we're getting one book published. I can adapt myself with ease to anytime at all that's most convenient for you, provided you have any at all.

* * *

The MSS arrived this morning. What a lot we are going to have to talk about. I'd better get this in the mail, and then me to the drawing board.

Ted.

Mr Peter Neumeyer,
12 Powder House Road Ext.,
Medford, Mass. 02155.

7.x.68 [Monday]

[EG to PN]

Thank you for your splendidly clear and complete directions. Now I shall have only myself I can blame when I get hopelessly muddled, and stumble over your house by accident because I have a thing about asking anyone where I am . . .

A quick trip to Hyannis produced *Siddhartha* (I am ashamed to admit I have never read a word of Hermann Hesse, why I don't know) and a volume of Heinrich von Kleist that Signet put out, which I have bought before, but also never read. *Peter Schlemihl* I have in a book from my childhood, but have not read since then. He is the one who loses his shadow, is he not? Because it seems to me he turns up in a story by Heinrich Hoffman about a man who loses his reflection, which I read not too long ago.

Indeed, I suppose Sir Thomas Browne[30] is my favourite prose writer in English, and the final passage of *The Garden of Cyrus* beginning 'But the Quincunx of Heaven runs low . . .' almost my favourite bit of all, though I am also very fond of various bits of *Urn-Burial*. Somewhere I have the *Pseudodoxia* and have dipped into it from time to time but never read it straight through. Ditto Sir Richard Francis Burton, because I get giddy from looking to the footnotes for the translation of all the foreign quotations.

Another bit on the same line I cannot forbear passing on:

The sound of the bell of Jetavana echoes the impermanence of all things. The hue of the flowers of the teak-tree declares that they who flourish must be brought low. Yea, the proud ones are but for a moment, like an evening dream in springtime. The mighty are destroyed at the last, they are as but dust before the wind.

They're the opening lines of the *Heike Monogatari,* a medieval Japanese chronicle.

* * *

I <u>must</u> get back to the very last bits of Donald, because tomorrow I have to clean the house.

I suppose it's too much to hope that our readers will be even as remotely amused by our efforts, as we seem to be by each other.

See you Thursday (D.V.) [Deo volente, God willing]

7:33

I feel this historic moment deserves to be noted by hand: Donald is finished. May I add that I think you are a genius, and that I even rather like my drawings.

Ted.

---

30. I had undoubtedly written to EG that Browne (1605–1682) was among my favorite English authors.

Monday afternoon [October 7, 1968]

Dear Ted,

The mail just arrived with your two letters from Friday morning, one pre, and one post Winslow—both pre Harry. And the package, or books, you wrote of have not yet arrived, but I think we needn't worry yet. I'm just very curious—that's all. I'm going to answer yours of Friday, and your long one from last week, again rather perfunctorily I'm afraid, because I've been having bad bouts with my neck. [. . .]

But I am glad to have the letters, and thank you. The nice, frog hatted, benevolent beast of yellow has such nice flippers. Which reminds me that last night I again read carefully *The Tuning Fork,* and saw for the first time the hand-like flipper on <u>that</u> beast, and admired also again his wonderful shadow. As for the pious infant—I'd never seen his hammer in his hand before. Fun, how much new is visible each time. But what does Satan seem to be holding in his left hand? It looks like either a mouse or another hand.

* * *

Donald's Dream I will be thinking about. I have no very complicated or Teutonic theories of artistic composition, suspecting each man does each work as he happens to do that work. But I do know the manner in which I've done every Donald (though not everything else). There's a fairly long time between Donalds—and no conscious effort brings one on—but when it comes, it comes quick. Both *Donald Goes Away,* and the one about the splinter, *Donald Has a Difficulty,* came to me, half in sleep, as I was riding the Greyhound back from Barnstable, having first met you. Both, I wrote down the next morning. The Rats took a little fidgeting with. I've tried to bring on another Donald, but haven't been able to. Perhaps after we have talked. But one thing! Your *Donald Makes a List* is just superb! If you meant what you said once about jealousy, I know now what you meant. It's glorious. I'm sorry I didn't think of it and leave it for you to admire. But above all, I'm glad it's born. It is grand. [. . .]

Your envelopes are making a beautiful exhibit. I keep thinking they will lend themselves to something—though I can't imagine to what.

* * *

Tuesday afternoon [October 8, 1968]

Dear Peter,

You are a very lovable nut to sit down and write a long letter to someone you are going to be seeing in the next couple of days, especially if you are having trouble with your neck, which I hope you are no longer.

Fortunately there was a copy of the PI [*The Pious Infant*] lying around to look at. You are quite right about Satan's left hand; alas, it is only bad drawing, and he is holding nothing at all.

I am once again at the teacup, waiting for my cousin and entourage (there is also going to be somebody's Labrador retriever, whom I shall no doubt like better than anyone else) to arrive, having rushed about today trying to make the house look presentable, and shopping, in the course of which I ran across Irish Breakfast Tea which someone I know swears by, so I bought some, and had it for elevens. It turns out to be incredibly strong, though quite good, and very dark, and I was reminded of the phrase, who knows where it comes from? I don't, 'Tea strong enough to trot a mouse on' and a children's book to be written by <u>somebody</u> occurred to me about a mouse who was kept to test tea in this manner. I think he perhaps has a chronic cold from getting his feet wet when the tea isn't up to strength, but nothing else comes to me further . . .

Do you by any chance have the Edward Upward (I have always had a sneaking desire to have that name rather than my own)? I've always meant to read him but somehow never found a copy. Now that I think of it, or rather can't, is *Journey to the Border* the novel from the 30's or the one he wrote what I think was about two or three years ago but was probably in reality at least ten, not that I have read that either, but if I recollect was supposed to be the beginning of a trilogy or something.[31]

I sat up last night reading as it were at your beheast (-hest?) Neither looks right, not to mention the fact that it doesn't look either way as if it could possibly <u>mean</u> anything . . . Anyway—but before I go on, a delicious bit from M. R. James popped into my head, which possibly you may know: 'Be careful how you handle the packet you pick up in the carriage-drive, particularly if it contains nail-parings and hair. Do not, in any case, bring it into the house. It may not be alone . . . (Dots are believed

31. The proposed trilogy, begun in 1962, was published as *The Spiral Ascent* (Heinemann, 1977).

by many writers of our day to be a good substitute for effective writing. They are certainly an easy one. Let us have a few more . . .).'

Again, anyway, I read *Siddhartha,* Thomas Mann's absolutely awful introduction to Kleist, which put me off utterly, and *Peter Schlemihl,* which obviously had a whole section missing from the middle of it, whether inadvertently or not, I can't imagine—it was in a volume from a series of various kinds of children's stories from the turn of the century, rather haphazardly edited.

* * *

Your mention of Donald's name having something to do with his character reminds of the bit somewhere in Jane Austen's juvenilia to the effect that someone was a worthy man although his name was Richard.

I seem to have got even more side-tracked than customary.

Peter Schlemihl is not at all what I expected; I guess I tend to think of stories like that as being boringly allegorical or whatever, and this is so horrifying simply because the loss of his shadow is nothing more than that, and yet you can feel just how awful it would be just because it wasn't. (Help. They have arrived.)

Hours have elapsed.

I somehow suspect that this letter is not going to get what you might call finished. What is going to happen is that I am going to arrive with my file labeled P. Neumeyer, among other things, under my arm. At the moment all I can wonder is when I am going to get my dinner, even though I shall be cooking it myself, but then it all depends when the infants have been put away for the night.

> Some, for renown, on scraps of learning dote,
> And think they grow immortal as they quote.   [*Love of Fame,* Edward Young]

Hm.
Or possibly—
But I have run out of paper.

Ted

9 October 1968

DONALD AND THE ...

Trim page 6 7/8" x 6"

Text/drawing page 5" x 4"

Head margin 3/4"   Outside margin 3/4"   Inside margin 1 1/8"

Foot margin 1 1/4"

Centre block of lettering for each page on longest line on
text page width

Sink 1 1/16" from top of text page to top of first line of
lettering on each page

Dedication to be flush outside on text page width; sink 1 1/16"
from top of text page to top of line

Copyright flush outside on text page width; sink block to foot
of text page

Endpaper art in two pieces. 1/8" bleed has been allowed for on
all four sides of each piece, including gutter just in case.

Jacket art in four pieces: picture for front, picture for back,
spine lettering, and border design which is to be used as is on
front, and flopped on the back. Centre pictures within white
area. Sink spine lettering 11/16" from top of jacket trim. Bring
border design only to edge of spine front and back.

Page break up:

1 Pasted down   2-3 Endpapers   4-5 Double page title page

6 Copyright   7 dedication   8 first page of text   9 first drawing

etc to 42 last page of text   43 last dr... blank

44 46-47 endpapers 48 ...

Tuesday AM, October 8, 1968

Dear Ted,

STOP: read no further if you think inspiration becomes clogged by introspection. Otherwise, below, some insomniac musings.

1. Virtually all the stories (Donald, Lionel, etc.) are about states of mind.

The technical problem following from the above is not to write in the first person, and not to write, "it seemed to him as though . . ."

2. Donald—the Donald who evolved—is your creature as much as he is mine. To elaborate: my original Donald, as my illustrations bear witness, was nice, flat, square. Beginning with the garbage can, a rarer Donald was born. The setting became exotic, there was a whisper of a whisper behind the heavy curtain of something that was not to be clarified till some years later in Vienna.[32] And Donald heard the flutter of a moth. Ernest Dowson. Oscar Wilde. And Donald's mother, a beautiful lady, was beautiful now, not only in the eyes of the little child (as in the first version), but became indisputably exceptional, secret, and beautiful, to the eyes of anyone.

Donald is, in his waking hours, in a world of women. His unwaking hours are shaped accordingly.

3. Lionel—August, Leo—reverts back to the first Donald somewhat. He has a father, only. And in "Alternate Ending I," even the humor is a shade of locker-room backslapper.

At least in semi-waking early morning hours I was impressed by the above thoughts, so I've made a copy to give Harry sometime, in case it may shed light on the matter for him, as I think it has for me. (I emphasize, I knew none of this before.)

* * *

Today I have classes and office hours all day—except for 5:30, when I may venture to Boston Common with camera to catch George Wallace.[33]

yours,
Peter

---

32. By Freud, of course.
33. George Wallace, the segregationist governor of Alabama, who ran for the US presidency four times.

I have managed quite inexcusably to very nearly put this in the mail without ever having thanked you both for having me, for the wonderful food, the bed, your company and anything else I haven't thought of, but should have. I do so now, utterly inadequately.

The dollar is for the phone call I made to the Cape.

Wednesday morning, 7:30ish [October 9, 1968]

Dear Peter,

It was not only dear of you, but also right (I expect you usually are) to have written me anyway. It somehow seems a good idea for me to begin a letter before I see you tomorrow that you won't get until probably a few days after. I expect all sorts of things will come out of our talking together—how odd it seems that it will only be for the third time, but then I feel in a way as if I had known you always, an experience I have had a few times with the best sort of children's books when I did not read them until long after I was grown up but at once they seemed to have been part of my childhood—and I hope that if you are coming to the Cape for the weekend I shall see something of you then, perhaps in some other way, where we all just walk on a beach together and perhaps not even talk about our joint concerns except in the most desultory way.

And so, since I am suffering (not suffering exactly; on the other hand I hope it does not become permanent) these days from a kind of insomnia which wakes me up about five thirty in the morning, my head awash with Great and Splendid Thoughts About Life and Whatnot, Mostly Whatnot, and since no one else is up yet, and since I do not think I shall actually get frostbitten in my pyjama bottoms, and since there is an extra typewriter here in the attic, and since a set of galleys for a book providentially provided this sheet of paper—hence its curious texture and shape . . . I proceed.

Borders being the subject. I by no means understand all you said on the subject in your letter, but when I woke (one of my great remarks, in case I have not yet passed it on to you, is: If you want to see the sunrise, you have got to get up in the dark.), that was what was going through my head, and I began to relate it to myself as one will.[34]

I think I have always felt that I was living on the edge, and then this became crystallized so to speak all at once when I read a sentence to this effect in a book on astrology by, I think, Max Jacob, which as I remember seemed to give a quite remarkable analysis and description of the character I thought I had. (Why one

---

34. EG and I had talked several times about the idea of borders. I told him that I had a special interest in the subject of borders—all borders—including the borders between sanity and insanity, life and death, land and sea.

should derive pleasure from that I don't really see.) Which means of course that the centre is elsewhere, always, mysterious and unobtainable. Other people are at the heart of things. Sometimes I get terribly wistful about this in my weaker moments, or used to; I don't <u>think</u> I do very often anymore. Well, anyway, I suppose this is why I have such a passion for the seashore, reinforced by mutable water, as I believe the phrase is, being my element. Also, not so strangely I realize now, why I had such a passion for the desert in Utah when I was stationed there in the Army.

This all went through my head very quickly, and I don't suppose it is really terribly relevant. In any case, I thought about your saying that all your characters made these journeys to borders, and I began to look back on my own books in this light. Since I shall have brought you a batch of them you will be able to follow some of this, if not all, in case I mention something you have not yet seen.

The border of borders is of course death—or is this just a creepy remark on my part? Anyway, it is practically omnipresent in my work. Those poor little children, all 26 of them, crossing it in *The Gashlycrumb Tinies,* and Millicent Frastley [from *The Insect God*] whose physical journey leads her simultaneously across the border of several worlds. Someone is crossing the threshold on the title page of *The West Wing,* and the title the book does not have, but which is there in my mind is *The Book of What Is in the Other World.* There is that edge in *The Inanimate Tragedy* over which everything plunges, Henry Clump [from *The Pious Infant*] is on a Spiritual Journey, *The Evil Garden* evidentally (cancel that extra 'al') is not precisely of this world, and once entered, there is no way out. *The Remembered Visit* has all sorts of borders, physical and mental. *The Gilded Bat* (which one sharp but hostile critic saw as only a feeble joke about birds in ballet) is (let's be pretentious) a journey among winged creatures and a fatal metamorphosis. *The Blue Aspic,* the opera book as yet unfinished, is a double journey to the borders of all sorts of things, as you will see whenever it gets done. *The Hapless Child* . . . I do not like to think of her. Few seem to return from the borders to which I've sent them. Friederich, Filda, Theoda, even the sock. Then there are other books which I feel fit into all this somehow, but in stranger ways: *The Sinking Spell, The Doubtful Guest, The Object-Lesson,* and perhaps my favourite work of mine, *The Nursery Frieze.*

How strange this all seems at first thought, so to speak, but then not really, because all these books have been written for you all along, and it just happened that we didn't meet until I had written some forty-odd of them. Written only, as alas, there are a dozen or so for which I still have to do the drawings one day.

I am beginning to get the shakes from the cold, so I expect I had better put on my clothes, and go and get a cup of tea inside me before lack of food nausea sets in.

Evening

I've retreated from the sounds of the vacuum cleaner and three small children to my somewhat chilly attic until it is time for, I hope, a drink and for me to cook dinner.

There's something very satisfying about typing a letter on a great long sheet like this; it makes me feel faintly medieval.

I fear I am not being very good about <u>answering</u> your letters; as I think I said, I am hopelessly out of the habit of even writing them at all, but I hope to improve, and anything that doesn't get covered tomorrow—I suspect there may be lots as so much new stuff will come up—I'll try to cope with when I get back to this again.

Thursday morning, 7:30ish

Onward and upward.

Saturday morning; one o'clock

The number of things words are not much use for saying has increased how many?-fold.

Saturday morning, 8 o'clock

Here I am shivering in my pyjama bottoms again. After I managed (and it was managed—I don't know when I have felt so wrung out) to type the previous entry, I fell into bed with the cats and did not wake up until six, at which time the book I said I would one day try to do from the Grotius quotation about notes began to emerge from my head. It is going to be very odd indeed I can tell. It is called *The Dislocated Shoulder*[35] and all the drawings are purprtedly (I think there should be an 'o' there somewhere) the work of one of the characters working from old photographs mainly made by one of the other characters. It is going to be without any discernible plot whatever, and really more mood than anything else (something perhaps akin though not like to *The West Wing*). The first drawing to come into my mind was that of a blank-faced gentleman doing nothing in particular with a note to the effect that it is possible at this time that he did <u>not</u> have a moustache (Paren: I think you should keep yours, not only because it looks very well and distinguished (how's that for a parody of the Neumeyer phraseology?), but because when we are becoming rich and famous and in demand, it will be much more impressive to those assembled to see one gentleman with an enormous moustache and the other gentleman with a beard than just one gentleman with a beard and one without, whether we are giving one of our famous antiphonal interviews about Life and Literature, or, even more recherché,

---

35. Recall that at our first meeting, on disembarking from Harry Stanton's boat (page 11), I dislocated Ted's shoulder.

our Readings from the Canon where you do that while I fumble with the lantern slides.) The second drawing that came to mind is the view from the window that one of the lady characters found so disturbing. Several cats will be postulated, but never more than one at a time, so that each note of necessity will read 'Florian looking at a grasshopper. Or possibly Olivier.'[36] You have perhaps guessed, clever sir, that this is all deriving in my own way from the past two days. Oh yes, and there will be something that whatever it is, could not possibly be what it was labelled (in the manner of the bluefish) and so forth and so on. I expect the first (very rough) draft of the book will get itself done today.

From a series of books which no one I have ever heard claim to be literature but which I have read more often even than Jane Austen, and which I may even try on you some distant day, I long ago took as an admirable way to do, the heroine's philosophy to be summed up in the phrase <u>On</u> <u>the</u> <u>boil</u>. I had the fleeting awful thought before I got up that perhaps all this boiling I am doing at the moment was not a reasonably natural outcome of our coming together, but a hint that this was my last chance. I <u>do</u> share with Mr. [Henry] James, the imagination of disaster, or whatever the phrase was. I <u>don't</u> believe this really for a moment, but I hope I can turn myself down to simmer, because when the drudgery (comparative) of getting the first fine raptures into some coherent esthetic form is necessary, it is very maddening to keep having these other things constantly going off in one's head with no hope of doing anything but jotting down the bits and having to put them aside for heaven knows how long.

Anyway, I do think we had an amazingly successful time work-wise (another splendid contemporary vulgarism to go with doing one's thing), and I besottedly like to think that perhaps my being there was of some help to you in bringing forth the absolutely magnificent modifications and revisions you did come up with on the Donalds.

I'm sure you will be relieved to know that I made it back to the Cape with-out (without is hyphenated because it was

EG and PN in Medford, Massachusetts, 1968.
PHOTOGRAPH BY HELEN NEUMEYER

---

36. My full name is Peter Florian Olivier Neumeyer. EG was able to incorporate this idea of using all our initials in the endpapers of *Why We Have Day and Night*, which wasn't published until 1970.

Grotius quote-

The drawings, with one (or two) exceptions were drawn by me & character
from photographs taken by another –

The Dislocated/Painful Shoulder

1 man who may not have had moustache.
   at such and such a time
2 view from window lady found disturbing
3 a child
4 the machine according to ——————
5 Florian or Olivier?
6 the woods I
7   a lady
8   a gentleman
9   a second lady
10   another child
11   a third gentleman
12   whatever it was, it could not possibly be ——
13   The woods II
14   a group photograph of individual characters – one unidentef
15   the machine according to ——————
16   a group photograph - someone who should be there missing
17   Olivier or Florian?
18   The other house. whatever that may mean - elsewhere in
                                                  time (or space
19   a third child
20   an object (seen elsewhere, by induction in me & pictures)
21   The woods III
22   a diagram - schematic "too much"?
23   a third group photograph -
24   The machine according to ——————
25   one of the character's home like opposite gas station
26   a strange animal? injured bird?
27

28 the woods IIII
29
30 buoy source unknown

except for words,
same of action m
seen? excep
very briefly
lots of trees - fo

going to be on two lines and then I forgot) without (just forget it) losing myself; it is fortunate one can drive on one's reflexes alone because I really was in a kind of trance—I had the window wide open to keep from falling asleep, and even at the most bright and alert of times, I feel there is a dream-like quality about turnpike driving. I guess because you and Helen are so comfortable to be with (I could embarrass you with all sorts of further goo, but I won't), I did not have my usual reaction of 'ashes and sour grapes' (Daisy Ashford), and while I recollected that I had finished few sentences and almost no thoughts, I felt, perhaps untruly, that I had been only minimally stupid (I won't elaborate on this score either) . . . So.

Later

Everyone here, except for the animals, is running a temperature, has a sore throat, and so forth and so on. Fortunately I feel so godawful in so many directions at once that I couldn't possibly be coming down with anything. Knock wood.

I am also in a state of total bafflement. I idly picked up Dorothy Wordsworth's *Journals* which prints a great many of the poems by Wordsworth she mentions to let you know where the Splendid Bit (which of course I can't begin to remember) came from. And it is not <u>there</u>. And except for *The Stuffed Owl,* which I already knew you knew, so I would not have quoted from that, I can at the moment not think of one other book in the house that could contain any Wordsworth.[37] Am I going mad? Quite likely. But wait. Now that I have gone through all this blather . . . there was an anthology of the Romantic poets, but what have I done with it? It leaps not to the eye. I go in search. Found. The Penguin Classics *English Romantic Verse* with a marvelous painting of a horse frightened by a lion by Stubbs on the cover. It was from 'Extempore Effusion upon the Death of James Hogg.' A nice title, too.

The day has become beautiful. I think I shall go and stand in the shower for a while, and then tousled and freshly garbed, get the hell out onto a beach, who knows, even perhaps to think of creative endeavour, a crumpled bit of paper and a pencil stub should suffice.

I spontaneously intuited (can this possibly be what I mean? It sounds <u>very</u> peculiar.) while in the shower the Buddhist (I think) metaphor of Life, the World, whatever you want to call it, being a burning house.

Our Mr [Ralph] Hodgson says: The handwriting on the wall may be a forgery.[38]

More on, perhaps, *The Painful Shoulder.* On a book like this one is going to be the word dislocated is maybe too much. Anyway, there will be various versions of a black box called simply the machine. What people are shown will be as if posed studio

---

37. D. B. Wyndham Lewis and Charles Lee, *The Stuffed Owl: An Anthology of Bad Verse* (J. M. Dent and Sons, 1930).

38. Ralph Hodgson (1871–1962) was another of those obscure poets for whom we shared an enthusiasm.

photographs so there will never be any action they are involved in; the landscapes will all be untenanted, various monotonous drawings of woods, for example, where it will say something has taken place, and all the objects shown will be in so far as is possible shown in a minimum of surroundings. The last drawing in the book will remark that no one knows where it is, who took the original photograph, or made the subsequent drawing, or why. Very sad, this: it will be the buoy in Barnstable Harbor on which we stood. (Lapse of time) Art having removed the figures from the buoy, Life has removed the buoy, as I discovered to my consternation when my cousin's husband was giving me a sail in his new Sunfish this morning. Only for the winter I trust, the removal I mean.

Sunday morning, 7:20 ish

Yesterday seems finally to have gone. It was what can best be described as a trying day. Psychosomatic hooha eventually localized itself as a pain in the stomach; the visiting infants were being fairly tedious, even to their parents; the visiting Labrador kept running in front of cars when it accompanied me to the post office; my aunt came to tea; my cousin and I then rather hysterically embarked on a vat of paella for dinner which neither of us had attempted before—it came out rather well, finally; and the first movie to appear I hadn't seen for weeks turned out to be not very amusing which was what I had in mind by that time.

I finished reading Hermann Hesse's *Knulp* before I went to bed. You could hardly have chosen a time when I would be more open to what it has to say; far too open to have any esthetic judgment about it whatever; I could only relate it to myself, and was rather desperately moved. Apart from a few obvious awkwardnesses, your translation seemed to me to have more of a voice than the one I'd read of *Siddhartha,* which at this point is the only other Hesse I've read to compare it with/to?

Having got into bed and turned out the light, I quietly burst into tears because I am not a good person. As they came and went for some minutes, I was concerned with the words following 'because' in the previous sentence, rewriting them over and over in my head until they seemed to be as close to the truth as it was possible for me to make them.

EG and PN on the buoy in Barnstable Harbor.
PHOTOGRAPH PROBABLY BY HARRY STANTON

Rather stunned by having actually typed out the above paragraph, and resisting the impulse to destroy it at once by a lot of elaboration, explanation, and whatall, I am deriving sustenance of a sort from looking at the sort of thing I could never manage at all, a small botanical study of morning glories, individual blooms, buds, leaves, tendrils in watercolours done by my great grandmother, which hangs on the wall beside my desk. A framed diploma awarded to her by the New York State Agricultural Society for 'Very Superior Pencil Sketches' at the Syracuse meeting of 1849 hangs over my desk; she must have been thirteen or fourteen at the time. She supported an invalid husband and their children for I have no idea how long by painting mottoes and greeting cards.

At this point I would like to hear sounds from the rest of the house, which I don't, because we are having something called David Eyre's Pancake for breakfast, whoever he may have been, but it has to be eaten right out of the oven, and obviously I cannot put it in the oven until everyone is up and waiting. At the moment I am starving.

If this is ever to get in the mail with a suitable envelope and I can remember to copy down my compositional throes from it before irrevocably inserting and sealing same, I had better start considering anything else I have in mind as I see the end of the sheet is about to disappear below the horizon of the roller behind.

I did mean to ask if you could permanently spare the copy of *Knulp* as I would very much like to keep it, but if it would be inconvenient, please say so.

There seems to be no wind whatsoever, but today I think I shall do what I have been meaning to do all summer, and that is buy a kite at our general store in Barnstable.

Lady Murasaki said in her diary:

Yet the human heart is an invisible and dreadful being.

LA VIE est un pièce composée par des fous & jouée par des acteurs ivres.
[Life is a drama written by madmen and played by drunken actors.]

Attributed to Shakespeare on a French postcard.

We slip. Farewell.
I really do not believe this letter. Especially having reread it.

Ted

[EG enclosed the pancake recipe with this letter.]

David Eyre's Pancake
4 servings

1/2 c Flour
1/2 c Milk
2 Eggs
1 pn Nutmeg
4 tb Butter
2 tb Confectioners' sugar
Juice of 1/2 lemon

Preheat oven to 425 degrees. In a mixing bowl, combine the flour, milk, eggs, and nutmeg. Beat lightly. Leave the batter a little lumpy. Melt butter in 12" skillet with heatproof handle. When very hot, pour in batter. Bake in oven 15 to 20 minutes, or until golden brown. Sprinkle with sugar and return briefly to the oven. Sprinkle with lemon juice, then serve with jelly, jam, or marmalade.

It is presumably Craig Claiborne who advises that one serve this while listening to Benjamin Britten's *Ceremony of Carols*.

[October 11, 1968]

A Poem for Peter from Ted, Composed in the
Dawn by the Latter After Unsuccessfully
Trying to Read Himself to Sleep with
Certain Essays by the Former.

The world may think it idiotic,
Nor care at all we're symbiotic,
But I will say at once, and twice:
I find it nice. I find it nice.

11 October 1968

[October 15, 1968]

[PN to EG]

* * *

On the boil (I am still going through your letter linearly, though you wouldn't guess it) on the boil, do not imagine disaster, for as you know, you can cause things to happen. As you can make yourself simmer, which you must (I speak knowingly, i.e., purposely, avuncularly) since, in the long haul, you have less distractions from your own thoughts than I do, and since disaster is disaster and by no semantic game good, you must try to cause yourself not to have thought of dangerous and frightening paragraphs such as that one. Don't feel you should respond to this—but keep it in mind, even at the cost of one less shadow in a book. Do not have premonitions of disaster, even though we all have premonitions of disaster.

* * *

Yours
Peter

Monday night [probably October 14, 1968]

Dear Peter,

It was good to talk to you this morning. I did not realize it was you for just long enough to make me sound a trifle feeble-minded I expect. Anyway, it did cheer me up, as what with one thing and another, such as Three Trying Tots and Untalktoable Grownups (except for my cousin) and lots of Domestic Squalor over the weekend, I was toying with the idea of crawling back into my hole and saying the hell with everything.

Anent that loopy letter of mine [October 9], just because you know someone will understand what you have on your mind is no reason for getting it off it. A vulgar epigram I do believe. Anyway, what I think is bothering me these days is a sense of total confusion, as opposed to the chronic and partial kind.

I finished Jerzy Kosiński's *The Painted Bird* and it's now back to Elie Wiesel's *The Gates of the Forest*.

Wednesday morning

Do you always sound so jolly on the phone? How nice. I believe people usually wonder what I am so cross about.

I left the two ailing males of the recent houseparty to catch planes to Newark and Chicago yesterday morning and picked up Connie[39] in Boston while the two ailing females and the three ailing children and the retriever whose health seemed rude packed themselves into the station wagon to drive back to New Jersey. Connie and I dawdled our way back to the Cape via the coastline rather than Route 3, discovered abandoned lighthouses, walked out on breakwaters, and got caught up on things in general, and you in particular.

Your last name had not come up when I mentioned that your father [Alfred Neumeyer] taught at Mills [Mills College, Oakland, California], and I was quite startled by the warmth of her response when she found out who he was. She was only there for a year, 1943–4, but said he was the only person there worth bothering about, so to speak, and as I guess I said on the phone, one of her great regrets was that she had not stayed on to study going into museum work under him. She also said that a couple of years later she met him again while out walking in Guatemala (I rather like that phrase) and that he had remembered her. I shall now try and find something of your father's to read.

---

39. From childhood on, Consuelo Joerns had been a close friend of Ted's. The two of them flew kites and photographed together. Connie herself had illustrated a number of children's books. Unfortunately, to this day, she and I have not met.

I have showed Connie the Lionel and several Donalds so far, and she thinks you are a genius too, which I was sure she would, but then again you never know, and my usual instincts are not to try this sort of thing, because so often one draws a total blank, and there you are with one friend on one side and one friend on the other, and both are so to speak peering bleakly at you and wondering what you can possibly see in the other one, etc.

I have finally managed to pry loose from her several children's books she has had around for years and never done anything with to speak of, which I think Harry might like, and so I am hoping she will also fly up from NY the weekend you are all down. She's going to the Vineyard on Friday and back to NY before the following Thursday because she has a camera class. Since it looks like it is going to be a good day, we're planning to spend it with our cameras tooling about.

Thank you kindly for mailing back the letters. Why I had not missed them before I can't think, as I knew I was leaving something behind—it nagged at me so to speak, but I for the life of me could not pinpoint it. Anyway, I began tearing the house apart looking for the rejected Donald ending, which you can have if you want it, to show Connie to give her an idea of what the drawings were like, and then the whole extent struck me. Numb like.

Apropos of nothing at all except that it has been on my mind and I think I had better say it because it accounts for a good deal of my behaviour. There is a strong streak in me that wishes not to exist and really does not believe that I do, so that I tend to become unnerved when these curious ideas are proved to be not really true because someone (in this case you) has responded to something I have said or done just as if I were an actual person the same as you (especially) or anyone else. Some of it is, I guess, just the worst sorts of arrogance and irresponsibility, but not all of it, as I really don't think I exist a lot of the time, so I'm asking you to bear with it, me, whatever, for the sake of what?—friendship I suppose, which I want to be capable of, which is obviously not enough. More brains might help, but enough unseemly remarks for eight o'clock in the morning and the shivering in pyjama bottoms syndrome.

I trust you to send the latest Lionel before too long. Not hope, trust.

What is Lionel going to look like? I ask myself. How will his looks differ from Donald's? In subtle ways only I expect, as I have this basic child figure which is the only one at my command, and then but fitfully. I think Lionel's hair is darker perhaps, and there's the slight possibility his eyebrows meet over his nose. Of course he can always wear a turtleneck sweater with a large L on the front so that he is Unmistakable. Obviously his sturdy father's moustache will Fiercely Turn up at the Ends. Don't panic; they will probably look not at all like this in the end, when it is too late and the drawings are all done.

* * *

I have just purchased lots of pristine new file folders. They await such things as neatly typed copies of revised Donalds, new Donalds, new Lionels, what else?

Thank you for the quotation from Oscar Wilde which arrived in the mail this afternoon along with a check for an obscene drawing I did for *Playboy;* the latter will allow me to purchase one beautiful book on American tombstones and two beautiful books on Japanese Art that I have been coveting. Also pay my rent, eat, and so forth. I do not know what I am going to do with the quotation, because I don't understand what it refers to, if anything. I fear I am being obtuse; do you mind terribly?

Connie and I spent a charming afternoon taking pictures. Neither of us has been doing it long enough to know why we take them. Or what we are taking, as it were. I did have a fleeting idea that sometimes at least one was taking pictures of things that spoke to one, but that one had nothing to say back to. Would you one day let me look at some of the ones you have taken? It might perhaps help me to get some sort of ideas about photography, by which I mean my own in this case. I have very strong but ambivalent feelings about other people's, like say Cartier-Bresson's, Weston's, Lartigue's, etc.

I have started reading your father's book on meaning in modern art.

There is possibly some relevance to the Wilde quotation (it is now somewhat later, and I am registering yet another upheaval in my featureless existence brought on by friends phoning to announce she is going to have a first baby in April and they are buying a house and thereby announcing too the end of an era which has lasted seven or eight years, which I am all very pleased about, the baby and the house, but is nevertheless disconcerting because one sometimes forgets how at the mercy of other people's lives one is, and there is no point in pretending one isn't)[40] where was I? in remarking that me is the envelopes and not nearly so much so, the often foolish letters inside.[41]

To the post office and then to bed.

Ted.

---

40. The friends expecting the baby were Mel and Alexandra Schierman. See page 116, note 73.
41. I do not remember which quotation by Oscar Wilde I sent to EG, but in this paragraph and earlier he wrote about the theme of (his own) dubious existence, a subject he returned to throughout our friendship. Note his remark that he feels he is more himself in the envelope art than in the written letters.

October 16 [1968]

[PN to EG]
Ted, I know we were not satisfied with *Donald Has a Difficulty,* but I have a difficulty too, and can't remember what we decided to do with it. What it is now is an infinitesimal miniature, a tiny still-life. Probably that cannot go out into the world as a story—not till we are very very famous.

so

would you like to venture an allegorical epic, a very big one?

After Donald recovers, he searches the house, finds all sorts of things, and constructs a Machine so that never again will he have to use his calf to push a tree. Then we can make it Tolstoian. Peasants, kulaks, sleigh trimmers, woodcutters, roofers, priests, guards, the taxidermist, barbers, a surgeon, printers, street-boys, etc. can all come and stand in awe of the Machine, realizing that it can be used to push, not merely a birch, not only pine trees, but even the mighty oaks by the moat. And when one has begun to push mighty oaks by a moat, it is more than one can imagine how many creatures are unhoused: the grub, the ant, the worm, the sparrow, the squirrel, the moth. And the roots, after all—who knows how far they may go, under the moat, and even close to the walls of the Palace. And if a palace wall should crack . . . !! The peasants, the kulaks, the sleigh trimmers, the woodcutters, the roofers, etc., etc., etc., all look at each other with a fog of fear over their eyes. The wall of the Palace. They look at Donald, and they seem to implore. But the Machine is so grand. And the splinter in the calf had hurt Donald so much. But Donald knows. His mother so gently takes his hand, and together they go to fetch the saw.

Could this be our big, colored book?

Oct. 17 [1968]

Dear Ted,

A wretched morning. If things are to get written, I have to be well under way, in good Teutonic manner, by 9 AM. It is almost 11, and I got hooked watching the Prohibition party candidate for President on television this morning, and inanely watched for about an hour, and then tried to work on "Tom's Vote," but got nowhere—nowhere at all. Pleasurable things, like writing to you, I save for afternoons—but it is good to get on with it now, since if I put it off any longer, I'll be seeing you, and the circularity and syntactic and logical convulsions of this letter are not to be taken seriously—at least not to this point (who knows what follows), for this is simply a bad day. So

Let me try merely to respond to that great, long letter

* * *

Yes, indeed, your books are about borders, so often borders already crossed, for the visit is in the past when it is remembered, and after the title page of *The West Wing,* one is already over (and you've set yourself the almost impossible task of rendering another perspective, as in the inside backwards of *The Evil Garden*). I haven't read everything of yours, for we're doing them together, several a night, sometimes repeating, for there is much to see.

* * *

I'm glad I didn't know [*The Remembered Visit*] before, because if I had, I couldn't have avoided copying "Mr. Crague asked Drusilla if she liked paper." I would have copied it all my life. I shall now have to try to remember it and forget it too. [. . .]

Why does that book keep coming back? Because it's a remembered visit, of course. One I never made, having only corresponded with the old ex-clippership-sailor for a couple of years, promising him a visit in the Sierra where he lived in a shack, in very modest straits for all his O'Henry short story awards and his fine book, *Ships and Women*. He wished Helen and me well when we married, and quoted in his letter the "Helen, thy beauty is to me" passage,[42] which was not camp when it was spoken true. And then one day he was dead.

---

42. When I was about twelve, I was befriended by Bill (Bertram) Adams, who had been a seaman and a second mate on clipper ships going 'round Cape Horn, as he recounted in *Ships and Women* (Little, Brown, 1937) and several other books, some of which won awards. Bill taught me how to construct squirrel traps, and in several ways he became, for a short while, a sort of surrogate father to me. The quoted passage is from Edgar Allan Poe's "To Helen." I treasure Bill's letters still.

As I am certain you know, the more delicate the nuances, the fuzzier the Borders in your books, the more they affect, the more poignant they are. Unless you set out pure and simple to be funny, which I can't imagine you ever do—though some, like *The Wuggly Ump,* with even a healthily Alpine interior decoration, seems rather Ciardiesquely hearty.[43]

All this is stream of semiconsciousness, and I'm rambling on making only .007% sense, I'm sure. But again, he said hollowly, 'it's that kind of day.' [. . .]

Your favorite, *The Nursery Frieze,* I have not seen, but I will scout around for it.

I'm intrigued by your Grotius book. It's (not as you describe it, but only as I think after your first sentence about it) a 27th cousin to Nabokov's *Pale Fire.*

Random thought—where the dickens will librarians classify our books? How do they classify yours now? Simply from a bourgeois business point of view—after all, I hardly think children will be insatiable in their appetites for our enigmas? Perhaps we should advertise in Rosicrucian periodicals. "CROSS THE BORDER WITH BLACK POWER" (not racial). By the way—have you ever illustrated a Gorey Olympics?

What you write about our beards and moustaches is persuasive. Did we talk about it though—my feeling it's fun to be square—and did you add (or did I dream) the extension, a la Borges, of that,—to be odd so that one is thought to be squarely and conformistically odd, and thus square, while in fact one is really what one looks? This can go on—perhaps into a book. [. . .]

God, I must keep confessing my illiteracy. You have driven me to check Firbank out of the library, he having been one I'd always said, "Oh yes . . ." etc. about, but had never read. I have now at least dipped in. At the same time I . . . well, hell, well, that wasn't going to be any sentence whatever.

---

43. Gorey and his friends had taken a poetry class at Harvard with John Ciardi. Not long afterward, EG illustrated several Ciardi books.

18.x.68 Friday night

Dear Peter,

A sane, sensible, sober letter perhaps? We shall both see.

Firstly, I hope the wretchedness of your morning did not prolong itself into the rest of the day, and that after all you were not coming down with something. Miraculous recoveries have been known to take place after lunch, or tea, or whatever.

Secondly, you are all most welcome to stay here anytime between now and the time I go back to New York; there is more than enough room, and I should be pleased to take the necessary trouble. Really.

To answers, comments, whatnot, as I munch my way through a plate of paella, my first onslaught on the leftovers I am destined to work my way through from the last ten days. Also some splendidly wilted salad. [. . .]

I [. . .] read through the piece [in *Look* magazine] on Leonard Bernstein, who I have always rather loathed, and finished it thinking, he really sounds much nicer and more intelligent than I had thought—have you noticed how people, no matter who, always say the right sort of things in interviews these days?—and what nice, warm photographs, etc., and then I suddenly thought, but there is only one way to get photographs (have someone take them), and from there one transfers the whole thing to one's own life, say, and one (at least me) revolts at the public calculation, etc. necessary to give this idea of private coziness, which therefore cannot really exist.

To return to the bishop for one last bit;[44] apart from everything else, I came away with a feeling of sadness because I do not doubt the bishop tried to reach his son, even if it was not the way the article makes it sound, and the obvious (I think) futility of any attempt on the part of anybody to reach him. I got the impression that nothing could have prevented him committing suicide. Not that this is a belief I would ever act on if I knew it; perhaps one has to try more than ever simply because there aren't going to be any results.

This leads to your article on the English teacher. Connie read it too, and the main point seemed not at all elusive to either of us. Both of us were, in fact, very moved by it. To be terse, I think anyone who has you as a teacher should be as grateful as he is capable of; I hope I am.

To quote from a favourite author (p. 29 of the above-mentioned essay): 'Just for example, consider the number three and the theme of the deceptiveness of appearances.' As usual, you have already said what I was trying to, in this case what

---

44. A previous section of this letter, deleted in the interest of brevity, related to an article about Bishop James Pike from the same issue of *Look*. Pike was a controversial figure in the Episcopal Church; after his son's suicide in 1966 he experienced otherworldly phenomena and tried to communicate with his son clairvoyantly.

I had in mind about "Rapunzel" and "The Three Wishes." It is all there, waiting for you to mine in a suitable form for the talents of an unfavourite illustrator, in that sentence and the references following.

I hope, incidentally, that the books which have probably not reached you yet won't prove redundant. Your Japanese quotations make me wonder; I was labouring under the delusion, carefully fostered on your part obviously, that you were not particularly familiar with such.

I feel the Nobel Prize has for once been given to someone I think is a good writer; what can they be thinking of? Anyway, Connie and I were sitting at breakfast talking about Kawabata [the Japanese short-story writer and novelist Yasunari Kawabata], whose name I can never remember, and usually recollect it as being Watanabe, whoever he may be, when the radio suddenly announced that he had been awarded the Nobel Prize; at first I thought it was some aberration of sound in my head. He was the one I was complaining to you that he was so little translated, which will now change as I expect at this very moment the minions of Alfred A. Knopf are arranging for a great pretentious Collected Works or the like, which in this case is fine by me. Connie filched my copies of *Snow Country* and *Thousand Cranes* to take to the Vineyard to reread, else I would have sent them to you, but I think they can still be come by—Berkeley has them out in paperback.

My mind has gone temporarily blank as to where I was going from here. I temporize. If I hear one more word about JK and AO [Jacqueline Kennedy and Aristotle Onassis] I think I shall go mad. (The news is on.)

This is not where I was going, but anyway. Variation on a theme: a person is told that a piece of paper can be made to go up a kite string; in making the attempt he inadvertently uses for the purpose a list he has with him of physical objects; the paper <u>does</u> go up the kite string, much to his surprise, to the kite itself; later, as he begins to reel in the string, the objects from the list begin to come down the string—rather rapidly I think, and eventually doing him a physical injury, perhaps, or even burying him under a mound of things, but perhaps this would not be necessary. It would depend on the objects which I have no idea of whatever.

This came to me, not surprisingly, while Connie and I were kite-flying most of the day, though alas, it ended in the various demises of both our kites. Also I seem to have got extremely red in the face. Well.

I don't <u>think</u> I said anything about it in my last letter, which I have no recollection of whatever, except I <u>think</u> (again) on the envelope there was a (possibly) overcome or (possibly) just upturned small beast under a stilted version of The Machine on the envelope. There is no need for you to verify this fact if indeed it is one, but if you have not seen this envelope, illusion and reality have merged for me and you will henceforth have to come to the all-white place on alternate Tuesday afternoons armed with paper and pens and tell me what to draw. You are now, I hope for your sake, wondering what I didn't say anything about in my last letter. In a word, and thank heaven you repeated it in your letter today, because no way of spelling it looked right, or like anything for that matter: monofilament. That first day I was flying a kite, for the first time in about thirty-five years, I lay on the beach for hours with it attached to my toe; it happened that the wind was such that it was almost in front of the sun, and I could only catch a glimpse of it, absolutely motionless some six hundred feet up, by carefully shading my hand over my eyes, and the string itself magically disappeared into the blue of the sky, it seemed only a few yards above my head.

And then today, when the wind was more fitful, at the risk of sounding remarkably silly, though I don't think to you, the kite at the end of the string was all sorts of things: a marvelous metaphor (not the right word but . . .) for art (?) in that from the movements of a visible object one can deduce the invisible ones of the wind, a remark that could hardly be phrased less elegantly; then obviously, but nonetheless touchingly on that account I felt, the kite as a bird, and from that the bird as a soul (vide Henry Clump), with confused bits of the Chuang-Tzu/butterfly notion,[45] to the point of wondering who is the flyer, who the flown (dear me, I am getting tackier

---

45. Chuang Tzu (399–295 BC): "Once I, Chuang Tzu, dreamed I was a butterfly and was happy as a butterfly. I was conscious that I was quite pleased with myself, but I did not know that I was Tzu. Suddenly I awoke, and there was I, visibly Tzu. I do not know whether it was Tzu dreaming that he was a butterfly or the butterfly dreaming that he was Tzu. Between Tzu and the butterfly there must be some distinction. (But one may be the other.) This is called the transformation of things."

and tackier in my expression). After this little tangle, I hope you aren't going to feel irrevocably insulted by my saying I felt I understood your monofilamental feeling.[46]

I am of course pleased by your comments and thoughts on my books, and the probable spottiness of my response is for two reasons. One, as I think I said, I have given up reading my books in the same way I gave up smoking, so that my recollections of some of them are fragile indeed and at best probably more than a little inaccurate, and two, I am coming more and more to realize that, at least so far, [although] I have eventually managed to understand what you are saying, there is often a fairly longish stretch, where without being aware of it, I do not understand. This is put very badly indeed, and it is a thing I have worried over for years without ever having been able to express it to my satisfaction. It is not so simple as misunderstanding a thing, but rather having a limited understanding that seems quite adequate until one has a sudden intuition of what is actually there. Anyway, I have made so many awful mistakes already of this sort in reading your things, that later on in this, there are only going to be a couple of very minimal indeed comments about the revised and new MSS.

To touch on one or two things you said. I seem to have wrought better than I knew with *The Remembered Visit*. It is a story from real life, the germ anyway, and the visit itself took place when Connie was introduced to Gordon Craig[47] in the south of France, and the paper collection is true.

We both felt it was a very tenuous little book, and were quite surprised when my editor at Simon & Schuster took it, and since then a few people seem to have become fond of it. Since I haven't the least idea what my usual vein is (except that I do not think it is very perceptive to mention me with Charles Addams), I am naturally enough not sure what of my work is not in it. Innocence? All I can say is, it is a thought which has arisen. Not that I am sure what it is (I'm planning a major attack on Blake one of these days which may help), but I have a sneaking suspicion that all my work is in some odd way very much so. It needs something, perhaps thinking about? I don't know. At the risk of sounding potty, the sentence 'Mr Crague asked Drusilla if she liked paper' was something I felt strongly at the time I was incapable of, that it came from somewhere else. I don't think time much enters into the effect we have on each other.

* * *

---

46. EG was referring to a comment I made in a letter about monofilament fishing line. I occasionally went fishing, and the thin singleness of a nylon monofilament line demarking itself from the whole vast surrounding ocean was something I was thinking about, and I related it to our ongoing discussion about borders.
47. Edward Gordon Craig (1872–1966), the English actor, director, and scenic designer.

Gordon Cairnie[48] possibly has *The Nursery Frieze,* but if I know lovable old Gordon, he is selling it for its weight in gold dust, and I'll send you a copy as soon as I get back to New York. To continue in this crass vein, I don't think librarians are ever called on to classify my books because I don't think libraries ever buy them, the clots, he added acidly. I'm counting on you to change all this. (I am zipping up and down as it were in your letter at this point.) I don't really much care for Mr [Vladimir] Nabokov; ought I to read *Pale Fire?*

We did I think talk about your feeling of it's fun to be square, and while I'll go along with the Borges-like ramifications, I don't think I was the one who thought it up. In the past my justification for my self-conscious oddness of appearance (by now I figure this is the way I look, and it would not only be more self-conscious but also uncomfortable to change) was that people would think their impression of oddity came simply from the way I looked, and eventually become (hopefully) pleasantly surprised that I was not nearly as much of a nut as I looked, and was really quite ordinary, which is also true I think. It seemed preferable to people thinking 'Well, he looked perfectly ordinary and then it became apparent there was something wrong with his head . . . ' Of course now practically everybody to my middle-aged way of thinking looks too peculiar for words, and only <u>very</u> infrequently attractive at the same time.

A Little Firbank goes an awfully long way, and as the years go by, I am less and less in sympathy with his manner. [. . .] I have to confess that technically I have been influenced by him to a vast extent, or at least when I first started writing, so I suppose something has persisted all these years. I guess he was the one who showed me how much you could leave out, though I think by now how I leave out things is pretty much my own. His unfinished novel about New York, which he never saw, called *The New Rythum* (sic), seems strangely a propos even today.

* * *

I also sent you off another book. Don't feel swamped, or that you have to read them. Also, I suppose it would have been more sensible to have memorized your bookshelves before I started sending you items, but somehow there was never time. Anyway, of the things I sent, all are for dipping, really. The Bashō is translated very peculiarly, or so it seems to me, if only because the English is so odd, so has to be read around the translation so to speak. *The Pillow Book* [by Sei Shōnagon] has long been one of my favourite things to dip into before going to bed. Though I have been waiting several years for the complete translation by Ivan Morris, now that I have had

48. Gordon Cairnie was one of the founders of the Grolier Poetry Bookshop, near Harvard Square in Cambridge, Massachusetts.

it for months I still have not begun it, probably because it is in two volumes, the text in one, and in the second, and infinitely thicker, all the notes. Mr [Reginald] Blyth is one of my idols, though one of the newest ones; I hope you find him as lovable and provoking as I do; his books, of which there are many, are for the most part anthologies of Japanese poetry in his own translations, interspersed with lots and lots of commentary. Alas, he died a couple of years ago, without having finished a nine, I think it was, volume history of Zen, again lots of translation and lots of commentary; four were finished, and his Japanese publisher has managed to eke out a couple of others since he died; eke out is not correct but you know what I mean.[49]

* * *

Harry is back from California, as I was told by the next Mrs Stanton who was shopping for the breakfast she was about to cook him when I ran into her in our local general store. She told me this, so I am not jumping to scandalous conclusions.

I am alternating between writing this, staring blankly out the window, and pottering about in an attempt to get the house and me into a tidier state. Wicked animals tipped over all the trash cans last night and strewed (does this word exist?) their contents all over the back yard. This has been dealt with, but both the washing machine and the dryer are making their curious noises, and will ultimately have to be emptied. Folding up sheets by oneself is extremely awkward and tedious. The dishwasher has been emptied after several days, but on the other hand it will sooner or later have to be activated with the results of those several days. What life would be like without these aids to domesticity I do not like to think, considering my general incompetence in the realm of real life, except for cooking. Something I think is about to go wrong with my rented car, or already has, in that it sometimes does not wish to start, and I somehow also suspect, unless I had a lapse while supposedly rewinding, that my last roll of film never passed behind the lens at all. Earlier, it being utterly grey, I went out to take some hopefully almost totally muted pictures. Connie and I did a good deal of photographing while she was here, and I am beginning to get some glimmerings of negative ideas at least about photography (for myself): no people, at least not yet, animals possibly, no angles, but only what one sees wandering around with a camera without leaping up on things, or lying down on the ground, etc, no photographs of things that are photographs already so to speak, no fiddling around with purposefully over- or under-exposing or blurring, and so forth along this line. It all sounds fearfully austere, doesn't it? Or do I mean dull. Even no obvious subject if possible.

---

49. About this time EG sent me a number of volumes of Japanese poetry, including Arthur Waley's *Japanese Poetry: The 'Uta';* R. H. Blyth's four-volume *Haiku;* Matsuo Bashō's *The Narrow Road to the Deep North, and Other Travel Sketches,* translated by Nobuyuki Yuasa; and Lady Murasaki's *Tale of Genji.*

EG sent photographs he had taken around the Cape.

I've just dismantled a jigsaw puzzle, so I can start on another one tonight. We developed a mania around here two summers ago, and now we have literally a closet full of them.

Have you read Mircea Eliade at all? I've been working my way through him since last spring from time to time. It is now time to fold sheets as all sounds have ceased from the dryer.

What we decided to do with *Donald Has a Difficulty* was to omit the next to last sentence. However, I suspect It Is Too Late Now. The mind boggles at 'an allegorical epic, a very big one', pleasurably, dazzledly, breathlessly . . . but it <u>does</u> boggle. All I can say is Gee! Are you serious? Yes, I think you are serious, or if not, you will be. How can I possibly rise to all this in my drawings? Or will it have to be murals? I don't even know what a sleigh trimmer is, much less what one looks like . . . On rereading, I burst into helpless laughter, with a tear or two. How noble Donald is, along with everything else. Do you think I could possibly apply for successive Guggenheims to work on the preliminaries, and the Ford Foundation for a grant to do the final art work? Help.

Donald Goes Away:

Did you purposely omit old paragraph 4: Donald properly turned his attention elsewhere. He picked up a trowel. I am very fond of it.[50]

One slight point: in the next to last paragraph you now have: Donald told his mother of the encounters . . . I think in view of the fact that the great pipes are filled with winged insects, and since this is what he does not tell his mother and since they could be thought of as encounters, I think it should be clearer that what encounters means is the encounters earlier with the worms and beetles, yes?

My mention of the monsters in October was only before you had decided what was down there, and had originally been mooted in September as a possibility if the story were going in another direction.

I think with the one slight qualification above, the MS is ready for Harry, don't you?

Surprise for Donald:

At first I was sorry you had decided against Donald building a machine to assist mother as she recovered from her vertigo—I still think it's a rather charming idea—but you were wise I feel to go back as close to the original concept as possible. (Second thoughts seldom seem to be very good I've often found, though sometimes they help you get back to a more satisfactory rendition of the first ones, as I think may have happened in this case.) Anyway, I think as it stands it is now right, and, not at all incidentally, deeper and darker. As Donald and his world grow, I watch awestruck. I mean this quite seriously. How I am to even begin to get any of it into my drawings I can't think.

I don't expect I am going to be able to say a thing about *Lionel Does Science* for weeks.

[. . .] I'll also send the rejected Donald drawing for you to have. I looked at it again when I was showing it to Connie to give her some faint notion of what I'd done for the book, and I shouldn't have. It wasn't very bright of me to think that because they weren't for a book of mine, I wouldn't suddenly loathe them, for of course it's much worse because it's a book of yours, or ours. Anyway, just bear with me when I am unable to look at *Donald and the . . .* from now on; I'll have to of course when I

---

50. See the original storyboards on pages 40–41.

start on another, but then I can narrow it down to technical considerations and not really take in what I am looking at.

Agrippina, my Abyssinian cat, is staring at my foot in a peculiar manner. She is excessively amiable and not very bright, but still . . .

I keep forgetting to ask after the robin. Has it recovered? Is it still with you?[51]

Your father's book gave me all sorts of things to think about; also some splendid quotations, both his and others he quoted.[52] The two of you sound alike every now and again; there were even a couple of sentences that might have emerged from Donald's ambiance.

This may not after all be the sensible, sober, sane letter I premised—I have yet to reread it—but it has the advantage that almost nothing in it requires an answer.

Yours, Ted.

Mr Peter Neumeyer

12 Powder House Road Ext., Medford, Mass. 02155.

---

51. When EG visited us, we were looking after an injured robin.
52. Alfred Neumeyer, *The Search for Meaning in Modern Art* (Prentice Hall, 1964).

Page from *The Unstrung Harp*
(1953) (left) and title page from
Donald and the . . . (1969).

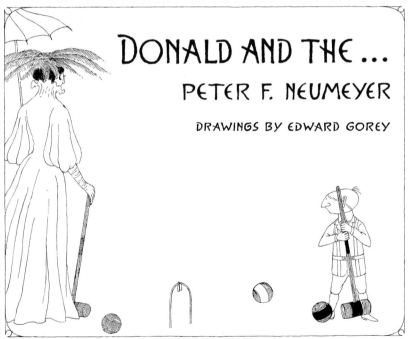

DONALD AND THE ...
PETER F. NEUMEYER

DRAWINGS BY EDWARD GOREY

Sunday maybe Oct. 20

Dear Ted,

Just again thanks for the books. I have spent a while with four more just now and am as impressed as always. Especially interesting was *The Unstrung Harp,* and very curious to see what you were doing so long ago. The croquet on the first page—I'm so glad, it's an omen, that it appears on our first together too. And by the way "studying a game left unfinished at the end of summer" is one of the finest sentences you have written, and most poignant, and . . . well, back to borders, which is not irrelevant, since Mr. Earbrass goes to the other side. I'm just delighted with that book, not because it's a masterpiece, though it has masterly strokes, like the Austenian conversation with Col. Knout (a kind of conversation you seem to have given up in your books), but because it's rich and warm and represents directions which are potential in your writing which you may sometime, when life has taken you there, draw on again, after perhaps a year or so more of the strange syntax in the minuets which you favor now frequently. Those are good—but the suggestion of alternatives—in this instance a rather hearty one for all the nostalgia—is nice.

The Sinking Spell is very good—and I think fittingly produced in its paperback. And the back cover is wonderful, and to my mind presages some of Donald's underground territory. Uncle Ogdred with the chicken egg in an egg cup is nice. (I think without reading into things, I see the most remarkable connections between things you have very expertly executed, and things I have imagined—e.g. the back cover). I keep being amazed by this.

The Gilded Bat—again someone goes who knows where. What a sad little girl, and her good, buff parents—unsuspecting of the intricacies which a delicate spirit can emesh itself in. Especially good the pictures of her in her tedious mundane life. It's a book I greatly admire, though I feel greater instinctive sym/empathy with some others.

Cobweb Castle [by Jan Wahl, illustrated by EG] is a funny thing. The story is in its details really very bad, trivially told—and yet in its entirety it is a good plot—of course, he <u>would</u> imagine that the little old lady in tennis shoes was a witch. I like the way the two on the island write their names back to back. And what an entirely different quality color gives your work—blithe, light, and things stay on the surface. You have surprising talent with big trees and meadows. For that reason—to see again the potential for diversity, and the non rut (that sounds awful) what do I mean—the way you are <u>not</u> really either limited or predetermined—promises much and is exciting to see.

I have been called to help move a large object which is in a room low in the house. After that has been moved I must attend to corners—so more another time.

[perhaps later that day]

As you now know, yes, certainly the upturned beast under the machine turned up. He had no ears, so I didn't know whether to attempt to whistle him upright rightside up, but I thought I shouldn't. He is very beautiful and very yellow.

I am in complete accord with your kite sensations.

The clippership sailor [Bill Adams—see page 69, note 42] was not a great writer, but only—not only, that's cowardly—but a boyhood idol, and a man I corresponded with and whose letters I have kept. I would guess his book would not thrill you (I, myself, haven't re-read it since then—sort of I suppose what happens to Sherwood Anderson or Thomas Wolfe on re-reading, at least with me, might happen). But then, maybe I'll bring along his book, of which I've tried everywhere to get other copies, but which is out of print as all the best things are.

No—you needn't read *Pale Fire* (I have only read sections). It's, as I recall, a mock 18th c. poem, with voluminous fake scholarly footnotes.

The paragraph has the words "Shoulder dislocated" because the inversion fits the ailment better than would normal English word order. (i.e. dislocated shoulder).

* * *

Never heard of Mircea Eliade. Who?

As for *Donald Has an Epic Difficulty*—yes, I'm afraid I was sort of manically serious, not stopping to think what a demand, a selfish demand on my part, that would make of you. I confess, I like it—but your job would not be enviable, and I apologize. Besides—well, actually, I was thinking of your saying once we should do one perhaps in color—and I thought some sort of Russian pigments—made from oatmeal and mosses perhaps—BIGOILY paints, would be appropriate. I don't know. Simmer it. We can talk. I don't know whether I'm serious or not. Largely I must rely on you for help to decide that.

Robin died. It was generous and selfless of you to ask after him. He died at the house of a neighbor who knows much about dinosaurs and is six years old.

Time to go. Be happy   yours,

Peter

21.x.68 Monday night

Dear Peter,

While waiting for the boeuf bourguignon (another leftover, this time from Alice B. Toklas via Connie) to heat up for supper, I start a letter.

How layered or simultaneous or something things are at times. I stopped off at the post office late this afternoon to leave a roll of film and found your letter of Saturday, which started several things going at once: *The Unquiet Grave*

(it somehow seems to have got to be nine o'clock. I am hungry again, but I'm having a gin and tonic instead, and in the meantime I have written down, more or less, where and when 360 (approximately) photographs were taken; where was I? where, indeed)

which goes back more than twenty years for me; your father's book, in the present; the machines on the envelopes which are first gropings towards the drawings for *The Painful Shoulder,* who knows how far in the future [. . .]. These in my head, I headed for Scargo Tower in Dennis [Cape Cod], which you may or may not know; anyway, it is from there that Drusilla is called upon to admire views, this several years ago now, in order to use up the rest of another roll of film on the sunset; on arrival there was such a gale blowing and it was so cold that I kept having to retreat to the car where I read André Schwarz-Bart's *The Last of the Just* in five minute bits until I was warm enough and the clouds had changed sufficiently to warrant another picture. Not to mention various other things that flitted through my head, everything quite clear in itself but having no connection with anything else. I wonder if this observation has any point whatever.

How you always surprise me. After I'd sent Cyril Connolly's *The Unquiet Grave,* I thought, Oh dear, it is not really his cup of tea. I could try and explain why, but I'd only get involved in a terrible muddle that wouldn't at all get across what I meant, so I shan't. Instead, I'll add *Walden* to the pile, since I've been meaning to read it for years, and especially this last summer. Anyway, I'm very pleased (that is <u>not</u> the word I want, but I can't find the one I do) *The Unquiet Grave* appeals to you.

Is there <u>anything</u> you haven't read? This is occasioned by your mention of Sarban;[53] I have a feeling I got rid of his collected works, all three or four of them, after some thought, when I was getting rid of books this last spring. Without wasting a speculation in passing that you could be anything but familiar with Isak Dinesen's brother's—is it Thomas?—*Twilight on the Betzy,* I am now perfectly prepared to discover that *Sir Richard Calmady* by Lucas Malet and *The Heavenly Twins* by Sarah Grand are as familiar to you as your own thumbs (I rather like this comparison,

---

53. Sarban was the pen name of the British writer John William Wall (1910–1989).

which just now occurred to me), and that Anne Thackeray Ritchie has always been one of your favourite authors.

But *is* one familiar with one's thumbs? I mean if one were suddenly confronted with them, detached as it were, would one recognize them? In looking at my own, they do not somehow seem terribly identifiable. Even two blue spots under the skin which I think must be ancient wounds involving pen and ink I only notice because of scrutiny, and presumably they must have been there for years. What an abyss I seem to have opened up at my feet? Are they my feet? They are looking rather red and podgy and boneless, and I would just as soon they weren't mine. It is necessary to go into French. Au secours!

An ingenious idea came to me in the shower. (It is now Tuesday morning.) I do black and white drawings, quite small,* for *Donald Has a Difficulty*'s first version, and The Fantod Press publishes it in an edition of no more than 500 copies. Then it's our full colour epic with a tiny note on the copyright page to the effect that it's a revised second edition. I want you to ponder the ramifications.

Afterthought: perhaps even the silhouette idea, under the circumstances.

Later. After getting your Sunday and Monday letter. One more cup of tea, or possibly two before starting to draw. I have got to finish the opera book. These letters are a terrible self-indulgence. It all comes of having found you to talk to.

* * *

The Unstrung Harp I privately classify as juvenilia (I was twenty-eight at the time); mostly because I dislike the overly eccentric style of the drawing, which I did for years and years and thought I would never get out of, and then I think despite the fact that it was in a sense written to order, though no one told me what to write about, it is somewhat maudlin, by which I suppose I mean personal, even if it is only about being an artist. I suppose it has a certain truth; I remember an agent who didn't want to take me on once said he thought it was the best book on the subject ever written. The whole anecdote is typical.

However I shall henceforth feel much better about it because of the croquet. My mind's eye sees a shelf of Neumeyer/Gorey works. Will Harvard have a room devoted to our memorabilia? It had better.

* * *

To get back to (you didn't know that's where we were, did you?) *Donald Has an Epic Difficulty*. Now I can't seem to get out what I mean; I'll try anon.

Tea time again. If I'm to get this into the mail sometime tonight, perhaps I'd better get on with it. There is a sentence from *The Aunt's Story* by Patrick White which I have always remembered: 'Life is full of alternatives but no choice'. How true! I say to myself every time I think of it (I do the same with Gauguin's 'Life being what it is, one dreams of revenge', but that is somewhat irrelevant here). So, having had no choice in finding myself in a wholly new situation (there's a vague phrase for you), I feel I can at least try to choose the positive alternatives rather than the negative ones.

As for concrete particulars, apart from the unillustrated MSS you have seen, there are nine others, all rather longer, which I'll show you one of these days, not to mention that I can fiddle away at the succeeding volumes of *The Secrets*[54] until my brain gives out, all of which means that I hardly need write anything at all otherwise for the next twenty years before catching up with the drawing involved. All of which means that you are keeping me from nothing at all of consequence because drawing does not present the same problems to me that writing does.

And there's no need for you to feel it is a selfish demand on your part, now or ever, if only because it is on behalf of us (I can't think of a word to identify what we seem to have spontaneously created between us; the temptation to visualize a creepy but lovable monster must be resisted). My only worry is that I won't be able to make not unbearable pictures. Us is much more exciting and worthwhile than anything I might be doing on my own; this is all quite impersonal, although it perhaps doesn't sound it. It is not friendship that makes me think you are somewhat of a genius. And here we are at the bottom of the page, and not a moment too soon.

The envelope seems to be peculiar in some way I can't figure out; perhaps because the ocean appears to be made of sand and molasses? I am sorry that the robin did not live to fly again. I trust your children are more tough-minded than I was at that age, or am now for that matter; it's the kind of thing that reminds me how I think that at bottom life is absolutely unbearable. Enough of that too.

Eliade's field is comparative religion and philosophy and anthropology; most of his books are fairly short and are in paperback in Harper Torchbooks, and then there is a longer one called *Patterns in Comparative Religion,* which is Noonday or somesuch. I can lend you one to try if it at all interests you.

Gordon Cairnie, in case the reference wasn't clear, is The Grolier Book Shop. How have you managed to avoid it all these years?

---

54. EG's *The Other Statue* was published as volume 1 of *The Secrets*. Others conceived for the series were never published.

I trust you will let me know somehow if and when you are coming down, or something. Or if you hear from H_RR_ ST_NT_N. Of course if you want to, you can sleep in the yard in tents, bags, nothing at all, and derive sustenance from chewing on leather boot laces, but wouldn't you perhaps prefer beds and food? A simple warning in time for me to get to the supermarket would suffice, to paraphrase an old Thurber cartoon, I think.

I think I'll go for a brief ride in the car and plunk this in the mail. My spine and brain both are paralyzed from working on the opera book. Tomorrow, goody, I can draw the hero crouched on the floor in as dreary a lunatic asylum as I can think of. At least there won't be any wallpaper to draw. Wallpaper is my bête noir. I put aside *The Hapless Child* after about three drawings for several years because I couldn't face the notion of drawing any more wallpaper.

If you don't understand most of this letter, you may ask questions.

Ted.

[verso]

We often imagine we are being educated, while we are only being amused.

Samuel Smiles [*Dr. Smiles's Works on Self-Help*]

30.x.68, Wednesday evening

Dear Peter,

A few things enclosed, among them the versions of the Bede I have.[55]

I have been feeling rather doom-and-gloom the past few days, so perhaps some of it may creep into this.

I'm slogging my way through the last drawings for the opera book, which should be done by sometime next week. Several days of pure awful blank will then ensue, they always do. I then thought of amusing myself for a day or two working on *Why We Have Day and Night*. So if I get to the Lear,[56] etc. at all it will have to be the week between the 11th and the 15th. Whatever day <u>during</u> the <u>day</u> is good for you is okay by me at this point. I won't come to dinner, stay over, etc; I have intruded on your time much too much already.

As for your invitation for Christmas, I am very touched by it, but I won't take you up on it.

If you actually do have lunch with Harry on Monday, if indeed that is when it was to be, try and prod him (a) about a blueprint of *Donald and the . . .* and (b) contracts for *Donald Goes Away*.

I'm sounding quite insufferable; I think I'll stop.

11:15

Not exactly evening either. I took myself off, as a Cultural Duty, to see Olivier's film of *Othello*. [. . .] Somehow the play came across as being terribly silly, perhaps because Mr Olivier chose to paint himself blue-black, stain the inside of his mouth a flaming red, and to play it more and more like a calypso number as the evening wore on.

On the way home I absently minded (you know what I mean) went through a stop sign in Hyannis so of course there was a police car to apprehend me. A soft answer turnethed away wrath, fortunately.

* * *

Several questions before I forget entirely. It may be too late. I mean I had them written down on something and now I can't find it. Hm. One was about William Morris. What am I supposed to be reading? I picked up a Pelican of *Selected Writings and Designs* (lots of wallpaper) but in the front it says his collected works are in twenty-four volumes; surely not all . . . of . . . them . . . ? And which translations

---

55. EG and I had been talking about the Venerable Bede's *Ecclesiastical History*, "The Conversion of Edwin," which I had translated for him from the ninth-century Old English.
56. Edward Lear's *The Dong with a Luminous Nose*, a sequel to his book *The Jumblies*. EG illustrated both.

of Rilke? There seems to be a collected in two volumes published by Hogarth, but the poetry volume is [translated] by Leishman, which I gather you did not think particularly good, or rather who, etc. I picked up the *Duino Elegies* translated by someone named MacIntyre, but I haven't looked into it yet.

* * *

Thursday, pre-breakfast

Two other things I wanted to ask: Chekhov (<u>no</u> way of spelling his name looks right to me): whose translations? Are we all still feeling nasty to Constance Garnett? And Montaigne: ditto? The Florio (the name comes to me out of absolutely nowhere so it may very well be inexplicable in this context) translation, or is there some superior new one?[57]

Have you done any more thinking about Lionel making decoys? Not to press; it's only that decoys run through my head. There may even have been one on the envelope. A metaphysical sentence.

How would you feel if we had to publish our books for adults rather than children? I foresee our having the same trouble that I do on my own, but maybe not.

I expect (my chicken egg intervened)—now I don't know what I expected. Non-metaphysical sentence.

Ted

---

57. The Florio translation of Montaigne would have been from the seventeenth century.

4.xi.68

Dear Peter,

This will be one of those installment-type things, and very scrappy I expect. 'Say not the struggle naught availeth', whoever did, for I am on the next to last drawing for the opera book, but it <u>has</u> been a struggle, and last week was so to speak knee-deep in mud.

I did feel I wanted to clarify what I meant about our stories right off the bat however. Your paragraph on the subject is unanswerable because I don't quite follow it. All I meant was that my own experience has been that although at least half of my own books have been written, albeit vaguely, for children, only with *The Wuggly Ump* did I actually get one published as such, publishers being very stupid if you ask me on the whole. Perhaps I am being alarmist without any necessity, but it occurred to me that we might run into the same difficulty, and that everyone would start telling us Donald, Lionel, et al were really for adults and want to publish them as such, and I wondered how you felt about that. In the long run I don't think it matters, because children eventually find what is for them, as I think in some slight way my books have, at least with children of the people who have bought the books for themselves, but with labels being pasted on everything in such profusion these days until you can hardly see what is underneath them, if any, it gives one pause. I should be inclined to fight for them as children's books, at least for a while (how's that for prepared backsliding?), but it is really up to you. [. . .] *Why We Have Day and Night* is no problem, and anything else in that same untroubled vein. It is the 'images of the evening' (a phrase I came across in Dorothy Wordsworth last night) that editors and such are going to feel are not for their tiny readers. (I went through the Children's book section of the *Times* yesterday, growing more and more annoyed and gloomy; I could find maybe five books, and those by authors I was already familiar with that sounded even worth looking into, and as usual most of the artists on the ten best list are the sort that drive me up the wall. (Incidentally, should you ever wish to add a note of extreme acerbity—a word I have never to my knowledge used before—to a conversation of ours just say watermelon pickle; I think we could have a real knockdowndragout on the subject.))[58] What are all these (())?

* * *

---

58. EG was referring to Stephen Dunning's groundbreaking children's poetry anthology, *Reflections on a Gift of Watermelon Pickle . . . and Other Modern Verse* (Scott, Foresman, 1966).

I enjoyed the Elizabeth Goudge book[59] very much, though I could have done without the descriptions of the Good People, but then I can always do without descriptions of the Good People; some things are better left to the imagination, and that I've always felt was one of them. And the whole thing was a bit too optimistic perhaps? I suppose the best books of all somehow manage not to falsify things, do not tell plain little girls that they will suddenly become pretty and so on. Still, it was what I think of as a good, cosy read. While doing so, various other books came to mind. Do you know *Moonfleet* by J. Meade Falkner? A very good period story of smuggling for boys; I can't guess whether Zack is old enough for it or not. (He also wrote two other novels, *The Lost Stradivarius* and *The Nebuly Coat,* neither of which I can remember a thing about, although I am terribly fond of them and reread them every ten years or so.) John Masefield's *The Midnight Folk* and *The Box of Delights*? Having only read these after I was long grown up, I have no idea of what age children like them; they are rather special in any case.

While I'm on children's books, do you and/or Helen know the Paddington books (he's a small bear from Peru) by Michael Bond? One of them is now out in a Dell paperback series for children. He ought to be good for reading aloud I think. Do you know James Reeves at all? He's done a splendid anthology for children, poetry, called I think *A Golden Land;* also various writing on poetry, etc. and several books of verse of his own for children: *The Blackbird in the Lilac, Prefabulous Animiles* (sic).

* * *

A possible favour, as if you had nothing else to do. If you are in Widener [Harvard University library] for some reason or other sometime, could you see if they have a copy of *What a Life!* by E. V. Lucas and George Morrow, Methuen, 1911, and if it can be taken out and if you think it could be Xeroxed (I have no idea how long it is), let me know. It is one of the grand frustrations of my existence that I have never even seen a copy of it.[60]

Thank you for the "Transfiguring Vision" article.[61] I hope it's good for my character that you make me feel as if my mind (by comparison) is a Peculiarly Insensitive Lump.

---

59. British writer, 1900–1984. I don't recall which book EG referred to here.
60. E. V. Lucas and George Morrow, *What a Life!,* first published in 1911 and well reproduced by Dover Publications in 1975, is a delightful nonsense book purporting to be a biography composed of catalog illustrations from a contemporary British department store. The book is charming, and stylistically it very much prefigures the tone of Edward Gorey. It's of interest that EG had not been familiar with it.
61. An article I wrote on Thomas Hardy, published in *Victorian Poetry* 3, no. 4 (Autumn 1965): 263–266.

Well, the last drawing is finished (tomorrow I have to letter the text: ugh) and a sort of dismal euphoria has set in. I mean at least it's done, though what is another matter. I carefully looked at the pictures and read the text, but only pure bafflement was the result. Since I never intend to look at the thing again, perhaps I shall never know what it is about. This is known as a Small Loss. Do you think it is too late for me to devote my life to something to do with String?[62]

I just drove down to Chatham and back to unfog my head, not that I particularly succeeded, but at least it was a change from my drawing board.

On the way back I was trying to think what to say, if anything, about Stony Brook and all, and I decided that I hope you feel you can afford to go to Washington because it is what you want.[63] Which I feel is mildly noble of me. It wouldn't be if we had known each other for years and years, but our friendship is so new that I can't really believe in it yet, and I have a strong sinking feeling at the thought of you being at the other end of the country. And so to bed.

9:30, only now it's Tuesday night

Well, the stupid thing is all finished, and packed up for the publisher. I feel very brave to have been lettering since dawn. I don't know which I loathe more, lettering, or reading my own work, and when the two of necessity have to be combined . . . I do not think it is going to be one of your favourite works of mine, but people who go to opera are very strange, and it may send them into convulsions. So here I am, mind gone, amid a litter of unfolded sheets, unpacked cat food, and a pair of sneakers I bought today from which the 'Keds' have been sandpapered off the little blue rectangles on the heels; this seems very mysterious.

* * *

The care package arrived this morning, for which my usual thanks. I don't know James Dickey at all, though in paging through one of them briefly I came across 'The Heaven of Animals' which I remember being moved by in *The New Yorker*.

Before I drivel off into whatever I'm about to drivel off into, if any, is the 14th, Thursday, still free? If you don't head me off, I'll come up that morning, D.V. Your admonition in capital letters noted; you are right as usual/always. One (me) sometimes gets quarrelsome in a vacuum, if that explains anything.

---

62. This thought materialized later in *Donald Has a Difficulty*, in which Donald thinks of "Strings" while having his splinter removed.
63. I was job hunting at the time, and the two main choices were in Stony Brook, New York, and in the state of Washington. I was emotionally inclined toward Washington, but New York was more practical and obviously would have allowed me to work more closely with Ted.

Also please thank Helen for her nice letter, Zack for his no longer mysterious message, and Chris and Danny for their spirited drawings.

As a matter of fact, I don't think I'll drivel off into anything. If I am going to get something on the envelope and this into the mail tonight, I had better get to the integument, if that is the word I want.

Before I forget, and I am only asking, do you think possibly *Donald Goes Away* is misleading as a title?

Ted (I think)

[excerpt from undated letter]

Thursday, somehow

[EG to PN]

From Spokane Public Schools Library booklist, Winter Supplement 1968–69, printed in its entirety:

> *The Jumblies,* written in verse form, is rather weird and the illustrations do not help any to change one's opinion. There is not much sense to the verses and the vocabulary includes some rather hard words. The frequent repetition of 'going to sea in a sieve, having green heads and blue hands' leaves one with a cold feeling. Examine before ordering.

Are you sure you want to end up in Washington?

Tuesday AM [November 5, 1968]

Dear Ted,

A hurried note before I go to work. Had lunch with Harry yesterday, and he will be writing you a letter that, I trust, will represent the gist of our conversation accurately. In sum—he balked at *Donald Goes Away* as it stands now, finding with it—for his children's books purposes—the same fault he finds with my others: they take you up, and then they leave you there. He feels children will not like that, and that *Donald and the . . .* is not like this at all and does come 'round. I'm obliged to say, I agree with him. That is not to say I can change stories—maybe I can, maybe I can't—but I do agree 1) *Donald and the . . .* differs from the later ones in this regard, and 2) Children might well feel like Harry says they will. I also think it reasonable for Harry to say that he is concerned that he has specifically children's books. This leads to the question I have asked before when I asked how librarians classify your books, and which you asked in your last letter—are ours really books for children. Harry wanted changing around on *Donald Goes Away*—and I just didn't like his ideas at all (finding arrow heads, etc.). Zack thought of finding a dinosaur egg—but something similar already exists in a children's book. Then I clarified something for all of us, I feel. I said to Harry, "Look, I think the inconclusiveness characterizes all the Gorey/Neumeyer books, and that they are not directly children's books—except *Donald and the . . .* Why don't Ted and I have the liberty of these other stories: I will either rewrite one for your criteria, or I will write another Donald of the *Donald Before the Fall* kind. The other books then, possibly with the hero (when Donald) renamed, will be Ted's and mine to take elsewhere, where Ted's sort of books perhaps are the purpose." Harry seemed pleased that I stated it for him—and I must say, I do understand, and I feel no particular feeling about the matter—unless it's some concern that you may be displeased. But I would be pleased if you granted that Harry ought to have a happy, healthy Donald—and the others can spin their precarious webs in other aethers. Which reminds me—Harry is delighted with *Lionel Does Science*—thinks it's the best, and in fact has a good idea for it—ending it with a final picture with the animals actually sitting around chuckling. I think that's first rate, since it even heightens the ambiguity—since, for those who have eyes to see, it is very sinister, doubly so for the fact that they will see that actually most people will NOT have eyes to see. By the way, Harry says the animals, the various ones Lionel picks up, might be depicted sort of hounded, hunted, nervous, anxious, etc., as animals may be in their lives, to make the soothing elixir more a point.

I've got to get to the office. Don't be angry. I think it all is ok. We can more freely do the other books (if you want) if we don't pretend they're what they are not. And I do have a couple of ideas for rewritten *Donald Goes Away,* one of which might please you and Harry. And if not, perhaps *Lionel Does Science,* and if not, I'll do something new. See you—we insist—soon.

yours,
Peter

later: Obviously—since writing the above
    I've tried a few more versions of Donald Goes Away—under new title.

7.xi.68, Thursday morning

Dear Peter,

I am not lying on the kitchen floor drumming my heels on the linoleum, but I should like to be. I am angry. I am enraged. I want to beat Harry Stanton about the head with a pewter mug. In an admitted state of frustration and incoherence, I shall start to splutter. Please, let's not try and make *Donald Goes Away* suitable for Harry; I love it so much the way it is. I got the old Housman chill up the spine when I first read it on the floor of Harry's office, and again when you thought of the insects in the pipe, and that is the way I want it to be. I'll fight. (Not that I don't think the new versions aren't rather grand, though surely large captive birds under beds are a little much even for me, and I howled over the various plaques, but couldn't we use them in something else?) I'm also at this point not prepared to see Donald split into two people, one for children and someone else for adults. Donald and his whole ambiance are very real to me. I don't know how much of a problem it would be to have him published for children by AW and for adults by someone else. In any case it doesn't arise as yet. I am trying not to feel as if somehow I had got you into this mess, if only because it's the same one I have been in ever since I began publishing. (A beautiful cock pheasant is stalking about our side yard; poor thing, I expect someone will shoot it presently, and I should not be terribly surprised if it were right in our yard, since people seem to shoot wherever they feel like these days; you can see what kind of mood I'm in.) Here we are, neither of us young, starting out, you for the first time, me for the second, and the prospect of all the nonsense about this not being a story, a book, whatever, and that it's not for children, or even people, causes me to meditate on futility. Also I could well have done without all this being thrown at me this morning, because I finally figured out how to do *Why We Have Day and Night* (I expect you'll loathe it, and say it is all wrong—I don't really mean that, but if you <u>do</u> feel that my 47¼% contribution is a bit much, I expect you to tell me so. I may be tiresomely difficult about myself, but I hope I'm impersonal about my work, I mean ours, which is another entity) and since I do not really know what I am blathering on about, I think I shall go out and buy some black paper and white ink and begin work on a dummy for WWHDAN.

Anon

Reading Marcus Aurelius, whom I am about to thrust on you, as I have been doing, has not noticeably affected my thoughts, more's the pity. I am still Seriously Annoyed. However. Working on WWHDAN has produced a rather curious family, all of them unprepossessing-looking and practically sexless. There is a boy of perhaps eight or nine, a girl a year or so younger, and twins just out of infancy who seem to have no sex at all. There is also an orange cat and a stuffed animal. Everyone wears black stockings, well, not the cat or the animal, and I think everyone is going to have to have curious and archaic names, and I think the dialogue needs some recasting in the Donald vein. Perhaps you will want to beat me about the head with a pewter mug? They're who're on the envelope I just decided (to put them there I mean).

So I might as well put this in the envelope, and it in the mail, as my mind refuses to function any further at the moment.

Ted.

Why We Have Day and Night

1 Title page

2 Copyright

3 For goodness sake!

4 It's all dark! Ouch. Oh.

5 Can you see anything? What happened to the light?

6 Here. Take my hand. Mom, do you know what happened to the light?

7 Tommy, you know. Do you know, Tommy?

8 Could a squirrel have chewed a wire?

9 Did the ink spill?

10 Did our eyes burst?

11 Did the curtain drop?

12 Are we still asleep?

13 Are we in a cyclone?

14 Is the world finished?

15 Are we bats?

16 Are we snails?

17 I know, we're underwater.

18 Aren't we born yet?

19 It's pitch BLACK.

20 Why is everything black? Dan, do YOU know?

20 Sure, I know why everything is dark. It's a long story. Why is it dark?

21 Tell us! Tell us! Tell us!

22 Remember when I asked Dad why the sun goes down?

23 He said 'It just looks like it goes down.' But really the sun does not go down.

24 'What really happens is that the earth turns round,' he said. He turned on a flashlight and you held an orange—just like this.

24 'Pretend you are a bug,' he said.

25 'And you are on the orange.'

26 'Now I spin the orange just the way the earth spins. Now you see how the light shines on a different part of our earth all the time. First the bug is in the light-See!-and now he is in the dark.

29 But why is it dark all over now? Because this little bug on the spinning orange got hungrier and hungrier. The hungrier he got, the more he would spin. And the more he would spin the hungrier he got.

31 And finally he got so hungry that he ate right through the outside and and into the middle, and he crawled deep down inside and it was all and

32 all, all....

[undated, November 1968]

Dear Ted:

Regarding the Donald revisions: fact #1 is that what I once said, and you may not have heard or believed, is absolutely true—I have not the slightest perspective or judgment about the merits of the various Donalds or Lionels (in contrast to my poems, where I can certainly tell the worst from the best). Thus, what must look to you like incredible wishy-washiness is, in fact, attributable only to this blindness, and the unsureness that comes from it.

Speaking practically, what does one do. I suppose least offense is given anyone if I simply offer to do another Donald. You see, part of the difficulty, and I don't want to go into it all now—is that I agree with Harry to the extent that the children do, that a simple bucolic tale coming to an end pleases them better. But which is the better story, I don't know. I want to support you against Harry in this, but (and I don't even know if Harry likes the new versions) I can't really, because what little feeling I have about it all is that, for Harry's purposes, Harry may be right.

I JUST DON'T KNOW. WHAT CAN I DO TO MAKE THOSE HAPPY WHO ARE UNHAPPY?

I can't tell you how pleased I am that you are doing Day and Night. I didn't, till the wonderful envelope came, really have any real idea whether it really (a hell of a sentence) appealed.

See you long before this gets to you undoubtedly—so farewell.

10.xi.68, Sunday morning

Dear Peter,

'Let us then be up and doing, etc' he remarked to himself, leaping from bed
at five-thirty, and pausing only to heat the teakettle, he then addressed himself to
rewriting the ending of *Why We Have Day and Night;* that done, he typed this—
what a vast long letter of answers to your last three or four, not to mention various
whatnots, I owe you—and now it's up to the drawing board to try and do a few more
pages of WWHDAN before you all turn up (hopefully).

As I tottered off to bed last night I kept wondering why I said it would be helpful
if you could spare me an hour today, until somewhere along the line it came to me
that unless we get the rewriting done, I won't have a finshed dummy to show you on
Wednesday. It is often a relief to find out why one has said something. Sometimes
not, of course.

Alas, for Sunday. All I can get on the radio are inspirational messages interspersed
with hymns.

9:10 P.M.

A really superb gale is raging around the house. Having just come back from
seeing one of my favourite old Walt Disney movies, *The Parent Trap,* I feel I had
better start typing away on the long letter I owe you for as long as I can hold up
before sinking comatose to the floor. I won't start answering the several of yours I
haven't until tomorrow when I trust my brain is in better working order, but I might
as well blather on for a while; perhaps there will even be a stray thought here and
there; perhaps . . .

After you all left and I had managed to eat something, I drove down to the
coast guard beach to see what the wild waves were saying. Their utterance was most
impressive. The tide was high and they were chewing away at the fences and the
cliffs, and I've never seen quite so much surf there before. Stupidly I forgot to take
along the camera.

I might as well admit right now, since it is on my mind, that I have had my last
talk session with Harry if I can do anything to prevent it; if anything resulted from
all the muddle, irrelevance, and confusion I always end up with—yes, I know I am
not being fair—I might not mind so much, but nothing seems to, at least nothing
that would not result without it. I'm sure he really does want us to do another
book as soon as possible, and I want to do it, but I am absolutely going to have no
conversation with anybody but you about it, and then on a one to one (if that is the
current loathsome phrase) basis. My tendencies to feeling rejected were certainly
not helped by being invited to dinner at the hour I was on Saturday, but since

Harry's world is not mine, I am as it were only impersonally depressed really by the various invitations which do not materialize and the chronic lateness involved in any appointment that actually gets made. I know this sounds positively paranoid, but then, I really did not enjoy the weekend, all things considered, and could have done without it, really because I feel I have been stupid again about WWHDAN. Nor did I mean to throw the amount of time I had spent on it in your face which was quite inexcusable, especially since it was a perfectly meaningless remark as far as anything I would ever feel and was only made because I was feeling so baffled in about thirteen directions, and my mouth was open at the time. Some minutes of staring into space have gone by, and I have figured out WWHDAN to my satisfaction, and when I am feeling stronger, I shall look over the dummy and see if there is anything salvageable from it, but I now have logical reasons, instead of merely intuitive ones, which are the ones I believe in, I could trot out for your not trying to rewrite it.

I <u>did</u> take in what you said about being no judge of your own work, and after today I <u>do</u> believe it whole-heartedly, which I didn't quite before (there's for you), all of which doesn't really matter, as long as you stick by what you've done, which you do in a way particularly your own, so I am not worried about what is still useful of mine for WWHDAN, as sooner or later you will tell me.

I am also suffering at the moment from double vision, i.e., how you are in your letters and how you are yourself, and while I still know the former better the latter is just at the moment sufficiently familiar to blur everything.

What a struggle everything seems to have become for me of late, but then I suppose therein lies the point, however much I loathe it all. Even as I pot away at this, I am busy trying things out for WWHDAN in my head. The children I think should be eating oranges throughout in the present, another turn of the screw so to speak. Do you see what I mean (I'm not at all sure that I do) when I possibly suggest that 'Remember when I asked Father why the sun goes down, etc.' to 'Remember I told you I asked Father, etc.' by which I guess I mean that it came to me while I was staring into space a while back that the really sinister thing about the story was not the explanation, which is pretty sinister, heaven knows, but the real and the presumed source of the explanation. Perhaps even the cat constantly trying to filch the stuffed whatsit fits in with this, at least emotionally if not rationally.

This may not be making much sense, but it is making me feel more in touch again and less uncomfortable about things. I am really about to fall apart. Goodnight, or something.

Monday morning

I woke up feeling rather more cheerful, but somehow I am depressed again. However, I shall try and put down the various things I was mulling over when I woke up. Yes, what were they?

One was that WWHDAN simply should not be changed, whatever its ultimate fate. It is really vintage (to coin a term of approbation) Neumeyer, possibly the strangest and most intricate of the lot, and the most difficult to see what it's about. I know you said you thought it was just a simple little story, but I can't agree. In parentheses, how odd it is that we so seldom draw the same conclusions about ourselves and about others, or even think of making comparisons, or maybe it's just me. This was occasioned by my thinking 'But how could Peter not see what WWHDAN is about (apart from the idea around which he built the story)?' This is a simplification, but what a lot of more subtle questions boil down to finally. And it was a long time before the thought occurred to me that I haven't the faintest idea what any of my books are really about. And so forth.

Anyhoo, I feel my drawings are not the catastrophe I was envisioning yesterday afternoon, and after I have made the changes you want and the ones I want, there will still be a lot of it left, and by making the drawings somewhat more sophisticated—the word should be in quotes—it can be made more ostensibly adult and we can take it elsewhere, though I do not think all the things that bother Harry will bother many children in the least. I had, I think, a dream inspiration for the stuffed toy—it may very well have turned into something else—a mandrake root wearing lederhosen (spelling?) and embroidered braces for example—but I can't recollect it at the moment.

The outburst of petulance and hostility on page 2 I hope you realize not directed at Harry, who I am terribly fond of, but only at the ambiance or whatever that surrounds him whenever I happen to see him. Of course the chief source of annoyance, and it is always one with me and I should, and usually do, avoid the occasions when it is going to happen, was that of seeing someone, who when they are around is the only person one wants to talk to nonstop, only in a group who consequently drives one up the wall. I could rewrite this sentence, but why bother? Even you, I'm afraid, would have come galloping around to ask what was the matter if I had said in a letter last week that I didn't want to see you all last weekend, which wouldn't have been true in any case really, but, but . . . and then if I had said that and you hadn't come galloping around, I should have been even more annoyed . . . there are times you can't do anything about anything. I fear my behaviour is never graceful about same.

I should be answering your letters, but the kitchen table is such a shambles. Gee. I mean the said letters are strewn about.

An only too apropos quotation: 'Now there's talking,' Rat said. 'A lot of persons talks, and what good does it do? I ask you, what, and echo answers where.' (John Masefield's *The Midnight Folk*)

Addenda to WWHDAN: Why has no one remarked that ostensibly the title has nothing to do with the book whatever? Perhaps because it is the perfect title, and that is the sort of thing that does not get questioned, however peculiar it may seem. No one would have questioned the ending if any of us had got it (I don't think Harry has yet; perhaps I am wrong, but he is I think <u>dismissing</u> it by labeling it as a metaphysical idea), but then that is not your fault.

(Coping with the shambles) *Donald Rewarded* I & II. My favourite plaque I think, though they are all great, is PAINTERS COME BACK AT TWO. I like the atmosphere of cosiness it presupposes at the centre of the earth.[64] Did Harry say anything about either of the two new versions? What did Harry and you talk about in connection with the stories, or was it all more of the same like when you were over here?

Version I: the wings really are haunting, now that I have been disabused of them being attached to a bird. Mythic. Not difficult to draw perhaps, but to convey the grandeur . . . (I am now musing) I wonder if, knowing your penchant for coming up with new ideas all the time, perhaps we couldn't do one book with a whole series of alternate endings? If, say, one did all the endings so far for *Donald Goes Away/Rewarded,* would the drawings that lead up to the parting of the ways to the various ends have the proper tone for each ending that succeeds them, if you follow me? I guess the tone of my drawings is usually so ambiguous that the answer is probably yes, even if the endings diverged more widely than the *Donald Goes Away/Rewarded* ones do.

What gave me this thought was a sudden recollection of a Paul Dehn poem ["Alternative Endings to an Unwritten Ballad"] I have always liked. [. . .]

I don't seem to be answering your letters, do I? They are here somewhere, treasured possessions.

The hunt has now produced Harry's folder of your stories which he seems to have left behind. Never one to mind my own business, I have rummaged through it for comments and such. There aren't many; various curious underlinings. There is a note from possibly someone with the initials M.N.?K. It begins: 'The string on the balloon which I used to feel reassuringly tugging me back to earth when I read Peter's work seems to have busted; I'm airborne and afraid, in a world I never made.' It goes on to

---

64. In the book we were planning, to be titled either *Donald Goes Away* or *Donald Rewarded,* Donald would go down a hole to the center of the earth. EG and I discussed at length what Donald would find there, and the answers ranged from a heap of wings (bird or insect?) to a series of signs or placards, one of which would read "Painters Come Back at Two."

a thoroughly banal idea of how to change *Donald Goes Away*. In case you have not got there yet, a thought from *The Unquiet Grave:* 'Birthday resolution: From now on specialize; never again make any concession to the ninety-nine percent of you which is like everybody else at the expense of the one percent which is unique. Never listen to the False Self talking.'

1:30

I went out three hours ago to walk up to Harry's with your MSS and have been there ever since, having found him at the end of breakfast, and have now had about seven cups of coffee and thus achieved a fine case of the incipient shakes. Perhaps lunch will counteract the effect. He is a very nice man; I hope that by the end of Thursday we shall have a nice simple story for him, so he will give us contracts, etc.

I had a thought as I was walking up there that I don't know what to do with: you know far more about me than anyone else in the world.

The attic produced a copy of another Favourite Book for you; it becomes increasingly obvious why I kept acquiring extra copies of them through the years. It is mere happenstance that you seem to be getting them all at once, and after all, a small bit of a shelf of books is not much to have to show for years and years of friendship, so just shut up on the subject. Please. I feel I should be polite to you, whatever happens.

4:40

I shall expect you to be even more charming and amusing on Wednesday than is your usual wont because I have just turned down an invitation to attend the Barnstable Comedy Club's dress rehearsal of *The Madwoman of Chaillot* Wednesday night. I've just been down to the coast guard beach again where the wild waves were saying less than yesterday though the cloud effects were grandiose. This time I took the camera, although the roll of film in it may have already been used once, in which case . . . I'm developing a tree obsession, especially for the ones in the red maple swamp by Nauset Marsh; I could quite easily spend months in there photographing them.

Why am I not answering your letters. Probably because it is a moral duty at this point.

The thing is I want you to have got this, at least by Thursday, so I should really get it in the mail tonight, and I am being drawn to see *Barbarella* a second time, or at least the possibility has suggested itself, and I can't obviously do both, or I'll be up all night.

The first letter that comes to hand from a Tuesday AM, a week ago tomorrow, fortunately needs no comment except to reiterate that of course I want us to do a simple Donald for Harry and that I was only displeased when I was by Life and not any of its various components in the shape of you, Harry, etc.

[. . .] The Cezanne book[65] told me a great deal more than I have ever got from any other source on Cezanne, not that I have ever read that much about him but I can't help having not read some; he's one of those painters who I have ever so slowly become more and more impressed by over the long years, though I still can't quite take him to my heart, but then perhaps he simply isn't a painter anyone can do so with.

At the risk of I'm not quite sure what, I should like to quietly remark that those who type sentences in capital letters that read WHAT CAN I DO TO MAKE THOSE HAPPY WHO ARE UNHAPPY? is not going to be happy himself very much longer.

Your letter of October 29th has long since been dealt with.

* * *

I hope you are not sending out these bits of new Lionels etc. without keeping track of them, preferably on teeny bits of paper which you keep in an old sock that never leaves your jacket pocket.

Thank heavens I don't have to feel queasy on the subject of watermelon pickle any longer.

I've begun the new Paddington, who I find as amusing as ever, but there's no reason why you should that I can think of. I tried to pretend I liked the Moomintroll books [by Tove Jansson] once, but had to give up, partly on account of the drawings I think.

* * *

The radio says another gale is coming in half an hour.

With the second appearance of the beast on the envelope I come to the conclusion that it is a STOEJGNPF, unless you can think of a better arrangement of the letters.[66]

I was rather surprised by the enclosed thing on Hesse which perhaps you haven't seen, not that I had the faintest idea who the college bunch <u>was</u> reading. So far I much prefer *Siddhartha* and *Knulp*—incidentally I think your translation is still the best of the four I have read, and Harry said he thought it was only because they had

---

65. I had given EG my father's book *Cézanne: Drawings* (T. Yoseloff, 1958).
66. The beast debuted on EG's November 6, 1968, envelope; see page 92. EG was using all of our initials: Edward St. John Gorey Peter Florian Olivier Neumeyer.

committed themselves elsewhere that FS&G [Farrar, Straus & Giroux] hadn't taken it—to *Demian* and *Steppenwolf.* The former I thought was great up to a point but then totally fell to bits with the Mother Eve thing at the end and the introduction of the war; *Steppenwolf* as a novel seems terribly silly to me, though otherwise one can't help but be caught up by all this soul-thrashing and philosophizing and finding oneself saying How True! and This Is Me! all over the place even if sober thought says Not Really. I can quite see, being in somewhat the same state again, how the young find it all such a 'gut' experience. Where is our language going?

I feel I have now achieved a letter of respectable size if not content and that I can stop and draw the envelope and put it in the mail and eat and go and see *Barbarella* again.

Will this reach you before I do?

Will it even fit in one envelope? I'll test. Just.

Ted.

* * *

reason, if you asked him, he could supply you with same. From my point of view, it will be nicer to have folded and gathered sheets as we say rather than blueprints to show Candida etc as the latter always have a rather tacky look to anyone not used to them. Whee! *May this inspire you to its companion piece.*

I was going to abandon an idea for a story I vaguely mentioned to you but it began to shape itself in my head this morning before I got up, so I fear I suppose I had better write it down. If it gets sufficiently down on paper to send along with this, I shall. If so, do be as harsh on it as you think you can, because I suspect it's a piece of inept mush, even before it's written. As 'We are having inept mush for breakfast, so perhaps you will want to open another jar of strawberry jam.'

An excessive number of something/s I may have mentioned in passing are on their way under separate cover. Their mad unsuitability for anything now may be a recommendation. The particular blue which is known as process because that is the blue you use for reproducing full colour was not my idea; I said a sort of ice-like blue green. Howsomever. *Perhaps you*
can start a neighbourhood great books co u r se.

Please thank Zack for giving up his room to me.

I knew there was something I was going to do this afternoon, and now I know what it was. This is known as giving one's letters a sense of immediacy.
                last line
The curious quality of the/handwriting, and spacing, above is due to the fact that I wrote it while this is still in the typewriter.

Space Needs Pressing

I was beginning to wonder if anyone else was ever going to notice how rumpled it was getting.

15.xi.68, Friday noon

Dear Peter,

Apart from 'thank you' in the most comprehensive way imaginable, I happily and comfortably feel there is nothing I feel I either have to or ought to say, which is your doing, not mine, not that it matters.

The house did not burn down in my absence. (I always feel the house has burnt down in my absence.)

Tomorrow I have decided to pull myself together and make preparations for my return to New York. Perhaps I shall have a little nap and then make the revisions on WWHDAN today. Tonight I can go and find out about the Boston Strangler on the silver screen, provided there is nothing else at the movies that would be more amusing, and I should think almost anything would be.

Helen mentioned the idea of a Donald bookplate for the boys for Christmas. Do you have any more specific ideas on the subject, or does she? We spoke about it only briefly. And what if any text to be incorporated (e.g., This Book Has Been Stolen From)? Discuss, at length, if necessary, and give me a reply soon, and I will send a sketch, and you will send it back, and I will take it to a printer (let it be my contribution to your Christmas cheer), and then it will no doubt be the middle of June when it comes back all done. I hope not, but if you have thoughts, send them to NY at once. And how many?

My semi-nap was interrupted by a call from Will Winslow. He said, I think, they were printing you know what next week, which means there will be press sheets as soon as that is done. Will said he thought they would be trimmed and folded—in other words the finished book except loose and no binding—and I asked him to send you some; however, I'm sure if you wanted any of the sheets unfolded and uncut for some mystic reason, if you asked him, he could supply you with same. From my point of view, it will be nicer to have folded and gathered sheets as we say rather than blueprints to show Candida etc as the latter always have a rather tacky look to anyone not used to them. Whee! *May this inspire you to its companion piece.*

I was going to abandon an idea for a story I vaguely mentioned to you but it began to shape itself in my head this morning before I got up, so I fear I suppose I had better write it down. If it gets sufficiently down on paper to send along with this, I shall. If so, do be as harsh on it as you think you can, because I suspect it is a piece of inept mush, even before it's written. As 'We are having inept mush for breakfast, so perhaps you will want to open another jar of strawberry jam.'

An excessive number of something/s I may have mentioned in passing are on their way under separate cover. Their mad unsuitability for anything <u>now</u> may be a recommendation. The particular blue which is known as process because that is the blue you use for reproducing full colour was <u>not</u> my idea; I said a sort of ice-like blue green. Howsomever. [. . .]

Please thank Zack for giving up his room to me.

I knew there was something I was going to do this afternoon, and now I know what it was. This is known as giving one's letters a sense of immediacy.

The curious quality of the last line handwriting, and spacing, above is due to the fact that I wrote it while this is still <u>in</u> the typewriter.

[clipping from newspaper]
SPACE NEEDS PRESSING

I was beginning to wonder if anyone else was <u>ever</u> going to notice how rumpled it was getting.

You will be spared the story with this. It is written, but far too long, and I don't see how to start cutting it at present.

A thought for today: 'Everything imagined is reality. The mind cannot conceive unreal things.'

David Smith, the sculptor

* * *

I picked up Jonathan Kozol's *Death at an Early Age* (what was the name of the one you said was better? Why does the number 36 come to mind?)[67] and *Selections from the Writings of Kierkegaard* in Hyannis this afternoon. (I can waste time better than any living human I decided.) Why I should feel at long last some sort of assault on Kierkegaard is in order I do not know.

Looking about the kitchen at the appalling amount of cultural debris that is going to have to be dealt with very soon indeed I am now going to hide in the bathtub.

You may get the story after all. (Quel suspense!) The bathtub proved fruitful. No, things did <u>not</u> come up through the drains.

9:30

The Boston Strangler was of an unbelievable tedium. At such times I feel perhaps I was wrong not to become a drug- instead of a film-addict. I shall now do what I might better have done earlier in the evening: retire to the sofa with a drink, Mozart, and a miscellaneous assortment of essays I suddenly find myself in possession of.

---

67. EG was trying to remember Herb Kohl's *36 Children* (New American Library, 1967).

11:07

Because I have had a shade too much dubonnet you are, at least temporarily, being spared a long diatribe. [EG originally typed this sentence: "Because I have had a shade too much diatribe you are, at least temporarily, being spared a long dubonnet." He then used arrows and circles to indicate the switch of words.]

Saturday morning

While the bacon is reaching a state of edibility in the frying pan (that is where I am planning to eat it, like Melippity (spelling?)),[68] I'll try and get back to where I was before tottering off to bed. I fear you may find my subsequent remarks a bit embarrassing, but it can't be helped. (Bacon consumed.) Perhaps if I don't use paragraphs it will all seem less glaring. Anyway, with the exception of the Kafka pieces I have read all the various things of yours you gave me.[69] As you know, I could hardly admire you more if you were gilded, but several things in the essays impressed me more than I can say. How's that for almost perfect inarticulateness? This is a digression coming up. I read them, apart from my specific reactions, with a very curious over-all feeling, so curious in fact as to be unique in my experience, which does not somehow help me in putting it into words. I should suppose we have both passed the point in reading each other's work where we are, at least partly, trying to find out from it what the other is like, and to match it up, to put it much too crudely, with the person we know. And certainly, though I can easily conceive us writing something together if the occasion arose, I have never written anything remotely like your 'scholarly' pieces, and would be quite unable to, I felt, <u>not</u> in the rather more abstract way that a paragraph from, say, *The Unquiet Grave,* makes one say 'I could have written this', very close to them, and is af (as if) the feeling went far back into the past. A feeling as if we were part of the same family, and I don't mean just metaphorically. I guess that even more than I think of you as a friend, I think of you as my brother. End of digression. Having struggled to get the above out, it's off to the post office, the hardware store, et al.

10:45

I've been wandering around with little heaps of things; the pile of what is going back to New York is nothing short of appalling. At these times I wonder whatever happened to my resolution never to go anywhere for any length of time with anything more than will fit into two Harvard book bags.

---

68. Melipety was our cat.
69. At this time, I must have given EG a number of "scholarly" essays I had written. These would probably have been on Hardy, Shakespeare, Thomas Mann, Franz Kafka, and Homer's *Odyssey.* It should go without saying that today I think he overestimated them.

After what I have said on the previous page I suppose it is a bit odd to be looking (at least trying to) at the assortment of things you gave me as if I had never even heard of you, but something clearly results from doing so, at least to me. Even the most special and/or brief pieces (e.g., Kafka, Painter Manqué, Undergraduate Training in Library Research (incidentally in that same Dec 1965 English Record there is a little piece called *The Japanese Way* which I think makes an excellent point about senryu being much better to write in English than haiku—I'll be sending you the R. H. Blyth book on same as soon as I get back)) and the short book reviews are always lucid and have a point, he said pompously, which I for one feel these things so seldom have either one. (What do you mean, everyone is always grammatical?)[70] And ditto for the things which are somewhat more substantial, whether literary or educational, e.g., the *Coriolanus* and *Odyssey* pieces. The implications of the latter lead to the ones that so excited me, and I would expect just from reading them if I did not know you that these were the subjects that really excited you. This of course does not take into account whatever this unknown author's private life is like, what its pressures, pleasures, and so forth are. Knowing you does not really help in this respect, since like everybody else you say a great many different things about yourself and your life (also I'm not very bright) and the varying thoughts you have on the importance of being somewhere like Bellingham, marking time, being in English or in Education, pursuing a career, other writing, and all sorts of other things. What this all is in aid of in case you have begun to wonder, is that certain things struck me very strongly, and I thought I would pass them along to you, I don't really know why but then I don't know why not either. So. To quote, so you won't have to stop and look it up, from your review of the Ginn *American Literature,* which I more than agree is one of your best things: '. . . literature represents a mode of experience and a way of knowing that is quite unlike any other, and one that implies and entails its own curious conventions, forms, and devices. These conventions, forms, and devices, are difficult and intricate. They must be taught. He who lacks the capacity to recognize and discriminate among them, perceives less, lives poorer, lives less for the lack. All the more reason, then, why instruction in the medium should be workmanlike, single-minded, disciplined, and intense . . .' and from "The Case for Literature": '. . . what this means is that every day, all the time, things happen to us and with us, and—unless we share the poetic sensibility—we are not aware of them, and we do not know the life, the element, in which we live. We do not know

---

70. My point, derived from Noam Chomsky, was that the grammatical structures of a language are inherent in native speakers—that native speakers generate (speak, produce) their native languages more or less grammatically, as it were by instinct. They may speak dialect, they may say things like "They don't have none," but they would not say "None they don't have."

EG at his house on Cape Cod,
November 1968.
PHOTOGRAPHS BY PETER OR HELEN NEUMEYER

that we fear, we love, we are happy; we do not know we breathe air, feel ground, or concrete beneath our feet, . . . do not really feel anything at all . . .' It is these two ideas which Peter Neumeyer, the teacher—or whatever other word you would find appropriate here—returns to over and over again, and how best to deal with the one so that the other will follow as fully as possible. Such papers as the "Not-Very Modest Proposal" and the "Structural Approach" seem to me to be the pragmatic and not too circumscribed/technical sort of thing that you do best as a result of your concern, and which I feel are the best parts of the draft of the HM [Houghton Mifflin] book. Not to denigrate your mind/brain/intellect/whatever (I wouldn't dare), but it is the passion of your belief and the goodness of your character which are so very impressive. How's that for a reference? I suspect that from the point of view of doing the most possible good, you would be most satisfied teaching literature and how to teach it to teachers, rather than literature to undergraduates,[71]

---

71. Whether to continue teaching future teachers how to teach, or to teach undergraduates how to read—that was an actual issue for me at the time, as I was teaching not in an English department but in a graduate school of education.

but then this does not take into account any of life's complications which as we all know are only too numerous, and nothing exists in a vacuum except the contents of a thermos bottle. I feel it's high time I stopped this and went with it to the mail. Alas, alas, by the time this reaches you I will be, D.V., at 36 East 38th, where one of the first requirements is a new file box to be labelled P.N.

Ted.

Story needs more work, even for first draft, but you may get it shortly, as otherwise I'll get cold feet, which is not really ever a good idea.

Back to N.Y. Monday : ugh.

Sunday evening

I would have sent a picture postcard, but then you would only have turned it over, and that would be that. I have finished the revised dummy of Why We Have Day and Night.

A small list you may look at from time to time and consider whether you want to do anything about anything on it. (A really choice bit of meaty-mouthed nagging, don't you agree?)

1. A companion piece to D. and the . . .
2. Lionel and the Decoys, or whatever it is called
3. The Three Toads/Bears/Caskets/Wishes/Princes/Princesses/Witches/Graces/Fates, et al.

Meditate on the significance of the inclusion of "F."

[November 20, 1968]

[PN to EG]
* * *

Yes, space does need pressing, but the great cosmic seamstress up above has broke her Iron.
* * *

Your paragraph on our kinship I am, I'm afraid, too congested in spirit to answer with the freeness that it requires. So accept my word that I answer that paragraph <u>to</u> <u>you</u> within myself, with gratitude, with devotion, and with faith.

I declined Bellingham yesterday. Stony Brook then phoned and made a rather low offer—and now we must choose (U. Mass. at Amherst called with a rather large offer, but with some very weird complications which we'll side-step for a while). [. . .] In any case, your advice is received gratefully. And I will indeed do what you see right—teaching both literature, and talking with teachers about the teaching of (and importance of teaching) literature. Both the present options involve that.

* * *

I'm resolving to write you about once a week, as I feel I'm being paid on my job under false pretences otherwise. We hope the trip was easy. The apartment welcoming. The ballet graceful. And above all that you are swinging as happily as is the marvelous dolphmouse on your last envelope. yours

Peter

Mr Peter Neumeyer,
12 Powder House Road Ext.,
Medford, Mass. 02155.

20.xi.68, Wednesday evening

Dear Peter,

Having managed, but only just, to lift the typewriter from the floor to the drawing board, I commence a letter. Then of course there will be the problem of getting it to a mailbox.

I had a very Japanese drive back on Monday: mist, rain, sleet, snow, smoke, etc., which was all very beautiful or would have been if I had not been driving at the same time. Then it took me the better part of two hours to get from the edge of New York to 38th Street, due to heaven only knows what detours and constructions that have appeared since I left.

I have been tearing around at such a rate that I have not yet had time to finish reading "Intention in Literature," for which thank you; it is open at page 10 by the side of my bed.[72]

It is obvious I should never have come back here, as Monday night I was walking up to Mel and Alex's for dinner[73] when I fell spectacularly on some sandy plywood beside a construction and in consequence am a heap of skinned knees, elbows, palms, etc, not to mention all sorts of wrenched muscles. Welladay, as they say. New York seems more than ever an Untenable Place. There is a certain oppressive interest to be derived from all the people who seem to be in evidence. The splendours and miseries of the human face and form, not to mention all the bizarre clothes, assail one on all sides; everyone (to one who has seen nothing but Hyannis to all intents and purposes for months) looks beautiful, sexy, bursting with money, health, ambition, nerves, and so forth. This impression will pass soon enough, it always does, and then one will begin to notice the limps, the missing fingers, and worse.

Speaking of worse, I expect the Francis Bacon catalogue[74] has reached you by now. At first the show seemed rather disappointing—no wild new departures such as the Van Goghs of a few years back etc, but by the time I left, I was feeling quite thoroughly discomposed by them. Connie [Joerns] and I are going to it again tomorrow, so I expect I shall feel other things on a second look.

---

72. "Intention in Literature" was a long and, in retrospect, tedious article I had written for a collection of essays published by the *Journal of Aesthetic Education* at the University of Illinois Press.

73. Mel and Alexandra Schierman met EG by way of Balanchine's ballet and remained close friends throughout his life. After EG purchased his home at 8 Strawberry Lane, Yarmouth Port, in 1979, the Schiermans and their small children stayed there for two summers. In the early 1980s, EG took up permanent residence there.

74. *Francis Bacon: Recent Paintings,* the catalogue for an exhibition of twenty paintings at the Marlborough Gerson Gallery. Along with Magritte and Balthus, Bacon was certainly among EG's favorite painters.

The two care packages which you will not have received, or perhaps you will have by the time this gets to you, contain all but two (I think) of the books you don't already have,[75] and then such oddities as the German editions, the Swedish, a couple of things I illustrated where the drawings aren't too terrible, various pamphlets of photographs and some postcards which for various reasons I thought you might like to look at, a Magritte catalogue, and Bunny Lang's poetry and plays which I mentioned once at least when we were talking about Sylvia Plath, none of which needs to be returned, as they are all extra copies I had lying about.

I have seen Candida briefly, and she is in great shape which I felt she might not be, if only because I hadn't heard from her, but I am seeing her again on Tuesday (some nit made a movie of *The Hapless Child* ages ago, and we are going to see a screening of it) by which time I hope I will have *D and the . . .* to pass along to her with the rest of the things.

When I was at dinner with Mel and Alex the night I got back, I was not entirely surprised to be told that they very much wanted me to move into the apartment on the top floor of the house they are in the midst of buying on 92nd Street. In case you do not remember, and why should you? she is the secretary to Lincoln Kirstein, the head of the New York City Ballet, and he designs textiles, and I have known them since before they were married some eight years ago, and have always felt vaguely avuncular towards them as neither one is yet thirty though by now nearly; anyway, Alex will be giving up her job as she is due to have a baby in April, not that this particularly has anything to do with anything. So if they can get the present tenant of the apartment out I feel fairly certain I'll move in. After all, it is a whole floor, with four rooms, and I can have some sort of domestic existence after sixteen years in this glorified cage for cats cum bookcases and pictures on the walls and no furniture. As Candida said when I told her about it today, she herself having just done similarly, from a tiny apartment, to a floor through in a townhouse, that eventually one reaches the age where it is better to live like an adult, and how much more bearable life in New York is if you have a place where you can be domestic.

Perhaps it would be a good thing for me to pause and eat something. Having discovered that I weighed two pounds less than when I went to the Cape in June (last year in the same situation as now I weighed thirty pounds more), I am being inspired to eat hardly at all, and having walked my usual ten miles a day for New York, after doing hardly any at all on the Cape, I feel faint and far away and <u>very</u> cross a good deal of the time at present.

There's a rather unlikely rehearsal of the "March to the Gallows" movement of the *Symphonie Fantastique* on the radio at the moment.

---

75. Ted wanted to be sure he'd sent me one copy of everything he had published.

Thursday morning

My early morning insomnia continues, which will be terribly handy if I ever get down to doing some work (next week perhaps; I had better, as there is another illustration job due the end of the month, which all too obviously won't be finished by then).

As I was sitting at the ballet last night, it not being a very good or interesting program for the most part, I began to wonder what I was doing there, not that particular performance—after all, there are many off nights in the proceedings and one hardly bothers to even notice, so to speak—but in general, and I came to the conclusion, perhaps because of recent contact with academia, that a great part of it at least, was as though I were taking some (endless) course, and while I don't take notes or write them afterwards, though I do know people who do from time to time, preferring to get it all out in talk during intermissions and after the performance— this sentence seems to have got out of hand—as an intellectual discipline. There I sit, usually watching people I have seen thousands of times before dancing ballets that I have often seen literally hundreds of times before, and so the whole point would seem to be an intellectual discipline directed at re-judging everything over and over again and trying to see it as freshly and objectively each time. I don't know quite what good this is doing my brain, but then. Of course this leaves out the artistic, aesthetic, sensual pleasures involved, which are going on all the time too (or their converses as last night when there was really some of the wretchedest dancing I have seen for some time).

I still have not been to a movie, a practically unheard of proceeding for me on first getting back to NY; I expect it will be remedied this afternoon as there is a Japanese film I can't live without seeing and it is the last week, and the weekend is already shot, etc. So everything is rather the way it always is around here. Instead of looking out at the Barnstable marina I see a bit of Thirty-Seventh Street pinched between the backs of two buildings. Forcing oneself to concentrate on the present moment only, the result at the moment makes the Cape seem a place I once saw some blurred photographs of perhaps; I feel I saw you last about ten years ago. Living from day to day in New York is a rather desperate business, however long one has been doing it; it gets more difficult if anything.

Since David Holbrook's *English for the Rejected* (hallowed title!) is too large to thrust into any of my pockets, it is becoming what I read before going to bed;[76] I expect to have finished it by June, say. I finished "Intention in Literature" while eating last night, but I seem to have somehow missed the point so will try again.

* * *

---

76. I still find it astounding that Ted took the trouble to read such books, which came to me by way of my job.

I was too wondering about a white line around the slowly growing smaller oranges [in *Why We Have Day and Night*]—I have not revised those drawings, partly because I think they are all right for the moment, and I haven't quite decided how much chart etc to put behind them; I don't want to get the whole thing too set in the dummy to leave room for improvisation and inspiration (ha!) when it comes time to do the final art work.

* * *

I also seem to have been pretty stupid about the bookplate; I hope Helen will forgive me. No one has yet told me what ideas anybody has in mind. Donald having a great folio about to shut him up inside perhaps? Further stupidity, if possible. Helen's note found on back of postcard inadvertently. Please tell her I certainly did not mean to snatch the project away from her; it was only that my drawing is so inadequate that if I can't keep on touching it up with fine lines in a way that make something like a linoleum block sort of impossible, that the result, my drawing, would be dreadful. It won't be expensive, so don't worry about that. I'll send a sketch sometime next week, I hope.

Donald and the Umbrella—I have only read it once so I can hardly be said to have read it at all, really—is beautiful, and I think maybe Harry will like it, who can say? I should love to do it in a slightly larger format than *Donald and the . . . ,* with flat colours somewhat in the manner of *The Wuggly Ump;* perhaps the drawings themselves, or perhaps the fantasy ones only in grey rather than black, and then have a paler grey for sort of misty rainy backgrounds with a sort of soft brown for the people, and then of course a glorious sun-yellow umbrella. This is all off the top of my head at the moment, and you may loathe the notion, if it is at all clear to you, which seems unlikely from my powers of description, and of course I may change my whole idea subsequent to various readings and rereadings. Anyway, do send Harry a copy right away.

* * *

One thirty (PM)

Well, I have somehow managed to mislay the first six? pages of this, along with your letter, but however I have just found them again, not that that gets any of us much forrader.

* * *

The sad, and it is, story of my cleaning woman's life is being rather incoherently poured into my ear as I'm writing this. Between her husband and her mother . . .

You'll be relieved to know that as I was trotting about on my errands, kneecaps, shins, and toes with various curious aches and twinges in them from all this unaccustomed rushing about on the pavements, I began to see *Donald and the Umbrella* in exceedingly simple terms; perhaps not even terribly many drawings. One question: how do you see the brown natives clothed? This is always a problem, clothes I mean. In this case do you see them as natives with quotation marks? Or are they fully clothed somehow and civilized? Or do you know? I might just conceivably have a sketchy and tentative type sample drawing to send along with this. It is obvious it won't get to you this week in any case, and so I may not put it in the mail until sometime tomorrow or even Sunday. Four, or five if you count tonight's, ballet performances loom over the weekend, and tomorrow morning I'm going to meet Mel and Alex to see the house, though not the apartment because of the tenant still in it, but despite the obvious attack of very cold feet about the whole thing I am shortly in for, D.V., I'll go through with it. And Sunday I have to go and be entertained by an old friend between performances. And I hate to think of all the illustrating I have to get done in the next few weeks.

Oh. This brilliant interjection occasioned by remembering something else I had on my mind. As I have perhaps fleetingly mentioned at some point or other, I have been toying for some time with doing three more Fantod books, and have not done (My typewriter needs help.) so partly because the MSS I vaguely had in mind were out being peddled. Anyway, one is coming out, so I'm told, in *Partisan Review* (a slight hysterical giggle at this point) and the other one maybe somewhere else, but in any case I know where both MSS are, which I haven't for over a year (neither have you seen—one is excessively dotty and macabre and reeking with plot—it all takes place on a Cape Cod marsh, and is filled with curious relations, sudden death, religious mania and heaven knows what else [*The Deranged Cousins*], and the other one is quite, quite poignant and Borgesian in that it is circular), and anyway, what would you feel about my going ahead with *Donald Has a Difficulty* as the third one? It's not even really publication in the large sense, but it would introduce PFN further to those rabid Goreyites who always find out about the privately printed things, and then the way would of course be open for the grand and glorious wide screen full colour second revised edition if and when.

Re carbons and originals I don't think it matters a bit as far as Candida is concerned, and I'll ask her about [it] for when she submits things. I do wish *Donald and the . . .* would hurry up and arrive, which of course is why it hasn't. Especially because until I see it again, I haven't more than an erroneous idea of what Donald and milieu look like.

* * *

7:40

Pre-ballet jottings (excuse handwriting)—

Donald and the Umbrella—a strangely wonderful and apt title. I read it several more times. You go, as the book reviewers say, from strength to strength. Seriously, it is a wonderful story, and don't listen to Harry if/when he starts suggesting things until you've told me what they are. I feel I am guarding your integrity when you are too amiable to do so. (Gorey, you are a pompous ass.)

Negroes? Are you mad?[77] Black is beautiful. Umbrellas are black. Therefore Negroes invented the umbrella. (LeRoi Jones) I'm in favour of gentle, brown, vaguely South Sea types. Once again, how are they dressed?

I see the whole book, which I think is a good sign; our empathy is in its customary superb working order. The rain, anyway, greenish grey, perhaps the drawings themselves. Black as a colour saved for Donald's umbrella. The people a mauvish brown, their umbrella the most wonderful bright yellow in the world. Again, the drawings absolutely simple, no elaboration or shading whatever. (There was a marvelous tiny (by comparison to the others) fresco in the Metropolitan show, which I caught the last day of on Tuesday, by, I think, Pontormo?, of a scene in a hospital (it had something to do with St. Matthew I think) where the architecture was all dirty mauve and orange, and the people were all grey-green. It haunted one.)

I think your influence must have improved me somewhat, as people have all been much nicer to me since I got back than usual. I don't think I much care for that sentence somehow; on the other hand it does seem to be true. (We have reached the first intermission, the company having made a hash of the Haydn Concerto, a fact that was only too [predictable?] from the casting. They will persist in a variety of such errors. The rest of the evening, alas, is not going to be any better and may very possibly be worse.)

I hope the various care packages are providing a certain amount of distraction, if not amusement. (Bacon is hardly amusing, though the one of George Dyer riding a bicycle induced (nervous) laughter. A second time around, the show was staggering, infinitely disquieting (the most being the triptych with the female? figures on either side and the gore with the luggage and the open door in the middle—it seemed to be taking place in outer space) with the strange dark oval spots everywhere and really ghastly streaks of white pigment streaking across the canvases, but the paintings themselves very beautiful and even in some strange way, serene.) The Magritte colour reproductions in the blue catalogue are sadly erroneous and do considerable damage to their charm, but the ideas come through of course. Oddly, it was by far the best Magritte show I have ever seen, even the one at the Museum of Modern Art. Another Balthus catalogue will be on its way eventually (they

---

77. In a postcard to EG dated November 20, I asked, "What if in this story, everyone were brown (i.e. Negroes)? Why? Why not?"

just had an enormous retrospective in London), but alas, the catalogues are hopeless at conveying the beauty of the pictures, though perhaps the strangeness comes across. I have three Balthus drawings, very minor, but good (I think) which I hope you will see one day. Anyway, for whatever interest is to be derived therefrom. Bacon, Balthus, and Magritte are my three favourite painters, along with Dubuffet, of the whole post-impressionist period, by which I mean that before them Bonnard, Vuillard, & Seurat are my favourite painters of that time. I am not making myself articulate and the lights have gone down, and they are going to wreck Apollo.

(They did.)

Saturday morning

Some attempt should be made to salvage this letter, like tearing it up into many tiny pieces and starting all over again, but I can't face the prospect.

I noticed that when I went out for the *Times* something called Smoke Watchers Inc. has moved into the block; they have a brass plate by the door which says so. An earnest young lady is reading a peculiar but very tedious story about a little Spanish boy and a whale that he keeps in his pocket (as far as I can gather) on the radio and I am too lazy to try and find another station. Addendum: the whale turned out to be imaginary, and she was finally abandoned like a wornout security blanket. Ugh.

* * *

I had other contradictory thoughts in passing about indicating that the oranges were complete spheres in the last pages of WWHDAN, not all that definite I hasten to add, but they go something like this. Actually the diminishing oranges I have drawn really have nothing to do with what is actually happening which is unillustratable, so that really they are an objective correlative (if that is what I mean), and to keep the oranges intact in the dark is not the same thing as having them devoured by the bug, and perhaps more confusing rather than less, but this can all be solved (your way) when we have a publisher. I just thought I'd mention it.

Perhaps I'll take my story off to the ballet and scribble at it during intermissions; at the moment, if nothing else, it seems dreadfully pedestrian.

I had a definite pang at the news you had turned down Bellingham. Possibly you will be able to supply the connection and even meaning of the following remark, since I'm not sure I can: it's perhaps not such a good idea to wish happiness for other people.

Talk about people rattling on, and boring other people to distraction . . . so I'll turn what's left of my attention to b--kpl-t-s and brown natives etc. Letter actually ends at *foot of page 6, which I expect you've already read.*

* * *

End of letter [. . .] A trip downstairs to see if the mail has arrived, in case Donald
. . . Nothing has arrived, not even the mailman. I feel I have surpassed my previous
record for incoherence with this.

I hope you are all right. This hardly sounds as if it were said from the heart, but it is.

Ted.

P.S. Mel and Alex's house is great, indescribable except to say that it is not [at] all like
New York, so I can't wait to get into the apartment, except it may not be till the end
of the winter because they do not get formal possession until the first of the year and
then they have to give the tenant two months' notice, but we're hoping the present
owner will give the notice now so I can get in sooner. All of this D.V. of course, and
one sometimes wonders.

P.P.S. No drawing for *Donald and the Umbrella* except on the envelope because I
think I want to hear your ideas about the brown people before I get some wrong
notion of my own, and besides, at the rate I'm going, this is never going to reach you.

[typed vertically, from bottom of page up]
What a heart-rending waste of space. . . . .

25.xi.68, 9:40 PM

Dear Peter,

I was thinking of beginning a letter to you while walking home, so I might as well anyway, regardless of phone calls. As I said when you suggested it, that I would never foist myself on you just because I happened to need moral support, but I fear I am not above doing it at one remove by letters. Not that at the moment I am in need of moral support, but you are the Solid Object as it were in all this flux; at least you can read these effusions at your leisure, or even not at all.

In case you should have occasion to call again and do not have any message to leave, the answering service only picks up after the third ring, and my apartment is so small that I always get the phone picked up by the second at most, so . . .

I looked at Mel and Alex's house Saturday morning, or did I go into this in my letter? I can not remember. In case I didn't, anyway I have decided to take the apartment, but it will probably be February before I can get into it, or even March on account of the incumbent tenants.

Just as I had decided Kierkegaard was not for me, I came across a few dazzling pages at the end of the selections from *Preparation for a Christian Life,* so I've at least decided to get through *Fear and Trembling* and *The Sickness unto Death* (such jolly titles). I've also picked up *The Wisdom of Insecurity* by Alan Watts and *The Perennial Philosophy* of Aldous Huxley, which somehow I never got around to. You realize what you have done is to put me well on the way to becoming a Religious Nut, don't you?

I've also started on Rainer Maria Rilke as I patter hither and yon in midtown Manhattan (as we call it, those of us who reside here); a great many of the selected poems are going straight into my commonplace book, and various bits of the *Duino Elegies.*

I'm scribbling Du musst dein Leben ändern [You must change your life] on a piece of paper to paste on my drawing board light, not that it will do much good, but still. (Last line of [Rilke's] "Archaïscher Torso Apollos," in case you flounder.) I must say the more doom-and-gloom ones strike all too many chords in my tiny head, and I get overcome. "Das Kind" must be just about the most heartrending poem ever written, but his whole selection is so good that there are no handful as it were which stand out. His notes and introduction incidentally remind me of Blyth, especially his really venomous remarks about the *Elegies,* which he then retracts in the last sentence of the introduction. I must also confess the last stanza of the eighth elegy rather had me on the ropes. It is probably fortunate I did not read him when I was seventeen, or I might have never survived into my twenties. The son of a friend of my aunt Isabel walked into the ocean in California when he was twenty, Rilke apparently having been his favourite author. Of course there may not have been a connection . . .⁷⁸

You tell me two new stories are on the way; I can scarcely believe it. I was thinking only today when I was going over them in my head at one point that I had been hitherto rather dense not to realize how remarkable your output has been this past three months, and would have been had you been doing nothing else at all, and as it is . . . ah well, we mustn't turn your head, must we?

Do you know *Language, Thought, and Reality* by Benjamin Lee Whorf? I got wind of it somewhere or other, though not anything you'd lent me. From a writing point of view lots of it is absolutely fascinating, even essays that have such titles as "The Punctual and Segmentative Aspects of Verbs in Hopi." According to Stuart Chase in his introduction, Whorf made two hypotheses: all higher levels of thinking are dependent on language, and the structure of the language one habitually uses influences the manner in which one understands his environment; the picture of the universe shifts from tongue to tongue. Excuse exposition if you already know all this/him/it. Anyway, it interested me because it somehow seems relevant to your/my/our work, all three. I was not being entirely facetious when I accused you of coming from another planet judging from the content of your work, and I have wondered if I wasn't trying to do something different than most people with the English language, and certainly our joint efforts are even more peculiar in this direction . . . Anyway.⁷⁹

Wednesday morning, and how did it get here?

Masses of Neumeyer in the mail this morning but no Donald from Harry. Neumeyer as always will take a good deal of thought before writing about in a letter.

But right away, thank you for *Lionel Leads* and its dedication. There's a really inadequate sentence for you. It will take many readings . . . and I can't even finish this one (sentence).

"The Faithful Fish" is a delight, and, I think, the most promising from a crassly commercial view to date. Let us hope Candida will agree when she sees it. Like the moustache story, not for me to illustrate (though I wish I could), but I'll insist that you insist on choosing your illustrator.⁸⁰

---

78. I sent EG several volumes of the poetry of Rilke. I wish I could recall whose edition, in order to reconstruct whose "venomous remarks" EG was talking about. Maybe the most striking line in Rilke's poetry is the last line of "Archaïscher Torso Apollos." EG had attached it to his drawing board, just as I still have it sitting on my desk.
79. Benjamin Lee Whorf is much more profound as a linguist and had a deeper effect on both EG and me than one would expect from his reputation today.
80. My story "The Faithful Fish" was eventually published with illustrations by Arvis Stewart (Young Scott Books, 1971).

4:30ish

I've just got back from seeing Marlene Dietrich at a matinee, a somewhat unnerving experience I'm not at all sure I'm glad I had, though I have been wanting to see her for years. She is uncanny, but that alas is the word. She looks, not fantastically well-preserved, but like a younger, not so well-preserved second-rate version of the genre she herself created. Heaven knows she went through innumerable versions of herself, all equally artificial, but one was always aware of the person behind them, but that is scarcely in evidence at all now, or at least for the moment—perhaps it will come back sometime—I've noticed that sooner or later every movie star goes through a period of not aging but losing their visual character instead, and that this wears off and they once more look like themselves only older—so now she might be anyone, except for the voice of course. It is just as great as it ever was; after all she never could sing in any narrow sense, and when she just does what she always did without strain, she is superb. Unfortunately she is also overproduced—and acts things out much too much sooner or later; also it is easily the least spontaneous performance one could ever hope to see; you know that it never varies by a millionth of an inch from night to night. Oh well, I suppose I am glad to have heard her sing "Lili Marlene," "Where Have All the Flowers Gone?," "Ich bin die fesche Lola," "Falling in Love Again," etc. in the flesh once, though I suspect I would have absolutely swooned away with rapture ten years ago, not that I wasn't wanting to this afternoon. Most of the audience did, so there you are.

There is a handy new Penguin containing [*The Castle of*] *Otranto, Vathek,* and *Frankenstein* with an excellent introduction by Mario Praz. He mentions as two modern novels of the Gothic variety, Mikhail Bulgakov's *The Master and Margarita,* which I picked up in paperback, and *The Golem* by Gustav Meyrink, the latter which rings no bells at all; does it to you?

While I'm at it, do you know Flann O'Brien's *At Swim-Two-Birds*?

* * *

A further thought on "The Faithful Fish"; I suppose you should show it to Harry, as it came up, did it not, the idea, when you were with him, and all, but from my selfish point of view, I'd rather you didn't until after he's agreed to take *Donald and the Umbrella,* if he's going to. This isn't very nice of me, is it? It does seem to me that if Harry balks at *Donald and the Umbrella,* provided it is the same old thing about not being a book or story or whatever, that we forget about him entirely for our kind of thing. I'm not being pessimistic about this, as I think he might very well feel *Donald and the Umbrella* is just the ticket, but I'm only saying this in case he isn't feeling that way. To quote a homely old saw: Kind words butter no parsnips. And speaking of butter, did you ever get the advance?

Shall I hazard another of my hopelessly wrong guesses and guess that of the books of mine I sent *The Hapless Child* will be the one to affect you the most? I can't even remember what the other ones were. The short, semi-animated film the young man made from it had its merits: quite straightforward, good music: bits of Beethoven, someone I can't remember, and some of the more sinister sawing away at the strings from Vivaldi's *Seasons;* he did however leave out the supernatural element, if that is what it is, entirely. Whether anything more will come of it—it needs revision for commercial purposes—depends on whether Candida can interest someone willing to distribute a revised version. It's all rather academic to me, except for what small amount of money I might conceivably make from it.

Thanksgiving morning

I discovered lots of this funny-coloured paper so perhaps I'll start using it up. I feel like I'm typing on oatmeal, especially with this typewriter.

I have just finished, subject to sudden recollections of other things, a little list of things I have to do. I have a mind to write SUICIDE at the top and forget the rest.

Having successfully resisted invitations for the day in various directions, I tell myself I am getting myself organized in order to better attack work. Ha. Even I can't make myself believe this really.

I hope you are all having a Thanksgivingy Thanksgiving.

Not to belabour the point, but I am obviously being awful about "The Faithful Fish" in telling you not to show it to Harry right away, simply because I so much want him to do another Donald, and I fear his seeing something else would only complicate matters further. On the other hand, while it doesn't improve my motives any, I <u>do</u> think since Candida will hopefully be involved as soon as I get the copy of Donald and show her the other things that it would perhaps be a good idea not to do any more with Harry, apart from *Donald and the Umbrella,* until we see how Candida feels about prospects, etc. My mind does not work very well on holidays as you can see.

When I was talking to Carla Stevens at Young Scott the other day I asked her to send you the two Brer Rabbit books I illustrated. I don't like them much, though they have been generally admired as they say, so why I had them sent to you was because of the way I used colour which was what I had in mind for *Donald and the Umbrella,* which may not have been clear in my letter. Anyway, see what you think of the idea of the drawings and text being in a sort of rain colour with brown people and one small black umbrella and one vast yellow one.

I just got a rather nasty shock. In looking for something or other I came across the fact that one of my cats is about to be nine years old, and that another of them will shortly thereafter be eight; I have been labouring under the delusion they were about five and six. And yesterday I happened to notice in the mirror that while I have long since grown used to my beard being very grey indeed, I was not prepared to discover that my eyebrows are becoming noticeably shaggy. I feel the tomb is just around the corner. And there are all these books I haven't read yet, even if I am simultaneously reading at least twenty . . .

Having organized like mad this morning, obviously real life holds no particular charm, so I'm going off to a Japanese movie (dubbed into Chinese with Japanese and English subtitles) entitled *Illusion of Blood*.

Illusion, indeed. One has seldom seen so much. It was all quite splendid. All about a samurai who was attempting to regain his place in society; after he gave his wife a poisonous draught which not only made her expire in agony but hideously disfigured her face while doing so, things went from bad to worse. She came back as a ghost causing him to hack up his second wife on their wedding night, and so forth. People had their faces cut off, supernatural packs of rats invaded the premises, and everybody ended up dead, all in the most ravishing colour like the best Japanese prints. They also have a totally different way with the supernatural than we do, which is fascinating. It was not, after all, dubbed into Chinese, but there <u>were</u> very curious titles in both Japanese and English, and I can only conclude the print was prepared for the use of the deaf, which does happen, because I have seen various American movies with English subtitles which maddeningly anticipate the dialogue in the same way, and that is what they were for.

* * *

I guess I'll have to read *Coriolanus,* as I don't think I can bear another article on the subject without having done so.[81] I think I saw it once, but it obviously left no impression. Why aren't you hipped on *Titus Andronicus*? Now <u>there's</u> a play you can get your teeth into.

All these attacks on linguistics I fear are making me very curious on the subject. I have purchased *Language* by Sapir to that end; was this a good thought?

* * *

---

81. I had recently published several articles on Shakespeare's *Coriolanus* and sent them to EG.

Sunday morning

Heaven knows what the rest of this letter is like; I'm not going to look.

It was good of you to write me as you did on Tuesday; in the same circumstances I probably would stupidly not have. If I am not trying to say all sorts of cheerful and consoling things, it is because I should not try saying them to myself, so why should I try saying them to you. By the same token I won't be able not to worry about you, again as I would about myself. However.

Keep me posted about whatever you don't mind ~~about~~ keeping me posted about. I think one of those abouts can go. It has. I won't ask questions because you might not want to answer them—anyway, I'm beginning to feel questions are hardly ever a good idea, that's provided they even exist, which sometimes seems doubtful. You'll tell me what you tell me.

Unless you want something stupid to worry about for a change, don't worry about writing (me).

Sputter, sputter, sputter, sputter, sputter (to paraphrase Shakespeare).

Ted.

* * *

3.xii.68, Tuesday night

Dear Peter,

* * *

I don't know why I didn't think of it before but if you like, Donald and his mother can be by a large window for the splinter removal to cover the very good light; what do you think?

Neither mine nor other people's prospects seem particularly pleasing just at the moment, and I have fantasies of going to Iceland, never to return. As it is, I tell myself not to remember the past, not to hope or fear for the future, and not to think in the present, a comprehensive program that will undoubtedly have very little success.

Whether I ever get into Mel and Alex's apartment (the day they moved into the house—Sunday—something went wrong with the boiler and the basement was flooded) depends on the status of the tenants in it now, and whether they can ever legally be asked to leave, which no one seems to have any clear idea of at the moment.

With the exception of *The Object-Lesson* in English and *The Listing Attic,* both of which may take years to find copies of, I think you now have virtually everything I care to acknowledge, which ought to be a relief. The latest care package contains a movie script [*The Black Doll*] that no one has ever shown the slightest interest in. *Les Liaisons dangereuses* is one of three copies of that edition I seem to have, not to mention an inferior translation hardbound and two copies in French.

* * *

Gerard ter Borch (1617–1681)
Man on Horseback, 1634

Thank you for the Xerox of the C. S. Lewis article; you are remarkably thoughtful. Also for the Gerard ter Borch "Cavalier." It put me in mind of a slightly curious idea I had for a visual anthology in which all the subjects would have their backs to the viewer; I have several Japanese prints of poets, and at least one of a puppy in this position, and I'm sure a quite respectable book could be got together from all times and places. What it would all be in aid of is another question; I do <u>not</u> see a knowing little psychological essay-introduction.

As of Sunday night the ballet is over for the month of December as far as I'm concerned, as they do *Nutcracker,* which I shall probably see three or four times spread over the next month, so I am free to indulge my cravings for the cinema, or would be, if I could find anything I particularly wanted to see, which I can't, not that it is preventing me from going off to them, but either movies are worse than ever, or I am losing my passion for them, which I don't think I could survive; after forty years . . . no, I couldn't.

Among all the other things I am reading at the moment, I've been reading Voltaire: *Zadig, L'Ingenu,* and *Candide,* all of which I must have read before if only at Harvard. *Candide* has its moments, but I'll still take Samuel Johnson's *Rasselas* over all three. Has it occurred to you that Donald's adventures, among their other aspects, are chapters in a sort of Borgesian *conte philosophique,* or better perhaps, *metaphysique?*[82]

Wednesday morning

Speaking of Donald, one wonders whatever became of chapter one from Addison-Wesley? I could see my copy of the unbound book being delayed in the mails, but you have not mentioned it either so I take it you haven't seen it. I don't want to see it; I only want to give it to Candida. Drat, to put it mildly.

* * *

It is pouring rain, and I am wondering whether to go out and walk in it until I have contracted pneumonia in all probability. Surrounded by things that I should have done weeks ago, a sort of adamantine paralysis has set in, and I resolutely allow myself to get further and further behind while my mind gets blanker and blanker. If only I could think something sensible and creative was going on beneath this tiresome surface behaviour; but it don't seem likely.

* * *

Thursday night

I didn't really mean to send you <u>another</u> book at this point, but after I'd marked God knows how many bits in the first ten pages to pass on to you, I thought it would be far easier to simply get a copy for you (this anent the Renard *Journal*).[83]

I just got back from *Hot Millions,* which I apparently enjoyed rather more than you did, as I laughed madly throughout and also found it very touching. I've always had a predilection for English films that are the latter and something else entirely different at the same time, my favourite in this genre which no one but me knows exists is *The Ladykillers,* since the [something else] entirely different in this case was violently macabre. To go back to HM, there was one definitely Neumeyerish line

---

82. Eighteenth-century technical term for a short tale exemplifying a philosophical or, here, metaphysical idea, applicable to some Borges pieces.
83. One of EG's favorite books was *The Journal of Jules Renard,* edited and translated by Louise Bogan and Elizabeth Roget (G. Braziller, 1964).

where Peter Ustinov was explaining the window to Maggie Smith and said something to the effect that it let the darkness out.

I have the most brilliant opening for a story (filched I must confess from something in Alan Watts) in which a little boy turns on the tap, takes a quantity of water, wraps it in brown paper and string, and sends it off to a friend; somehow I think, perhaps because it has rained for several days, the package accumulates a lot more water than there was in the first place so that when the other child opens it he is swept out of the room on a small flood and into some other world entirely . . .

Friday morning

At last! Donald arrived in a large tube this morning. After I have gone to look at some coffee cakes (explainable later) I shall come back here, cut it up into pages and take it to Candida, along with the other things. Excelsior!

Noon

Well, things are in the hands of Candida. She was in a busy state but flipped through *Donald and the* . . . and WWHDAN very quickly with cries of glee, so I expect mature reappraisal of them and all the other things will only confirm her opinion. Let us hope, though I don't believe in doing so as a regular thing.

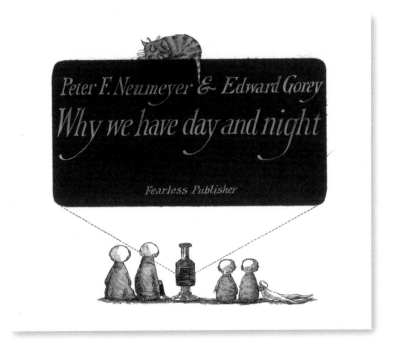

Peter F. Neumeyer & Edward Gorey
Why we have day and night

Fearless Publisher

Saturday evening

* * *

I had one of Harry's letters this morning, which told me nothing except that you'd sent him *Donald and the Umbrella,* which he thinks he likes but isn't sure because he read it when he was more than usually distracted. Hm.

To quote: 'I keep hoping Peter won't throw away each of his stories, systematically, rather than changing them. He seems to feel quite unfeeling about thus disposing of his children, once they are said to have any flaw.' He then goes on to wish for a revised *Donald Goes Away* which ends with him putting together a prehistoric skeleton of some sort. At the moment I feel life is too short for much more of this sort of thing, but perhaps you don't.

I hope you like the press sheet of Donald. The text is not placed on the page the way I wanted and presumably specified, but then only I can see this, and something like this always seems to happen, and there's nothing to be done about it now, but perhaps this accounts for the slight edge to my voice, as it were. And if it's my fault because I gave the wrong instructions, THAT ONLY MAKES IT WORSE.

It is time to hie me to five or six hours of shadows on the silver screen at my friends, the Eversons.[84]

This is another one of those letters that seems reluctant to allow itself to get to the mailbox. Perhaps tomorrow.

Sunday evening

* * *

To be repetitive, it was very good of you to call this morning.

* * *

I have, surprisingly enough, been fairly successful at not thinking about where you might be going, so if I sounded a bit dazed at the news of Stony Brook, that accounts for it. As the Unitarian thought for the week has it (I passed it on the way to the Eversons last night): Our ideals are our possibilities (anon), but then so is the converse true, and SB seems much more possible than California from my point of view, so I needn't say more except that I very much hope that whatever is not ideal about SB will be closer to it than you expect and that the compensations will be more and greater too. Much as I hate both of them really, New York, like life, does

---

84. William and Karen Everson. William was a noted film historian and, later, professor of cinema studies at New York University's Tisch School of the Arts.

have them (compensations, in case you are wondering where I had got to), cultural ones at least, and for example, by the time you are in this neck of I hope not totally non-existent woods, it will be time for another Bacon show no doubt. I saw it for the fourth or fifth time yesterday, the last day, and by this time I was absolutely swooning away at the sheer beauty of the painting in them, and could even imagine (had I the room and $150,000) being able to live with the triptych where something horrid has taken place in the middle panel; all that gore and even the zipper on the bag are superbly painted.

Apropos of nothing in particular, I had an odd experience earlier in the week which I don't think I have set down as yet. I saw a rather simple-minded but amusing private eye type movie with Frank Sinatra called *Lady in Cement* at the beginning of the week. Anyway, there was a rather flamboyant character actor in it whom I had never seen before and have no idea even what his name is; before the movie was over he is murdered, the whole movie taking place I forgot to add in Miami. So, several days later one noontime I was walking up Fifth Avenue and saw said actor crossing 57th Street; my first thought was, But that's impossible, he was murdered in Miami two days ago.

I have just reread Harry's letter, and he _is_ ecstatic about *Donald and the . . .* , and I feel he really _does_ want to do another book. His fatal defect is this mad urge to think all the time, and roll things around in his mind, until they disintegrate into crumbs. I seriously more and more find thought and the necessity for it a terrible mistake or the indication that one exists, and I think (oh well, let it stand) that what annoys me so about dealing with Harry is that the only way to do it (when you are so lacking in character as I am) is to start thinking and rolling things around too, and I just don't believe in it at all, at all, at all. I don't mean things like thinking up painful ribs[85] instead of what was there before, but I do mean things like totally recasting stories until they are about something else entirely. And in the case of *Donald Goes Away* I will fight for the insects in the giant pipes until you tell me not to, which I hope very much you won't do. Oh well, why blather on at this juncture? Let us wait and see what Candida has to say, and while I don't really wish to deprive Harry of his fun (and maybe yours, I don't know really), I do think she might be useful in getting Harry to finally make up his mind. After all, he has seen God knows how many manuscripts and he knows you're not a one-book author and he's seen enough of my drawings to know what _they_ look like and so forth and so on. I do not precisely look forward to your comments on *Donald Has a Difficulty* because I am _very_ fond of it as is (your text, _not_ my dummy) and _I_ don't think it's pointless at all.

---

85. I had for some time mulled over what could ail Donald, before I came up with the idea of "painful ribs," in *Donald and the . . . .*

[. . .] I seriously consider getting a vast trunk, writing ANTHOLOGY in large white letters painted on the top, leaving it open and throwing in poems, postcard reproductions, and anything else that comes to mind as the spirit moves me; then every now and again I could lift out a few handfuls and peruse them when in pensive mood.

I really must get this into the mail tomorrow morning . . .

And accomplish, or start to, a few pressing items, like whole books that have to be illustrated. I finally managed to beat something out of my pillow-like brain yesterday, if only an outline I can actually put down on paper of a book I have been supposed to be writing since last spring for someone else to illustrate, a sequel to *Fletcher and Zenobia,* which it occurs to me you don't have, but I'll pry a copy out of the editor tomorrow as we are having lunch; all I did on it, was to take the original plot, change Zenobia to a doll (as a girl it was fairly ickypoo-Freudian) and rewrite it. The sequel is going to be about them saving a small circus.[86]

* * *

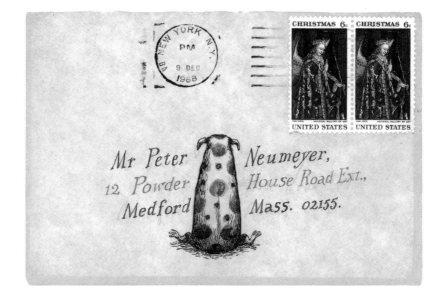

---

86. *Fletcher and Zenobia* (1967) and *Fletcher and Zenobia Save the Circus* (1971) were illustrated by Victoria Chess.

December 9, 1968

Dear Ted,

* * *

Main point 1: This is a horrible thing to say at this point, but I just think *Donald Has a Difficulty* is a very weak story. This didn't become clear to me really until I saw it with your rough sketches. They are so much better than the story itself is, or than the story deserves, that they merely underline the lameness of the story. Actually, if you look at the story on one or two typed pages as I just did, it doesn't look so bad. It seems to hang together—but just slightly—if you can look at the whole thing at one glance, get the total Gestalt. But when one has to look at the story page by page as it would actually be in a book it just strikes me as being extremely lame. I think my first choice would be to work on it some more (if this is the story you really want to do next) in a week or two. I don't think you would like me to put a Harry Stanton kind of ending on it, but I just feel very strongly that the story is too weak to stand on its own now—even as a small practical joke in anticipation of the big Donald epic.

Main point 2: I think the first few pages of the drawings are superb. I think Donald's mother is very beautiful and Donald is fine, as is his clothing. (My only reservation about Donald's physiognomy is in anticipation of the umbrella story. In the umbrella story, I think Donald should have very definitely a child's, not an adult's, face. The same essential Donald, but a face not to be confused with that of his elders. [. . .] Margret Rey[87] came to visit me [. . .] and looked at it and her first and immediate comment was, "That's not his calf, that's not his calf, that's his shin he's pushing with." Now we've got to correct that. There are two possibilities: we could say, "Donald pushed the tree with his shin," but that doesn't sound very good, or—and this is a little difficult on you perhaps, I'm afraid—we could keep the text as it is and have Donald actually pushing the tree with his calf. I don't know how one would do that short of going into a yoga bend, but perhaps it's worth a try. [. . .]

Yours,
Peter

---

87. Margret Rey, wife of Hans Rey, was the author of a number of the *Curious George* stories.

[December 17, 1968]

[PN to EG]

* * *

15. re Harry's quote "I hope Peter won't throw away each of his stories . . .
disposing of his children . . ." etc. I suppose immodestly and debonairly and
cavalierly, were I to think of a character, a story-writing Peter N whom I liked,
I would invent him as a man who puts down what he has to put down and goes
on to the next, and the fixers and arrangers be damned. And this writer couldn't
care less. That's a sort of nice image I think. Whether it fits the facts, I haven't the
foggiest. Sometimes for some stories maybe, and for others not so much. Re *D Has a
Difficulty*—after half an hour concentration, I can't really think of other endings. So
in a way you're vindicated. That is—the story as it is. Period. But that, I'm quite sure,
does not make it a satisfactory story for a potential buyer. I'm shy of pawning it off or
whatever on someone. It's not that good. If it were by someone whose thoughts were
big enough or good enough to be of interest to the world, it would be an interesting
entrée to a corner of his mind. But really—we haven't reached that point. I don't like
it, but taking your idea and giving it words, one could end "only later would Donald
learn that with his calf he had indeed succeeded. The tree was down." By the way,
re-reading the epic Donald—that, I think, is really something. I think it is full, big
worthwhile, good. I do look forward to that. (In vistavision)

16. Do you know the artist (18th c) Carl Wilhelm Kolbe? He, from the one
picture I just saw, is very for you.[88]

---

88. I was probably looking at an engraving by Kolbe (1759–1835) illustrating the Latin phrase "et in
   Arcadia ego," which was the subject of an essay written by Erwin Panofsky—see page 172, note 110, for
   more about this.

17.xii.68, Tuesday evening

Dear Peter,

It was more than good of you to call this morning, and I must admit it made all the difference in the world, as they say, not that I mind (admitting it), but if my postcard sounded like a cry for help, I can only apologize like crazy. I honestly don't think I meant it to, but then as Mr Auden has said, 'the desires of the heart are as crooked as corkscrews' and, well, . . . (incoherent dots)

He also said, which sprang to mind when you were telling me about the crack in the ice, probably wildly misquoted, 'The glacier knocks in the cupboard, / The desert sighs in the bed, / And the crack in the tea-cup opens / A lane to the land of the dead.'[89] One of my favourite cold chill bits.

I began this on the separate yellow sheets (for business), and it is now time to go off to the Theodore Huff Memorial Film Society to see I forget what, but it is an eerie experience at the best of times, so I'll get on with this later.

Wednesday morning

Things are not what they were. This profound thought was occasioned by the movies at the Huff last night, which was a sort of ordinary program which brought fewer out of the woodwork than usual. But there was a superb early Keaton two-reeler with a prefabricated house put up all wrong, the front door on the second floor, the windows all askew, etc which was finally demolished by a freight train driving through it. Then there was a splendid bit of 1927 romantic sludge called *Surrender* with Mary Philbin who was incredibly beautiful and a Russian actor named Ivan Mosjoukine who was not only one of the great actors the movies ever produced but had a face of the kind that apparently no longer exists, at least not on the screen. (Keaton's has always struck me as having been the most fascinating of any actor's— that sort of deadpan is somehow far more mysterious and evocative than any amount of expressiveness—and among actresses, dearly as I worship Garbo and Lillian Gish, for this same quality Louise Brooks, of whom you may well have never even heard, since her American movies are negligible and not easily seen, and her only three good films are two German ones directed by Georg Wilhelm Pabst: *Diary of a Lost Girl* and *Pandora's Box,* the latter being Frank Wedekind's *Lulu,* and a French film called *Prix de beauté* at the end of which a former movie star in a projection room is stabbed to death by a jealous husband? while watching herself in a love scene from one of her old films on the screen. Very Borges.) I seem to have digressed. Anyway, the Huff ended up with a most amusing and witty *Bulldog Drummond* from 1934 with Ronald

---

89. The excerpt is from W. H. Auden's poem "As I Walked Out One Evening."

Colman, and practically every character actor living at the time. When I think of the new movies I've seen the past few days, it is all I can do not to despair. For what it's worth, I should advise steering very clear of such works as *The Charge of the Light Brigade, The Birthday Party* (unless you are a devoted Pinterite, which I confess I am far from being), *The Killing of Sister George, Candy, Charly;* did I say before that *Faces* is worth your attention if you can bear it? I felt about it the way you felt about the Mailer novel; *The Subject Was Roses* is more bearable if not as good and only if you are a great admirer of Patricia Neal, which I happen to be.

I fear my enclosed business remarks sound awfully abrupt, not to say snotty. I don't mean them to be, as I expect you know, but this tone always creeps into my voice so to speak when I try and talk about drawings, etc. Beg pardon, I'm sure.

Rapture, though modified: I find that *Duden* is available in all sorts of languages, including English. Needless to remark it is all madly modern now, and the drawings lack the precise charm of your edition, but it is obviously the single great reference work in existence anyway. Though I think I'll try and dig up one of your vintage somehow too. It is like the time in a mad moment I threw or gave away an ancient Larousse I had because I needed an up to date one at Harvard, totally forgetting that all the marvelous period illustrations would not be in the new one. It is one of the scars on my soul even today.[90]

Before I forget, I have perforce, if that is the word I want, been reading Borges's *A Universal History of Infamy* in a French translation, and Roger Caillois, the translator, has a note at the end of it which is rather interesting. I presume the German translation has the supposed list of sources for the first part at the end of the book?[91] The French one does at any rate. Anyway, M. Caillois investigated them, or some of them at least, and took as an exhaustive example the last of the accounts, the one about Hakim of Merv. The result being that nothing is to be found in the sources he mentions, and that he does not mention all the sources where the story is to be found. Or rather, the true story as it were, since apparently Borges' version is almost entirely made up by himself, and the denouement, which I won't spoil for you, is Borges' idea entirely and may have been inspired by a story by Marcel Schwab. In other words Borges more or less made up everything in these potted biographies, or at least changed them so that they are completely his. The only one I knew something about was Tom Castro, the Tichborne claimant, on which I have read fairly exhaustively. The facts he gives are fairly accurate as far as I can remember—there was a colored man named Bogle, but the whole thing about his being the evil genius behind the thing and his fear of being run down at a crossroads is again Borges' idea entirely.

90. I later gave EG my 1935 edition of the finely illustrated German dictionary *Der Grosse Duden,* of which the French equivalent would be the Larousse.
91. EG had given me a set of Borges's works in German.

With the next batch of stuff I send I'll include a book on Borges which you may not have seen; I don't feel it's terribly illuminating, but there are bits here and there, and some good quotations from him that one hasn't read otherwise. I wish someone would devote themselves to translating him in toto, including ephemera and his things written in collaboration.

Friday morning

I'll answer your letter of the 17th in my next; it just arrived, and obviously needs all sort of digesting, so I'd better get this in the mail without attempting much further, as a mild crisis of a deadline in the offing. is.

Did I make a mysterious reference to coffee cakes in my last, or was it among the innumerable pages I tore up in the last week or so? Anyway, me and *Woman's Day* got our wires crossed about some drawings for their recipe section on coffee cakes and buns for the April issue, so I had to whip up sketches yesterday, and if they like them this morning, I'll get them back this afternoon and have to spend the weekend doing the final drawings. If they don't like them, I don't care to think. Anyway . . .

The bookplates have been promised to be delivered this morning (syntax?), and so I'll mail them airmail as soon as they get here, so you should get them before this, but probably not. When you see them, you may wonder why the names appear to be reversed in order, but if you think about it, you will realize that they are not. I also thought, for what it may be worth, that the appropriate rocks can be filled in with pretty colours. This paragraph probably makes little sense to you now; will it then?

THIS BOOK BELONGS TO
DANIEL
CHRISTOPHER
ZACHARY
NEUMEYER

Thanks to you, I think, my mind is fortunately beginning to function again, and I have dredged up a story about a pig to work on again—another one of those things for children that will obviously turn out to be totally unsuitable according to everyone else by the time it's in its final form.

Your appendix story was already typed, obviously, before your letter arrived. Do you think perhaps it would be a good idea to put business on different coloured paper or at least on separate pages? My file is a vast muddle; I don't know about yours. Though I don't quite see what else it could be, considering.

Ted.

BUSINESS:

From your letter of December 2:

Story about passage of time, mutability, shortness of life, etc.

Little boy impressed by fact that all the things he anticipates or waits for that are in the future, move into the present, and are past before he knows it. Thus it is with birthday parties, visits to dentist, school assignments, visits from the boring uncle who talks too much, etc. Only one thing, it seems to him, does not fit the pattern— the upcoming appendectomy. That seems always to loom.

As he waits, sure enough, all those other things, good and bad, pass—but the appendectomy still is in the future, and he is afraid of it. Pictures and texts show all these things, good and bad, passing from the future into the past. Hints, perhaps, of the dreaded operation, in form of a page or two of ominous clouds. Then, after many things have gone into the past, there are two facing blank pages. Turn page over, and the next page shows the little boy, postoperative, happily sitting up in bed, toys on counterpane, appendectomy (even if it should be spelled with only one p) safely in the past now too.

Re: *Donald Has a Difficulty* and your letter on same: it is no doubt moderately futile to try and say what one intends with drawings and I never like discussing them, but just for what they may be worth when you get around to thinking about the story again—

First, I still like the story as is. I expect my last words may be these. However. Nor do I see it simply as a joke in connection with the epic second version. I will go so far as to admit that on the surface it seems to be without much point, but then I think that only makes it better underneath. I know I don't explain very well, or at all really, what I see in the story, but whatever it is, it is there, and not something I am perversely reading into it. The <u>finished</u> drawings would hopefully get it across in another way, or at least my feelings about it.

Re Donald's physiognomy. I had already sent off the press sheet to Candida so I had nothing but memory to go on as how Donald looked, so perhaps he looks more ancient in the sketches than before. You must realize I cannot draw realistic children by <u>now</u>, and my sketches are always, or almost always, terrible; I mean unless you have decided that Donald looks too old, or rather too unchildlike in *Donald and the . . .* , I don't think you need worry unduly. One point I would make at this point (sorry) is that I do not see <u>this</u> story as being for children at all; which fact <u>does</u> affect my thinking about the drawings, though I would be hard put to say exactly how. On the other two points: the text never says that he pushed the tree with his calf, but only that the splinter entered the calf of his leg when he pushed a tree. Actually, the front of one's calf is right there in front with one's shin, especially if one's leg is bent, and I have played around with Donald less in profile, and pushing with one side and shoulder, so that the splinter might easier reach his calf; on the other hand splinters always enter one's body rather mysteriously anyway and I rather like the ambiguity of it all the way it is now. Again, about the market, battle, string—the drawings were purposely conceived as an abstract threesome, and therefore as simple as possible (besides I couldn't draw a birdseye view of a market to save my soul) and really as three kinds of space—that inside the pots, the space through which rigid things like arrows pass, and the space in which string is stretched taut, hangs limp in various ways, and lies on a surface. I'm not saying this really has much to do with anything, but that is what the three drawings are about, and they either have to stay or go together, I think. I agree about the drawings in relation to real children, but then I don't think in this case that real children have much to do with anything, either from the point of view of them looking at the book, or with Donald, who I at least cannot see tying strings all over his room and the objects therein, not unless there was some great metaphysical reason for doing so. So anyhow, these are my vague thoughts on the subjects you brought up. You don't mention the pet at all. You hate him.

I'm not really trying to talk you out of or into anything, even if it sounds like I am. Just explaining why I was doing what I was doing, in case this may be of some use when you think about it again. Also what about putting it all next to a window, in which case all sorts of things might be seen through it. Also, what about back of jacket, you didn't mention that either? Is it too much to have the tree have fallen down?

[undated, December 1968]

Friday evening

Dear Peter,

 Your letter of Tuesday night only got here this morning, and I've spent the day rather numbly wondering what I could say that would be of any help. Very likely nothing, but . . .[92]

 If only somehow I could return the strength and happiness you have given me the past several months so they would be useful [. . .] as it is, what can I say but that all my thoughts and feelings and hopes are with you in this.

 Another long, stupid, inconsequential letter has been in and out of the typewriter the past several days, and will follow in due course.

 Forgive no picture on the envelope.

Ted.

---

92. I had written to EG about health issues that, at the time, were of serious concern to me.

25.xii.68

Dear ~~Peter~~, 潤夫

Happy Massacre of the Innocents (the 28th, in case you've
forgotten).

Thank y
Shirley Te
to drink t
mesmerized
haven't ha
(Ugh.) Th
your copy
I couldn't
you will t
began a co
in my hear
painted bl
The meal i
supposed t
'40's. Sc

Found o
remains tr
of Donald

Sorry I
with the f
his family
Christmas
couple of
pecially i
as I hear

The enc
why MacLei
I'd feel d
'So what?'

2

and rather ingratiating on that account, about its wickednesses,
but it has been photographed so ravishly by Walter Lassally (who
did Tom Jones) that one is constantly on the verge of swooning
away with visual rapture. Here too something somehow gets sets up
by the presumed depravity of what is being shown and the beauty
with which it is. I don't think I am being very articulate about
this, but perhaps you get what I mean. I suppose now that I think
of it, it is the thing about the subjects of Bacon paintings and
how they are painted. Yes, I _know_ we're not supposed to separate
style and content, but then.... Up Tight, too is a rather coldly
efficient remarke of The Informer with an all negro cast doing
their thing in Cleveland after King's assassination; lots of up
to date talk do not conceal the fact that the whole thing has no
more to do with negros than nothigg, especdilly as whole chunks
of dialogue are lifted from the old script when they aren't being
self-consciously _now_, while in the meantime the photography xxxt
by Boris Kaufman and the decor by Alexandre Trauner, who used to
do all those realer than real Paris Metro stations and lonely
hotels standing all by themselves in those late thirties French
movies of doom and gloom like Port of Shadows and Daybreak, says
all that the actors aren't. All of which proves as usual that
there are very few people around who can write anything, as always

Another day fraught with fruitless endeavour confronts me:
errands to be run (the snow is _still_ coming down; where has my
cleaning woman hidden my rubber boots?) hither and yon, yet another performance of Nutcracker to take in, and a party on the confines of civilization to judge from the address. I reelly, reelly
will answer your last umpteen letters in my next.

If you ask me, the world, except for the children, could very
well do without entirely the week between Christmas and New Years.

堯中斷麼

25.xii.68

Dear Peter ["Peter" scratched out; two Chinese characters penned in],

Happy Massacre of the Innocents (the 28th, in case you've forgotten).

Thank you all so much for the Christmas stocking and the Shirley Temple (be still, my heart!) pitcher, which I am using to drink tea out of, the latter not the former. The cats were mesmerized for some minutes by the water flowers, as was I. I haven't had any for rather more than a quarter of a century. (Ugh.) They also supplied the title for the enclosed story; your copy is not on carbon paper, or rather a carbon, because I couldn't find any. If you think it is about something, I hope you will tell me what, because I haven't the slightest idea. It began a couple of days ago when someone mentioned white sauce in my hearing and the ending came to me when I saw some ornaments painted black in the window of a chic boutique on Madison Avenue. The meal itself is, no doubt apocryphally, what was frequently supposed to be Sunday night supper at Radcliffe back in the late '40's. So much for my scavenging muse.

Found on an ancient scrap of paper: Only that which changes remains true. (Jung) (I do not think it applies to the endings of Donald stories.)

Sorry I have no news from Candida. Whether she is still down with the flu, or perhaps not even in town [. . .], I don't know. Since she knows I've called a couple of times, I dislike seeming to badger her further, especially if she's not well. I'll let you know by phone as soon as I hear anything. Not to worry, at least I don't think so.

* * *

I am come as Time, the waster of the peoples,
Ready for the hour that ripens to their ruin.

(Ch. XI, Bhagavad Gita)

Which reminds me that something must have happened to Thursday (but what?) for it is now Friday. Above is where I happened to have got to over my morning coffee in Mr Huxley's *Perennial Philosophy*. I don't know whether to recommend it to your attention or not. Or perhaps you've read it. If not, it's Religion rather than Philosophy. If nothing else, it's a great anthology, and Huxley himself is not intrusive. (I think it was Cyril Connolly who once said something to the effect that Huxley hits the nail on the head, and then hits it again and again and again.)

A small and sinister snow seems to be coming down relentlessly at present. The radio says it is eventually going to be sleet and rain, but I don't think so; I think it is just going to go on and on, coming down, until the whole world . . . etc. It has that look.

The Water Flowers

It began snowing in the early afternoon.

Jane settled herself on the sofa with a novelette in a yellow paper cover.

The wind rose and the snow came down harder.

Jane lay enthralled by the perils the heroine was subjected to.

The clock struck for the first time that day; she started up from the midst of a trainwreck.

'I must go and shop for dinner' she said, drawn to the window by the curious glare.

The snow was far too deep for her to get to the village.

She read to the end of the novelette and then asked herself 'What shall I do about dinner?'.

The kitchen yielded nothing but an unopened box of soda crackers in the cupboard.

Charles came in and said 'What are we having for dinner?'.

'Soda crackers,' she said 'but I'll make a delicious white sauce to go over them'.

She took flour and water, and mixed some of each together on the stove.

George came in, stirred the sauce about, and said 'It's too thick'.

Jane added a quantity of water.

Anne came in as George was tasting it.

She took the ladle from him and said 'It's too thin'.

Jane added an amount of flour.

William came in as Anne was sampling it again.

He stuck his finger in it and said 'It's lumpy'.

Jane poured in water to dissolve the lumps, so that it was too thin once again.

She dumped in flour, so that it became a second time too thick.

This went on until there was so much white sauce, it filled every available receptacle.

It was still lumpy, but they sat down to dinner notwithstanding.

In the ensuing weeks white sauce appeared at least once, and often two or three times, at every meal, even breakfast.

The last of the sauce covered some ill-mashed turnips.

Just after the meal concluded Henry suddenly died.

It was Christmas Eve as it happened.

Jane, Anne, George, and William painted all the ornaments a dull black.

Charles went to the village for black candles.

Snow was falling again as they finished trimming the tree.

Books just arrived, so I hope Borges has reached you by now too. Wonderful drawings in the Hudson.[93] Many thanks as always, he mumbled inadequately.

I meant to start this page with pleased remarks about Candida taking you on— she said all the right things (meaning she agreed with me) over the phone in what was passing for her voice at the moment—and then it slipped my mind, the surface of which is notoriously smooth and unmarked, like a blanc mange. Anyhoo, I was not surprised, and only mildly apprehensive only because I hadn't heard from her. [. . .] To recapitulate, I gave her *Donald and the . . .* , the dummy for WWHDAN, the other five Donald stories, the three Lionels, and "Snowflake Snowflake" and "The Faithful Fish." I'll drop by sometime after New Year's for a chat with her. Not to push, but a revised ending for the moustache story might be a good idea, as she would then have two stories of yours at least that would have nothing to do with me (except presumptuous noises from me in the background about who should be allowed to illustrate them). Also I'll see what she thinks about the Harry situation, whatever that may be by that time. Have you sent him "The Faithful Fish" or not? If you haven't, I wouldn't at this point; it just gives him another thing to dither over. If you feel awkward about trying to get him to commit himself, don't, for Heaven's sake, let me badger you into the attempt. After all, Candida can easily tell him she has all the MSS and would like to start showing them around, but realizes he has first crack at them, so to speak, and all that kind of jazz; it just might make him pull himself together, but I for one as a rule of thumb to be going on with am not inclined (where is this sentence going?) to look on him kindly or helpfully if he is going to start the old not-a-story,-let's-have-a-new-ending bit, on any of the Donalds. If I ever get myself up to date on my work, which seems fearfully unlikely, I'm going to start nagging you again to let me do *Donald Has a D.*

Another care package of a very miscellaneous nature seems to have heaped itself up in Neumeyer's corner. *The Listing Attic* contains my earliest published writing (how's that for a pretentious phrase) since most of the limericks were written in one of those bursts of creative endeavor in a couple of weeks back in 1946 (I think) and the rest were written to fill out the book; I fear this is my épater le bourgeois work (Clifton Fadiman once refused to quote from it in an article on limericks in *Holiday* because it was so horrid) and only of interest because of its extreme rarity, it being the hardest to come by of anything at the moment. *Fletcher and Zenobia,* as I thunk (think) I said before, is not my plot or characters, though I did a complete rewriting job on it. Alas, the pictures are hideously reproduced, which is sad, because they are lovely and bright, the originals. I guess I also mentioned I am writing a sequel where

93. I had sent EG books by W. H. Hudson, one of my favorites at the time, although I don't recall now who illustrated them. Among these was not the usual *Green Mansions* but rather Hudson's modest memoirs and observations after he moved from Argentina to London.

they save a small circus. Let's see, what else? The Isak Dinesen is to be returned at your leisure, everything else for your shelves, wastebasket, whatever. *The Metropolitan Museum Bulletin* for the della Bella.[94] It is a pity they did not do a catalogue because the bulletin only hints at the wealth and variety of the show. I've been doing the Flann O'Brien as bedside reading. I don't know whether Charles Williams will be your cup of tea or not.[95] Someone has apparently borrowed all of mine, or else I have put them somewhere else without noting same on my chart (everything is double-rowed around here, which is a Great Nuisance) which is why the paperback. There are six of them, and I suppose I've read each three or four times; he is not the greatest novelist in the world, but somehow they have always stuck with me, and why no one has made movies of them I cannot think, except of course I can because people never or seldom make movies of things that would make good movies, or if they do, they rewrite them completely. Grrrr.

Speaking of which I return the copy of *The Black Doll,* which was for your file anyway, and besides, who knows, you may meet someone with millions to put up for just such a project, and how can you strike while the iron is hot unless you have a copy to have one of the children rush to them in the middle of the night in a blizzard without even giving him, the child, time to put on his bunny slippers? The snow is coming down harder. Yes.

You may add *The Magus* to your list of films to be avoided whatever happens (John Fowles must be far and away the most pretentious living writer—I use the word loosely); seldom have I seen a picture where nothing works with such relentless thoroughness. I jumped on *Candy* from hearsay before, but desperation set in one evening and I saw it; it may only be because I expected it to be perfectly horrible, but I ended up quite enjoying it. It is a dreadful film, do not mistake me, but eventually its very ham-handedness and foolishness creates a sort of valid surrealist commentary, and it is marvelously cluttered with gewgaws and extravagances of decor that for some reason only the Italians are capable of anymore (witness their endless stream of ancient world bits of nonsense that were made for practically nothing that made Cleopatra look incredibly cheap, tacky, and unimaginative by comparison). I am beginning to think that most of the comment being made today <u>is</u> in the decor. I think I mentioned *The Touchables* to you with its plastic bubble pleasure dome, and then there's *Joanna,* another little English item, which is naive beyond belief, and rather ingratiating on that account, about its wickednesses, but it has been photographed so ravishingly by Walter Lassally (who did *Tom Jones*) that one is constantly on the verge of swooning away with visual rapture. Here too something somehow gets set up

---

94. The Italian printmaker Stefano della Bella (1610–1664).
95. He was not.

by the presumed depravity of what is being shown and the beauty with which it is. I don't think I am being very articulate about this, but perhaps you get what I mean. I suppose now that I think of it, it is the thing about the subjects of Bacon paintings and how they are painted. Yes, I <u>know</u> we're not supposed to separate style and content, but then . . . *Up Tight,* too, is a rather coldly efficient remake of *The Informer* with an all Negro cast doing their thing in Cleveland after King's assassination; lots of up to date talk does not conceal the fact that the whole thing has no more to do with Negroes than nothing, especially as whole chunks of dialogue are lifted from the old script when they aren't being self-consciously <u>now</u>, while in the meantime the photography by Boris Kaufman and the decor by Alexandre Trauner, who used to do all those realer than real Paris Metro stations and lonely hotels standing all by themselves in those late thirties French movies of doom and gloom like *Port of Shadows* and *Daybreak,* say all that the actors aren't. All of which proves as usual that there are very few people around who can write anything, as always.

Another day fraught with fruitless endeavour confronts me: errands to be run (the snow is <u>still</u> coming down; where has my cleaning woman hidden my rubber boots?) hither and yon, yet another performance of *Nutcracker* to take in, and a party on the confines of civilization to judge from the address. I really, really will answer your last umpteen letters in my next.

If you ask me, the world, except for the children, could very well do without entirely the week between Christmas and New Year's.

[signed with four Chinese characters]

Mr Peter Neumeyer,
12 Powder House Road Ext.,
Medford.
Mass.
02155

CHRISTMAS 6c — CHRISTMAS 6c

NEW YORK
PM
20 DEC
1968

UNITED STATES — UNITED STATES

Mr Peter Neumeyer,
12 Powder House Road Ext.,
Medford,
Mass.
02155

UNITED STATES WASHINGTON 5c

The Museum of Modern Art   20.xii.68.
11 West 53 Street, New York 10019, N.Y.

If my method and arithmetic
are not at fault, I have a notion
for a book that can, or rather
can't, obviously, be read in —

265,252,859,812,191,058, —
636,308,480,000,000² ways.

It's to be called (what else?)
The Boggle Book.

NEW YORK N.Y.
AM
20 DEC
1968

Printed in Sweden

Post Card

Mr Peter Neumeyer,
12 Powder House Road Ext,
Medford,
Mass.
02155.

Vladimir Tatlin: Monument for the Third International (finished model)
(1920) Wood, about 15' high. Destroyed.

December 27, 1968

Dear Ted,

Your card, your yellow business letter and your good letter of the 17th just arrived. But I was thinking last night just before going to sleep that I would write you today anyway—and I would write you, I knew, something very simple and without the convention of the sputter. I wanted only to say this: it was more than good to hear your voice on the phone, and to hear you happy. Secondly—you said some months ago something about a change, turnover, flip in your life. I listened. But I did not say "me too," because it would not have been the truth. But now I want to say, "me too." So—me too. So, for nothing describable simply or short of a poem, thank you, Ted. You are a blessing. And in the knowledge of that, you should——I don't know what. But your letters, the potential of our reunions, your existence has made something of this world that [it] hadn't the possibility of before. Let it go at that!

The mundane:

Even before your yellow letter "BUSINESS" I also felt bad last night talking business, sort of, with you on the phone. I don't like to do that, and I felt (briefly) badly about it, notwithstanding the fact that I am ecstatic about the prospects with Candida (does she have another name too?). Subordinated under that point is my awareness how incredibly selflessly (don't say, "oh for HEAVEN sake, STOP it!") you have been in this. If a student's work begins to hover imaginatively in an area where I have been thinking, I am very aware of rather low and vile feelings in myself which I must attempt to resist. [. . .] You have really acted very grandly, generously, selflessly, and I owe you (but we don't owe each other, do we) I somethingorother you, in addition to resolving to attempt to emulate you in that spirit, henceforth.

Which may bring this letter closer to the yellow paper.

1. The yellow paper letter of yours is very good. Let's not pussyfoot with each other in our work with each other. The directness of your disagreement is superb, and I shall try to talk likewise simply. For I trust we will for long have to do with each other, and talking about our work frankly makes all infinitely easier.

2. [. . .]

Now the points abt. *Donald Has a Difficulty*. No—actually—I somewhat agree with you. The story is not pointless. It does have a point. But I should guess only perhaps 16 people in the world, all of whom would have to love us dearly, would see it. You see it. I see it. But it is a zephyr of a point. Question: Does one print a story with a zephyr of a point? (Honest (not rhetorical) question.) For whom? Yes, yes, yes, there is a point indeed. But . . . And if it weren't a worthwhile point—say like the wind of a sea anemone closing—a real thing in a life that isn't very real—it wouldn't be a point. But again—but? but?

Interior (top) and back jacket illustrations for *Donald Has a Difficulty*.

The bovine (i.e. Donald's calf) correspondence is worthy of the *New Yorker*.

But if anybody but you and me read the story, the sideways pushing, making at least the possibility of a calficular injury conventionally conceived, is an improvement.

Physiognomy—main concern not yet, but later for the umbrella story. Donald is part of us. We cannot criticize his appearance. For the umbrella story, let's talk later. There, I think, there will be reasons.

No metaphysical reasons for strings all over the room. Depends on if it's "for children." If not, skip it. If it is, believe me, though there are not what you term metaphysical reasons, there are infantile reasons bred into the race. Most children do. Most parents would say "Aha, sure enough!"

Do I hate the pet,[96] since I don't mention him? I didn't mention him because I am thoughtless and gauche. I took him as one of us, as a member of the family, and so—awful as it sounds—I took him momentarily for granted, and only when you whatever you did, did I come to my senses to say what I felt. Absolutely, he IS. Nem numquam speratemus igitur.*

The back of the jacket is superb. And it leads to the Epic. And by the way, the back of the jacket says what the book didn't. So it i.e. the book has my original ephemeral point. And it has your, in this case much more solid, point.

* * *

Let me know immediately if you don't get this letter.

yours,
Peter

P.S. We got a big map of New York City. THERE IS NO 38th ST.! The streets go from 37th to 39th. ARE YOU A MIRAGE?

*not Latin, so don't try.

---

96. "The pet" was the stoej-gnpf—the creature pictured on a number of EG's envelopes, in *Donald Has a Difficulty,* and (sporting a red scarf) on the cover of this book. In a way, he became emblematic of our correspondence.

Wednesday morning, 1.i.69

Dear Peter,

* * *

If you want to think of me as being noble and selfless, go right ahead. I mean who does not wish to be thought noble and selfless by one's loved ones. Your evidence, however, seems pretty flimsy to me. For one thing, I said more than once ages ago that my usual first reaction to anything new of yours was to turn fierce green with envy and all uncharitableness; not any more I think. Any more than I have such twinges when I read Jane Austen, or Borges, or Lady Murasaki, to choose not entirely at random, from the idols in my cave (I know this phrase has something to do with something else, but the classification of Bacon's (?)[97] does not come to mind, and all I mean is that I live in a cave as opposed to a market-place, which is the only other one I can remember—you can obviously steel yourself for vast amounts of blather from here on out today). I mean, Gee, I think you are a Great Writer, Dr Neumeyer, and I have All Your Books at home, but I forgot to bring one today, so could you please write 'For Edward (I spell it with two E's and two A's like Mr [Eadweard] Muybridge—and aren't some of those photographs pretty strange, don't you think so?) with All Good Wishes' and then sign your name, legibly if you can, and don't forget the date, in a copy supplied at your own expense, I mean you must be making a fortune, I hear authors are very rich people . . . How did all that get in here?

The thought behind the above, though you'd scarcely know it, is meant quite seriously, and if as an author you were someone else, I should be sending you Donald books et al as touchstones in the same way as I send you Borges you haven't read, for example. In passing, it came to me that Borges is the first person we talked about together, practically as soon as we were under weigh (is that how it's supposed to be spelled here? and if not, why do I think so?) in Harry's boat. Perhaps he [Borges] imagined us both. So as it is, and not being one for doing things for people ordinarily, mostly through lethargy and lack of interest, but a little bit because I'm not particularly confident that anything I might think of would be good or of use, if in this case I have for once been in a position to do something, I have also felt so strongly on the subject, that no merit whatsoever attaches to doing what it would have been impossible not to have done. One would hardly guess from my correspondence that my simple declarative sentences have sometimes been admired for their inexplicable resonances and under/overtones, even by you.

---

97. Sir Francis Bacon classified the sorts of delusions that confuse human understanding under the heading "idols." His "idols of the cave" are those delusions to which human beings are subject because of their personal predispositions.

Why should you feel, even briefly, bad about talking business over the phone? You baffle me from time to time, as you know. So much for that.

I now take you to task about the point that only 16 people would see the point of *Donald Has a D* for having anything whatsoever to do with publishing same. The 16 people, for one thing, would not have to love us dearly, at least not personally, to see the point, and while I reluctantly admit that an audience has to ultimately exist somewhere, the moment you bring into question its numbers or anything else about it, the whole thing becomes invalid, if you see what I mean. Despite the fact (excuse presumption) that in some way I am you and you are me, nevertheless if no one but you ever read "The Water Flowers" as a recent example, still you are also not me enough so that the story has an audience and its existence is justified communication (how I loathe that word, but it will serve here) has taken place.

Also, after fifteen and a half years of getting myself into print, I still have all sorts of incredibly complicated and contradictory thoughts about doing so, but I have learned to disregard them, since somewhere at bottom I obviously wish to see the books I write in print, if only as a way of murdering them to get them out of the way, there is little point, after one has done the best one can with something, to think about it any further.

The rest of your comments on *Donald Has a D.* noted and mulled over; at the moment I don't have any further thoughts, not that any seem to be called for. It will depend a great deal on this and that, most of which is too tedious, frail, and filled with unknown factors to be able to be thought about, as to when I can get around to getting three items ready for Fantod Press publication, but I now take it, tentatively, that you will be able to be nagged into letting *Donald Has a D.* be one of them when the time comes?

I have been toying with the idea of reading the Peter Gay book;[98] I now take it I shouldn't? If I do not seem to be mentioning anything I've read lately, it is because I am in one of those periods of undifferentiated flux or something in which I am reading about fifty, at a minimum, books at once, so of course I seldom finish one. Eventually this phase will pass, and I'll discover I have about ten pages to go in all of them, and will sit down and systematically finish them, one after another. The seeming, or real for that matter, chaos in which I live, I am happy to say, no longer bothers me nearly as much as it once did. [. . .] I am a practically perfect example of Mr Connolly's rock pool metaphor, and it is at least interesting to sit here waiting to see what the next wave will bring in or take away.

When does the Kafka come from Prentice Hall?[99]

---

98. I had just reviewed Peter Gay's *Weimar Culture: The Outsider as Insider* (Harper and Row, 1968).
99. My book *Twentieth Century Interpretations of "The Castle": A Collection of Critical Essays* (Prentice Hall, 1968) had just been published.

What is this about 38th Street? Who ever said I lived on 38th Street? That's the mirage; not me.[100] Put not your trust in maps. There's a terrifying story that has haunted me ever since I first read it (I forget, alas, the title and the authors, it seems to me there were two of them) about some people boating on English canals and going off the map as it were and somehow ending up in the centre of a grey and windless lake, their view bounded by nothing but tall grass and No Way Out.

* * *

Missing unanswered letter found. A few oddments first. I think I'll send you two novels by Rayner Heppenstall to read sometime and return at leisure. I discovered him by accident with *The Greater Infortune,* in 1960 I see from the dates read in the front; he's one of those rather strange, isolated writers who haunts me.

I was sorry about Thomas Merton's somewhat unsuitable demise.[101] I read his translations of Chuang Tzu last spring I think, and I had just finished his *Zen and the Birds of Appetite,* which seemed most intelligent and sensible, which so much writing on Zen does not seem to be. I remember reading *The Seven Storey Mountain* when it came out, but very little since then.

Another small care package may have reached you by now. Arthur Waley's only translations of Japanese poetry and a small anthology in German, whose merit I cannot guess, though I thought the illustrations nice.

I fear you must expect various bits of Orientalia as the bookshops classify it from time to time. The Yasunari Kawabata, incidentally, is unfortunately not the complete novel, or rather, since apparently he never really finishes them in the sense that he is liable to publish a few more pages of continuation from time to time over the years, several more episodes have appeared in Japanese since this translation was made. One hopes perhaps Knopf will bring out a new edition incorporating them.

There is now a second *Personal Anthology* of Borges in Spanish; one wonders if someone will translate what of it has not been before—I only glanced at the contents and recognized quite a few things that have already been done into English—though by now it would be more to the point if the books, title by title, were systematically translated.

Bad literal translation from French edition of a bit from the Kenningar, describing them, but which put rather well for me what I think I have always wanted my own writing to be: They procure a satisfaction quasi organic. What they succeed in transmitting is indifferent. What they suggest is null. They do not invite to revery,

---

100. EG did, of course, live on 38th Street.
101. Thomas Merton died from an accidental electric shock as he was stepping out of a bathtub on December 10, 1968.

156

they wake neither images nor passions. They are not points of departure, but of arrival.[102]

Do you dream much? If so, how, what, etc. if you care to divulge? Some days ago now, I woke from one of my more spectacular efforts (it was an endless series of variations on staircases, all made of shiny dark wood like benches in railway stations, one flight of them also seemed to be made from them, very high, and curved, and slippery, and then at other flights they were wide enough to contain whole Kafkaesque offices filled with desks and chairs and people, and so forth and so on, God knows how many flights and different sorts, twisting and turning, until finally I was precariously perched on some baroque woodwork high, high above the world which was still nothing but all these endless variations of stairs) and began pondering on how while if I existed in the dream, I was recognizably myself, my daytime one, there were other times when I imperceptibly ceased to exist, or at least there was no distinction between the perceiver and what was perceived.

I dream incessantly, always in the most brilliant technicolor and either my dreams, the most vivid ones, when I am overwrought in one way or another, are incredibly intricate and diverse and tortuous things and plots in the world of people, or else incredibly grandiose and impersonal spectacles of both natural scenery and man-made architecture, though usually only one aspect, man <u>or</u> nature, at a time; they also tend to encompass all sorts of art forms and to slip from one to another and to reality and out again: movies, plays, books, paintings. I suppose it is all some sort of compensation for my creepmouse daily existence ('Close retirement and a life by stealth' (Creech: whoever he may have been)).[103] What this was all in aid of before I got to maundering, was the part about there being perception pure and simple without subject and object, though what there is to say about it beyond the simple fact I don't know.

At some point I think I was about to mention that my grand new German Cassell's arrived from the Book of the Month Club, and now here I sit, looking from time [to time] rather wistfully at a small pile of [Christian] Morgenstern in German I have bought over the years and wondering what if any headway I could make if I also purchased a German grammar. Since I have no facility whatever for languages, very little I imagine. It's a pity I can't share your mind enough to know German without having to learn it.

---

102. In this paragraph, EG was still on the subject of Borges translations. "Kenningar" refers to "kennings," Old Norse poetic metaphors or figures of speech that used two words (e.g., "sea road") to stand for one concrete word (e.g., "ocean"). This is a subject Borges wrote about.

103. "Creep-mouse" is a word I know only from Jane Austen's *Mansfield Park*. The quotation "close retirement and a life by stealth" derives from a translation of Book I, Epistle 19, line 42, by the Roman poet Horace, translated by Thomas Creech in the mid-eighteenth century. EG's literary wanderings were remarkable.

3:15

Since the thermometer says 11°, I've perforce had a brisk indeed six-mile walk.

To the other unanswered letter.

Don't know Panofsky's writings, except by name. Will add him to ever-lengthening list of people to look into.

I was so taken with the first few pages of the Jules Renard journal that I went out and got the complete one in French which is well over a thousand pages, so now I am in the dilemma of whether to go on with the English or wait until I feel I have the time and powers of concentration to work away at the other, which would obviously be a labour of months.[104]

You did not make any phony, pseudo sophisticated remark about the Ustinov movie [*Hot Millions*]; I don't know why on earth you thought perhaps you had since I have yet to hear you make a p,p-s remark about <u>anything</u>. Ever. If I recall you simply said you moderately or perhaps mildly enjoyed it, which is why I said I apparently liked it better.

The Ladykillers was Alec Guinness being a dotty master criminal in charge of a gang pretending to be a chamber music group and renting rooms from a dear little lady who lived over a set of railway tracks, and at the end everyone managed to murder everyone else, except of course for her. There was one absolutely marvelous scene where she roped the gang in to a tea party she was giving for all her ancient spinster friends and they all sang "Silver Threads Among the Gold" around the harmonium or whatever.

Re Salinger, it is just conceivable that at the age of 14 I might have fallen for *Catcher in the Rye*, though even that I doubt, since my favourite authors at the time were [Evelyn] Waugh and Aldous Huxley, but even then I do not think I could have taken all that ghastly self-indulgence and -pity and, to be brutal, slimy soul-searching.[105] When I do sit down finally to give someone a chance, I do think I can manage to be fair about it, even if I find I don't much care for it afterwards, but he I found to be everything I find most pretentious and dishonest. I don't think there are many immoral writers, but he comes high on my list. Let us argue about this some time.

Kolbe rings no bell at all. What was the one picture you saw? Elk Sinking into Swamp? Lady Flying on Black Pig? The Interrupted Obsequies? What?

Re great and good thoughts, yours and others. Once again I appreciate your

---

104. EG had enthusiastically sent me the one-volume edition of Renard's journals in 1968. I treasure it still.

105. Although EG was extraordinarily generous in his views of others, "self-pity and slimy soul searching" were always traits deeply offensive to him. Although he would occasionally exclaim dramatically in a tone of almost cosmic despair, he did that patently for humorous effect. EG indulged in less self-pity than anyone I've ever met.

hesitations about *Donald Has a D.* even if I do not share them. Now of course you see it all in time, as the other Donalds have not yet been published, and so on, but relatively soon, please the pigs (a secular equivalent to D.V. that I am fond of), this will no longer hold true, and there will be many Donalds for people to read, not to mention other things, and then it will only be graduate students and their ilk (misuse of word, but they are frequently ilky, don't you think?) who would know or care that *Donald Has a D.* came out second, etc. So that then, however minor you feel it is, it will be of interest to the world for ever afterwards. Of course I think it would be now, because it is the work, not the author in one way, and even if you never wrote anything else for me it would still have its exitsnece. God, my typing. Existence.

As to the intellectual hierarchy, I couldn't a. with you m. Anent this, Alison Lurie, of whom I have spoken somewhat I think, the author of *Imaginary Friends,* etc.—her new one is called *Real People,* which I have not yet had a chance to read, but she expects galleys fairly soon—has been teaching a course in creative writing at Cornell this year [. . .] and she says that at least half of every session has to be devoted to listening to the drearily same accounts of the students' latest trip on LSD, speed, whatever, and/or their latest sexual activities and/or their thought on Viet Nam, the world, etc. Also, that she cannot get them over the notion that to revise, or rewrite, or even think about what they write, is to be the worst sort of hypocrite, dishonest, ad nauseam. If it isn't whatever gush happens to hit the paper without any premeditation whatever it is apparently worse than meaningless, it is phony in great big neon letters. The authors they most hate are Jane Austen and Dickens, the former I can understand: she is much too uncompromising and tough-minded for them, but <u>Dickens</u>? One would have thought that things like *Bleak House* and *Our Mutual Friend* would turn them on like mad: what could be more contemporary to the present orientation of sensibility, the psychedelic bit not excluded by any means. What could be more hallucinatory and all the rest than the whole tenour of those books? Most peculiar. Several people who taught painting were there when we were talking about this, and they said it was the same thing all over again. Endless amounts of confession, with no interest in whatever their elders might have to say back, and no knowledge or respect for whatever anybody else may have done. One woman said most of her students were absolutely incapable of telling in even what century a painting might have been done; all of it was dead as far as they were concerned.

Re Schopenhauer, you use the phrase 'doubting the usefulness of my own mind'; not that I wish you to be in a muddle, but it so exactly describes what I sometimes think is an almost perfectly chronic state with me. If you have difficulty with him, think what it will be like for me if I try. Actually I should like to now, as I discover we share the same birthdate, along with Chopin. I can't tell you what a relief it is after all these years of thinking I had to have some affinity with George Washington, whom I have always coldly detested, though I was also told the other afternoon that he did have some human frailties, such as not dining out very often because he was embarrassed by his wooden false teeth. Somehow this is not yet enough to endear him to me.

Which brings me to the latest things washed into my rock pool by the tide, one old, one new. It is the first time in many years that I have had much of a chance to see Alison, which has been pleasant, as except for people like Connie, whom I have known for thirty years, she belongs to the second oldest group of my friends whom I have known for twenty, since my Harvard days. Anyway, many years ago she taught me to read the tarot cards, which I have now not done for years, but have decided to try and take up again with the aid of a couple of books on the subject; also, one of her creative writing students has got her interested in astrology, and she has done ditto for me so I have purchased the requisite texts, and I shall see how far I can get on my own in the next several weeks, and then if I am still interested, there is a class starting on Monday nights beginning the end of this month, which I rather think I may go to if it looks like my sort of thing.

As you know, I have always, if desultorily and spasmodically, been interested in what is loosely the occult, and believe in it to a certain degree as indicative of the nature of things and the relations between them, if not too much in the more specific kind of fortune-telling. I mean if someone tells me I am going to get a letter from a short blonde girl residing 423 miles in a southwesterly direction which is going to contain a request for one of my old bowties I am going to be very dubious, but things like the *I Ching,* the tarot, palmistry, astrology, whatever, do seem to me so many similar ways of by-passing the cause-and-effect, rational world in which we normally try to function, and by means of their various stylizations and symbols of the whole reality to show you things and clarify them which otherwise you might have much more trouble finding out. Ultimately of course one should absorb whatever the thing is to the point where it is no longer needed, the method, I mean. I know somewhere someone says in connection with the *I Ching* that eventually it should become so much a part of you that your conscious mind would no longer need to consult it at all, and that then you would directly be apprehending the Tao and acting in accordance with it without any conscious thought at all. As it is, however, who is going to achieve this very easily? Not I, for one.

Since your letter had just come the day before, I asked Alison to read the tarot in connection with the first paragraph for you and then for me. I had of course told her something about you, though not a great deal, because I find it difficult to try and explain our relationship(s), and otherwise all I said was that your letter indicated that something had happened, or rather come into being, and that in a way I knew what it was and in another way didn't know at all, which is true. Except for the fact that our collaboration seems very liable indeed to be successful (one supposes on the material or at least public plane, since it obviously already is as far as we are concerned) since the card working for us was the same in both sets of cards, and that's what it indicated, I won't say any more now, because for one thing it is impossible to say how much both readings were influenced by my subjective feelings, which are obviously very strong on the subject. What is remarkable, however, or rather isn't, since it is always true as far as my experience goes, is that in such readings, however the cards that come up may be interpreted by individual differences of opinion by interpreters, the cards themselves that come up in a reading are always perfectly relevant to the question, however specific or, on the other hand, generalized, they are meant to answer. To take a madly simple example, if one consults the cards about a private emotional problem, all the cards are going to be those which deal with this aspect of things, and one is not going to get a whole set of cards dealing with irrelevancies such as money, work, public things, etc. Anyway, I have kept a record of the cards that turned up for the two readings and will tell you about them one day no doubt. May I add that both were favourable, if a bit fraught, as I do not want you to think the reason I don't go into them further is that it was all doom and disaster. Quite the contrary.

I can't guarantee what progress I shall make in the next couple of weeks—after all, people spend lifetimes learning to read them—but if you would all, including the boys, like your horoscopes at least cast, send list of birthplaces and dates and times of day as accurately as they are known, and I'll eventually send back fascinating charts covered with mystic-type squiggles with some sort of commentary dealing with transits, oppositions, ascending signs, and who knows what all, and what it all means (What It All Means; WHAT IT ALL MEANS) in a rather rudimentary sort of way.

Since the ballet starts again tomorrow for six weeks, and since the correspondence columns of the theater section of the *NY Times* have been filled lately with diatribes against the vileness and immorality of the movie (*The Impossible Years* with David Niven) at the Music Hall this Christmas, I think I must get to it this evening.

9:40

Very odd. I am doing my astrology and have suddenly come across bits of Marcus Manilius's *Astronomica* translated by Thomas Creech.

Thursday morning

The movie, incidentally, was just another comic strip sort of thing, utterly tasteless and franker than it would have been ten years ago, but really quite innocuous and mildly funny from time to time; one wonders how people get so worked up; on the other hand, I did about *The Fixer,* which I found to be a really viciously sadistic piece of drivel (I did not read the book) while everyone else is talking about Dostoyevskian moral intensity. Ah well.

* * *

Please thank Zack for his note and Helen for hers and for the pictures, and give her my apologies for not writing her separately on some equally elegant stationery, which I don't have any of. I must say you could not tell from the rather owlish picture of us what boyish high spirits are ofttimes concealed within.

Will the plumber come <u>this</u> morning? I now realize this is an inexplicable interjection here, because the plumber's coming was only mentioned in hitherto mentioned destroyed pages.

I must to the envelope—what shall it be?—if I am to get this into the mail. This letter, whether there is any evidence in it of such or not, is a great triumph of mind over matter, in that I've been feeling that New York was having its usual effect on me and making me incapable of doing anything but coping with <u>it</u>.

Ted.

Forgive perfunctory answering of your last letters—masses somehow got left out, as always.

Jan 1, 1969!

Dear Ted,

Just a note regarding two matters:

1. Harry S. brought over last night his young lady, and the BOOK. The former was herself; the latter looked very very good—bigger than I had thought. The only flaw was that on the back of the cover, the picture is infinitesimally askew—the paper probably pasted a little bit off. Only the creators of it all would notice.

Harry was a nervous wreck. Has been trying for weeks to hire a girl to do promotion, public relations, whatever—space buying, etc.—at 12–$14,000. He's been on to this for weeks, I know, and still has no one. For all I know therefore (but he didn't say this) promotion for A-W's new endeavor may be sinking fast. Anyway, Harry was most definitely on edge, anxious, jittery, etc.

Then—Harry saw your beautiful envelopes on display on their black felt board. I don't know what he was thinking, but he was certainly emotional, intrigued, fascinated, admiring, sputtered something incoherent about borrowing sometime being sure to take care . . . etc.—end of subject.

Then, as he was looking at them, I pointed out the young man hanging onto the winddriven umbrella, and said, "that, you recognize, don't you, is Donald and the umbrella, from when Ted and I were corresponding about it." Bafflement on H's face. Repeat sentence with variations two or three times, till finally he looked sort of vaguely as though he connected. Then the animals, Lionel's, in semicircle. I identified these for him, and he took on a look as though being pursued by flying ants. Needless to say, when Helen pointed out the *Day and Night* children, he had no recognition.[106]

With all this snarliness above, I want to add ritualistically but truly—Harry is nice, human with human problems, and existing in a state somewhere ambiguously between friendship and business.

THEN, he started muttering about boxes in which to send out the books—all his books—and what they should look like. I don't know if you'll curse or thank me, but I instinctively said, "Why don't you ask Ted Gorey to design (eyecatching) boxes for A-W books?" He lit up like four star spangled banners, twitching for five minutes with excitement. So———I expect you may hear from him. It may be lucrative. It may be fun for you. Obviously A-W could bless its stars.

2. I have here your "The Water Flow(u)ers" (The blanc mange—see Chaucer's "Cook's Tale"—rather, the prologue, the cook.)[107] Two main feelings. It is good,

---

106. These envelopes are shown on pages 123, 79, and 97, respectively.
107. In Chaucer's *Canterbury Tales,* the cook, one of the pilgrims, has a running sore on his shin, the
    overflow of which, Chaucer implies, contributes to the substance of the blancmange, the white sauce,
    that the cook is stirring up for his fellow travelers.

The last of the sauce covered some ill-mashed turnips.

Just after the meal concluded Henry suddenly died.

genuine, in fact very high Gorey. Secondly (you may not like this) it would also—its central part, the adding more and more and more and more, till the sauce overflows everything—be an absolutely charming, winning, funny, favorite, perhaps classic, children's story—outside its frame. Could you do it both ways—one: with the Gorey frame, setting, novel, spawning cast, etc. And secondly, just, à la Grimm, which the idea is after all like, just as a sweet, winning, innocent children's joke. [. . .]

* * *

As for the way the story is now, it is one of the very good ones, it seems to my prejudiced eye. Two tiny things I wonder about in it.

1. "ill-mashed turnips": Except for the fact that it was snowing, and they were snowed in, there seems to me no reason why the inhabitants should be bare-ration type people. The settling on the sofa with a novelette even suggests slightly otherwise (as will, I'm sure, your characters' appearances). I figure they're more jasmine tea and wafer-with-cheese people, no? So then why the peasant fare (besides your liking the sound of the words)? [. . .] It's a little distracting from the main line, it's you allowing yourself a luxury, I feel (presumptuously, but with good intention)—i.e. not you, me presumptuously, of course!

2. More difficult point: There is a big, lengthy, wonderful, main-focus incident with the lumping and unlumping sauce for the central meal. Then there is, in one sentence only, the many meals of the ensuing weeks. ok. Then the last, the turnip meal. Then "Just after the meal concluded Henry suddenly died." In my reading, there is so much interest on the central meal, that there is confusion for me whether Henry died after that big one, or after the weeks of meals that ended with the turnip meal. I may be a poor or too simple reader. I don't know. My psychological processes keep me so hooked on the main meal, that I feel a little irritated at having to go back to see whether it's after that one or after the cursory meals that Henry died. One could, of course, say that "after the last, the mashed turnip meal, Henry died." Or one could try more intricate transplants. I don't know. [. . .]

BUT I DO LIKE IT VERY VERY MUCH. It's funny. It's subdued. It's moodful. Its main line is clear and clean. And the title is marvelous.

* * *

yrs,
Peter

P.S. To my surprise (I hadn't re-read it all really in p/haps a year) I think Donald and the . . . is UNDERLINE good. On both our parts. More on that another time.

THE MUSEUM OF MODERN ART
11 West 53 Street, New York, N.Y. 10019

8.ii.69, 6:00 ish

R: MT arrived this morning but the postman neglected to hand it to me when we met at the mail box, so I didn't find it until after I had mailed the letter. In any case, it needs thought, and several rereadings. Something of a shock to me, who had already done away with the past & future, and now... well, where am I?

Donald never need have got near that tree. I came in just now, felt a horrid twinge, and discovered not a splinter, but

Mr Peter Neumeyer,
12 Powder House Road Ext.,
Medford, Mass.
02155.

THE MUSEUM OF MODERN ART

11 West 53 Street, New York, N.Y. 10019

8.ii.69, 6:00 ish

R: MT arrived this morning but the postman neglected to hand it to me when we met at the mail box, so I didn't find it until after I had mailed the letter. In any case, it needs thought, and several rereadings. Something of a shock to me, who had already done away with the past & future, and now... well, where am I?

Donald never need have got near that tree. I came in just now, felt a horrid twinge, and discovered not a splinter, but a thorn in the sole of my left foot. I had virtually to break my leg to get at it with the tweezers. If you know how it got there, I fervently hope you will be kind enough to let me know.

✳

Jacques Henri LARTIGUE: The Beach at Villerville. 1908. From the Photography Collection of The Museum of Modern Art

lieve I have neglected to say that MT's

Mr Peter
12 Powd
Medfor

Friday morning [presumably January 3, 1969]

Dear Peter,

I have <u>got</u> to work (hollow laughter), but I thought I'd get a few first bits in reply to your kind two-page 'note' about Harry and the Flowers.

I take it he appeared with only one copy of The Book (if only I had a bi-coloured ribbon); as you know, I won't even look at it, but I do want copies to shower everyone with.

I would hazard a guess that your suggestion about me designing a box, after a first flurry of enthusiasm, will leave Harry's mind; or at least I will never hear anything about it, until long after they have got someone else to do it. I could be wrong. I'm not being bitchy, incidentally—you might find it hard to tell from the bald statement in a letter—just considering how these things go. Anyway, it is typical of you to have thought and done of it. If you see what I mean through that odd bit of syntax. Or lack of it.

Did you mention Candida? If not, I suppose we ought to let him know somehow. I can easily do it if you'd rather. Something to the effect that I'm so pleased etc. and that since I am months behind, and all booked up, all of which I am, that if by any chance he wants really and truly a book by us for next autumn, that he'd better tie me down, and then of course that Candida will be wanting to get started peddling so to speak and so forth and so on. And then of course I'll tell her all this when I see her, soon I hope.

I do appreciate very much your taking the time to go into your thoughts about WF ["The Water Flowers"] at such length. I'm also glad that you like it, as I didn't want to say so when I first sent it, but without you I don't think it would have been written. I know this sounds awfully vague, but I can't really put it any narrower without starting to say what I don't mean.

The first idea was of course simply the sauce <u>everywhere</u>, though not specifically as a children's story, but before I could begin to wrestle with what happens then to end it, the funeral Christmas tree attached itself to it, and that was that. There was an almost audible click as they fitted into place, not that I don't agree with you utterly that the other story is still there in the middle, which I confess I still don't see a solution to, without dragging in an endless amount of eating on <u>somebody's</u> part because you can't make it disappear like the water in "The Sorcerer's Apprentice," unless it magically melts along with the snow (random thought). Anyway . . . Also white sauce is really so ghastly; though I suppose a proliferation of brown gravy, however delicious, might be <u>worse</u>.

Re ill-mashed turnips. I fear you detected me only too quickly being self-indulgent; it started out as mashed potatoes, and then 'ill-mashed' came to mind and what else but turnips? I am not against them for the tone of the story or the people actually. I see them as middle-European vaguely, even Russian, like the Gololyov (sp?) family in their sea of mud. Not that the decor would be specifically anything, but they are definitely not jasmine tea types. The ladies dark, drab, hollow-eyed, the gentlemen with long moustaches, also hollow-eyed. The furniture dark, drab, hollow-seated. They are not impoverished, but they don't know too much about gracious living.

The pictures I think would make clear that Henry died at the end of the turnip meal, which will in turn be connected with the line about Christmas Eve, as the others will be shown bringing in the tree while one or two of them is either poking Henry's corpse or removing it or something.

Anent nationality, they can't be too un-English obviously, as all their names are those of English rulers, but . . .

* * *

One other point re Flowers. It is not clear from the text, nor may it be from the pictures for that matter, but in the ensuing weeks which I see as quite a few, five or six maybe, they are not all that time snowbound by any means. It is simply that there is a large snowfall at the beginning which prevents her from getting to village that night, and then it just happens that another snowfall occurs on Christmas Eve. This doesn't have much to do with anything, but I don't mean to convey the idea that everyone is trapped throughout and otherwise foodless, except for the fact that they have to get rid of the sauce, and no one thinks to throw it away.

Saturday evening
Not really a letter at all, but into the mail with this, with annotations on "Michael's Time."[108] If I sound a pompous old foof, it's probably because I am.

Ted.

---

108. "Michael's Time" was a children's story I had written about a boy and the idea of time passing.

6.i.69, Monday night

Dear Peter,

Not a letter.

The new Donald is one of the best yet: absolutely I don't know what.

Anyway. It is certainly just what Harry keeps saying he has in mind, as is the umbrella story, so there is just no real reason for his not making up his mind without further hooha whether he wants another book by us or not, is the way I feel about it. So he has human problems, so, even, do I. (We made a terrible mistake, of course, in letting him see so much, as I expect his dithery subconscious tells him that maybe the next one will be the perfect one that only exists in his anticipation, but then, he ought to see this as well as anyone else.)

So I feel he must be told this. I am trying to get in touch with Candida (did you tell him she was now your agent? I don't <u>think</u> you said anything in your letter to indicate that you had—it's temporarily buried somewhere) in order to have a small session with her on the subject, and she can of course do it as I suggested before.

How do you feel? What do you think?

* * *

For horoscopes[109] places of birth necessary, and as accurate times as possible, and if any were daylight savings or in any way not ordinary time include information.

Cupid driving four horses
(I mucked up the
impression a bit)

---

109. Ted was sending away for rather elaborate horoscopes for each of us.

Jan 9, 1969

Dear Ted,

    Having just talked to you on the phone about such things, I can now write you on white paper, and not on yellow. But your last letter is so long, has so many things to be answered, that again I'm going to have to be perfunctory. Should get a rubber stamp to say this, which seems to begin all my letters. Anyway—

    1. Thank you for the Borges. That is so typically thoughtful of you.

    2. The literary company you put me near, or as a distant poor relative of (I'm taking care of 2 children with the flu, so there's lots of interruptions during this writing)—well, what does one say. Only oneself knows fully how derivative one is. And as we were saying too, a proper sense of hierarchy—(children are vomiting at the moment).

    3. Later—other subject. P. 2 of yr letter

    4. re feeling bad about business on the phone—I guess when the chips are down I feel less bad about business on the phone than about writing business. Witness this morning's call, which was pretty crass and material (is there a difference) on my part. That was a yellow paper call.

    5. You have such writerly reactions to your books! What I mean by that, and it would take a long long walk to explain—is not that writers get their books out to murder them and never see them again, or whatever way one—or you—might put it. But what you say about yours, not wanting to see them again, or whatever, well—backpedal, that's not necessarily what writers say—maybe 6% of writers would say it. But it's what 6% of writers <u>would</u> say. One might see it in the collected miscellanea of 6% of the world's great writers. I believe you absolutely, by the way. But . . . I'm quite sure I'm not making myself clear. Anyway, not being published myself, I can only admire your attitude (though it's you, and not your attitude I'm talking of) vis a vis (I hate foreign expressions actually, so—face to face) with your own works. That's muddled—but perhaps we can save the subject for a talk.

    6. *Donald has a D*—I trust your taste—do what you like. WHO pushed the tree? Djuna Barnes, of course.

    7. I'm a slow reader, and am presently reading what I must to collect my paycheck honestly, so—what you have sent is piled up by my bed. I thought of taking the Evelyn Wood [speed-reading] course, but having queried six or so people around, decided I can perhaps teach myself. But what you send, one can't do that to anyway. But maybe to memoranda from my Dean, which run to 30 pp.

    8. [. . .] Made the Medford headlines again yesterday—having written long blast, and gotten signatures, about the library showing films of the glory of our

bombings in Vietnam. As I say headlines. So, last night I felt obliged to go to the library and see the film. I was the only one of the signatories of my letter to show up—but the American Legion was out in force, and in uniform, waiting at the library entrance, rather raucously. I felt a little timid. Just before the film started, they trooped into the little auditorium, took up the first four rows, I was reminded of my father's story—which could well be true—of the time he lectured near the end, ca. 1936, in Berlin, and the first rows were taken up by uniformed and stomping storm troopers (he was lecturing on the painter Max Beckmann). Well—so Medford goes.

* * *

9. Yes, Merton has died. I read only the first (Seven SM) [*The Seven Storey Mountain*] when I was an adolescent, and was at that time quite swayed by it.

10. Big stuff in the School of Education, BIG BIG, is Carl Rogers' *On Becoming a Person*. Read half of it last night—and my god, my god. The man is perfectly ok—but how awfully windy, poorly written, and secondary to the wonderful Orientals you send, or even to any poet like Rilke or whoever else you might think of as being close. What an education the educators are lacking. Rogers is perfectly good, humane, non-manipulative—but hardly the one one ought to be so excited about.

11. Merton—Westerners in the Orient—do you know the poems of Gary Snyder? [. . .] a nice and searching [. . .] young man who writes poetry—so if you happen to stumble across his name [. . .]

12. Will read Kawabata tonight.

13. Medford Vietnam will take a good deal of the next three weeks—so I'll be reading less.

14. Dreams: well, yes, I do. I used till recently always to dream formally. That is, I would enter a theatre, sit in a seat, the curtain would go up, the performance would begin, then it would end, I and others would applaud, then I would leave the theatre, then the dream would be over. In the last few months I've had many frightening dreams—they would frighten me at the time, to the extent that I'd call out in terror and Helen would shake me awake. But I never can remember them later. Never. I will start, as I've often resolved, to keep pencil and paper at bedside. Occasionally I dream hysterically funny (at the time) dreams, which then in the telling seem incredibly prosaic, mundane, unfunny.

15. I haven't read much Panofsky, but will by and by (did you know "by and by" is one of Mark Twain's favorite expressions?) send you a book in which are two

essays I have read. One on "et in Arcadia ego" is marvelous. And a Kolbe picture is in the book, and I thought of you.[110]

16. Did I tell you, Helen was in stitches telling me about when we saw *The Ladykillers.*

17. The Kolbe picture you ask what it's about. Could have been, but isn't in, Ruthven Todd's *Tracks in the Snow.* Two classical figures classically drawn, standing in grass etc.—BUT THE GRASS IS ABOUT 12 TIMES AS TALL AS THEY ARE!!!!!

18. Again to intellectual hierarchy—not only Thos Mann and such attest to it, if simply (though that isn't in fact all) by writing essays about their betters, but E M Forster too, in *The Art of the Novel,* or whatever it's called. Anyone who writes admiringly of other novelists, with the winning tone of dismay at never being able to write similarly. What is the matter with our students? That's an old man sentence, which fact doesn't invalidate it.

19. I'm more than excited by yr tarot, of which I'll know nothing till I read the Charles Williams, which is about 3 or 4 on the list now. Gosh I hope we can give you accurate enough information. I'm afraid the daylight saving time business (which I never understood in the first place—I never know whether we're on it or off it when we switch, nor did I ever fully figure the rationale of doing it in the first place) will be missing. Will that invalidate all? Anyway, as soon as I can get Helen to stop for a moment nursing the halt, the lame, and the blind, I will have her write down everything. Moments of childbirth are—oddly—stronger retained in her mind than in mine.

20. You are maddeningly—frighteningly—mysterious in about 12% of your description of Alison's workings with our cards. I hope you remember. I hope no disaster. I hope . . . what? . . . should one worry?

21. There is no 21.

22. *The Christmas Bower*[111] was enjoyed by 5 of us, I assure you.

23. Helen has to use up stationery given on occasions, before we move.

24. The New Year's envelope is wonderful. I should tell you, Harry cast a VERY covetous eye on the display of envelopes, and I saw commercial circuits sizzling. But I can't imagine where they might sizzle to . . . Can you?

25. Kings and things and sealing wax. Thank you.

---

110. The main essay by art historian Erwin Panofsky that I sent EG was "Et in Arcadia Ego: Poussin and the Elegiac Tradition." The engraving by Carl Wilhelm Kolbe reproduced with the essay, titled *I Too Was in Arcady,* shows two classically posed figures in front of a tomb with that inscription, standing in the midst of grasses much taller than they are. For the era of its composition, the image seems fantastical and surreal. (See also page 137, note 88.)

111. A children's book by Polly Redford, illustrated by EG (Dutton, 1967).

26. Will *Day and Night* ever find a home, do you think?

27. Yr scoffing at such tests notwithstanding—*Fletcher and Zenobia* was loved by all of us. The children were enthralled. The pictures are lovely—the balloon spacing, design, those wonderful circles. I can imagine the originals are joyous. And the story is perfect. That book, by the way, was exhibited in the Medford public library.

28. And *The Listing Attic,* thank you too. Mrs. Keats Shelley is great, as also Lord Stipple, thrums-eardrums, and the original poetical rhythm of "partition of Vavasour Scowles," as the great idea of the baby sinking into the font, as the picture of the bike—which is missing a critical member and thus could not really exist!!!!!! That is wonderful. [. . .]

29. I haven't forgotten your asking for the moustache story. Trouble is, it's a BAD story. There are nice touches in the middle, but the whole frame is shaky, I found out when I tried to fix up the end. It will take re-writing, and putting in a more plausible frame. I'll do that when I have a free weekend. (I did sit down ready to dedicate a morning to rewriting the end, and that's when I discovered the encircling weakness.)

29 [*sic*]. Conversation overheard in this house at 8:50 AM on Jan 6. "Well, Ted may already have received *Surprise for Donald.* Maybe right now he is wiring us 'am on third illustration—rest by end of week. Candida has sold, with film rights, for $2000 advance to Houghton Mifflin Stop Vacation Guadaloupe.'"

30. I'm touched by your many and thoughtful and kind and sometimes absolutely geniusical comments on "Michael's Time" story. P/haps the long written version is better. Will return the works w/in a few days, with answers to your comments.

31. Thank you again and againagain for your intercession or whatever it was with Candida. I'm delighted.

This is terrible, another letter that does nothing but touch on what you brought up in yours. Forgive me. Know your letters are welcome, anticipated, thought about far more than this perfunctory answer would suggest.

I've got to go to work now. It is unavoidable. Next week, I'm in the office all day every day, so I probably will not have much time to respond. But thank you again for all. For everything. I will write today or tomorrow a very brief note to Candida, addressing her Miss Donadio, and telling her I am so pleased to know she's there, and that the manuscripts are in her good care. Probably that's about all I should say at this point—just sort of, 'hello.'

yours,
Peter

What about graphology?

8.i.69, Wednesday evening

Dear Peter,

How thoughtful and generous you are. I don't think you should part with the Duden [*Der Grosse Duden*] but since apparently you have, what adequate can I find to say? It will be a Most Treasured Possession (capitals are of use in moderation), not least for reasons of sentiment.

* * *

Candida will deal with Harry. I saw her yesterday, just back to the office from a bout of pleurisy contracted after I saw her before. She says you can hear your lungs rattle with it. Anyway, I gave her the new Donald, and explained things. In the long run, this will save our friendship with Harry better than any other way, don't you think? Your letter didn't say whether you had told him that Candida was going to be your agent, but if he doesn't know, and he happens to be in touch with you, I suppose you just tactfully intimate that she will be handling things.

He ought to be in raptures over the new Donald; I am. In a way it's the easiest of the lot for me to illustrate, not that that matters one way or the other.

I think *Donald and the* . . . is going to be an instant classic with a certain adult audience, though how large that will be just at first and how it will fare with the children's market, I can't guess, but then I don't think anyone else can with any real certainty either. I think we're just going to have to wait and see what sort of reactions Candida gets in the beginning as straws in the wind.

Thursday morning

A page is a page is a page. So what if all this was gone into at great length on the phone?

Sunday evening

Heaven knows where this week went. Apart from the usual eight ballet performances, nothing seems to have happened or been accomplished. Ah well.

The George Kubler book [*The Shape of Time*], which I have read about two-thirds of and which I am very excited about, I presume you would have told me about if you know it. There's a sentence for you. Yoshida Kenkō's *Essays in Idleness,* apart from being a nice book, I thought perhaps might hold some technical inspiration as it were (as I also thought about Sei Shōnagon's *The Pillow Book*); I remember you once mentioned the impossibility of sustained effort with the life you led so I wondered if analogous brief excursions on the innumerable subjects that interest you, etc. . . . . And I have always been fond of the way the Japanese do it. The only other thing I seem to have <u>finished</u> of late is yet another Alan Watts that has turned up in paperback: *Psychotherapy East and West.* The thought <u>has</u> crossed my mind that the reason I enjoy reading him so is that I can understand what he is saying, which is often not the case with various recondite things I pick up from time to time. Apropos of nothing at all, except that I just found the copy of same I have been madly looking for for weeks, Balthasar Gracián's *The Art of Worldly Wisdom?* Also a.o.n.a.a., did you ever try Mervyn Peake, who also just died? I read *Titus Groan* when it came out—I got the impression that the whole thing was taking place under water from the style, and while I have the other two, *Gormenghast* and *Titus Alone,* I have somehow never got round to them; I see they too are out in paperback, no doubt on the heels of Mr Tolkien as it were. So much for literature at this end for the moment.

An example of Neumeyerisms in real life: on Monday I went to the dentist[112] who told me all my teeth were not coming loose, so Tuesday I went to the eye doctor with wild apprehensions about them because I have not had my eyes examined for three and a half years and the radio keeps telling you that if you are over forty you probably have glaucoma and don't know it, etc. In the interval the doctor I used to go to had died, so I was seeing his successor, a small, severe man about sixty named Perkins. He poked and prodded and shone bright lights into my eyes and then began testing me for new glasses. I hemmed and hawed and dithered because I can never tell which lens is really better, but finally he stopped and said nothing, so I said don't I need new glasses and he said we were dealing with minutiae and that while the right lens in my old glasses was perhaps a bit strong there was no point in changing it or I wouldn't need glasses at all, so I was subdued by this, but then I said aren't you going to test my eyes for glaucoma, and blithered on about being over forty etc, etc. When I finally subsided, he looked at me coldly and said: 'There is no need; your eyeballs are as soft as pudding.' I crept away. Having got myself worked up to new glasses, I felt very deprived so I decided to get an extra pair, which have teeny rectangular frames that for some not obvious reason (since I can't to my knowledge ever recall seeing one wear them) make me look like a German U-boat captain.

This is obviously one of those letters that is going to find it difficult to get to the mail because I haven't even begun to answer your last, and it is time to go to bed if I am to stir myself up early to finish a drawing that someone wants by one o'clock.

Monday morning

The week starts off with a leak in my ceiling. You have never said, not that I ever asked, whether you know/like Constantine Cavafy? And Giorgos Seferis, for that matter. I've got to draw.

---

112. EG was referring to my Lionel story *Do Not Fear a Visit to the Dentist.* He once said it was his favorite.

Monday evening

Not a good day for culture. Someone I was talking to at the ballet over the weekend began raving on and on about Nabokov so I thought I might give him one more try, but not holding out a great deal of hope, I picked the shortest thing I could find: *The Eye,* which is apparently his first novel. It struck me as thoroughly banal, frequently cheap, and vaguely unpleasant. Not a profitable hour spent all in all. This evening, having somehow got the idea *I Love You, Alice B. Toklas* was more amusing than one had been led to believe, I went off to see it. It was not more amusing than one had been led to believe. It was less. It was also very dumb. I don't wish to sound alarmist, but something really dreadful is happening to movies; they appear to be made out of lead rather than celluloid.

A cache—it is the only word for it—of your recent communications has turned up as a result of my cleaning woman, who loves to tidy up.

Maurice [Marcel] Schwab sounds familiar, but I don't know why. Enlighten (me). Mirko Hanak does not even sound familiar, but that does not surprise me, not being middle-European (me).

[. . .] I know back on the Cape I toyed with the idea of sending you my second copy of L. H. Myers's *The Near and the Far;* is that what I did? I don't remember doing so, but otherwise I am totally baffled.

I have Flann O'Brien's other novels, two in hand and one on order which I have already read, so any time you would like to read them, if you do, let me know. I realize I have been swamping you, but on the other hand I am hardly asking for a book report on so many a week; it is just easier to send things when one thinks of it.[113]

* * *

I trust the children have long since stopped vomiting and having flu. (letter of Jan 9)

Since you mentioned Djuna Barnes, what do you think of her? I should hate to tell you how many times I read *Nightwood* in bygone years. (I haven't read it now for perhaps a decade.)

I should like to hear in much greater detail sometime about the whole movie thing at the Medford library—especially since you rather cryptically say later on that 'Medford Vietnam' will take a good deal of the next three weeks. I trust you are not going to be incarcerated or the like. This whole sort of thing, I mean your taking a part in it, them, whatever, is something I'd like to have a long talk about sometime, as it was apparently wholly left out of my makeup. I suppose you can figure out what I mean, though on reading this last sentence over, I don't know how.

---

113. EG did send me Myers's *The Near and the Far,* and Flann O'Brien became a literary touchstone for us.

Remind me sometime to tell you about my experiences writing down my dreams. It was while I was in the army and reading J. W. Dunne's *Experiment with Time*. Creepy, and incredibly exhausting; I had to give it up. It is interesting, however, to find out that yours begin with being in a theatre, etc. I suppose we both bring in these formal devices in the way we would anything else since we are both so much concerned with art (in the widest sense) and its problems. Though I have never heard anyone else mention this factor in relating their dreams.

The Kolbe picture you mention, reminded me that one of my favourite engravings which I picked up once for a dollar somewhere and which I know nothing about is, presumably, 19th century—looking at again—it's on my wall—in order to describe it, it now seems to be eighteenth or even seventeenth—anyway, it's a winged, two-footed dragon with a great lashing tail going up behind, the only thing is that he is splashing in a tiny pool surrounded by cat tails which tower above him.

I did not mean to induce apprehension over the tarot cards and Alison's readings. No disasters were involved, and I only don't go into it in a letter because, as I said, I feel I rather stacked them as it were by bringing my subjective thoughts to bear on them, and I suspect my character is perhaps a bit stronger on things like that than it is in other directions, where I seem to have very little at all.

From what little I remember of *The Listing Attic* you seem to have taken to all the horrors, or were they all that way and I don't recall?

It would serve you right (awful pun) if I carefully cut out your repeated queries about graphology in your purposely dotty handwriting and forwarded them to an expert for analysis; then I expect we'd find out Things. In answer to your queries, of course I believe in graphology, also palmistry, the *I Ching*, the tarot, astrology, and all those other delicious things you can find in places like thesaurusi (can that be the plural? No, it can't, it must be thesauri), which turn out to mean prognostication by means of snail tracks or something.

Talk about terrible perfunctory letters, which yours never are, this one certainly is, but I feel I ought to get something in the mail, and this will at least save you from answering, because there is nothing to answer.

Did I tell you about an idea which flitted in one night as I was going to sleep about a work to be entitled *The Book of Awful Possibilities* or somesuch? Would you care to jot down random thoughts on this line; they could be practically anything I should think, though I envision so far truly awful things with the attendant circumstances so particularized, if you follow me, that it would be unlikely you were taking from life, and then the last one would be something to the effect that: Or, things will go on just the way they have always gone on, and you will live to be 103. (You can't get more awful than that. On second thought, not really.)

Tuesday morning

This is really a miserable excuse for a letter, for
which I do apologize. You have been spared a lot of aesthetic
maunderings (maunderings about aesthetics) which I meant to
try and organize before I forgot them, but that happened
first; on the other hand, you're getting nothing else but a
lot of scrappy fragments of nothing at all. You can (always)
assume various slushy expressions of friendships to make up
for it (if you wish).

Ted

道

TAO
(very ineptly rendered)

Years of curiosity are going to be satisfied, D.V., on the 22nd when a friend is going to bring in his collection of photographs obtained from Ruthven Todd of the complete Henry Fuseli drawings of which the details only appear in *Tracks in the Snow*. Prudishness will no doubt prevent me from hinting except in the most ambiguous terms what is going on in them. Tra la.

Refrain of a new popular song:

Now the wind just blows the past around
And this house settles deeper in the ground.

Bits of various interest (and varying) from the *Times* enclosed.

Tuesday morning

This is really a miserable excuse for a letter, for which I do apologize. You have been spared a lot of aesthetic maunderings (maunderings about aesthetics) which I meant to try and organize before I forgot them, but that happened first; on the other hand, you're getting nothing else but a lot of scrappy fragments of nothing at all. You can (always) assume various slushy expressions of friendship to make up for it (if you wish).

Ted

[Chinese character]
TAO
(*very* ineptly rendered)

Jan 16, 69

Dear Ted,

I don't consider myself given to hysteria or hyperbole—but Stanton is too much. I've had it. Too much.

Today I thought, since next week I've got to routinely see the orthopedist, I wanted to give him a small token of . . . and so, why not for his little children, a copy of *Donald and the* . . . . Hadn't H said once that Jan 1 we should all have "authors' copies"? but we haven't gotten them. And so—and so I made bold to call. Harry answered himself. I said "Hello." He said "Hello." We went through certain conversational conventions. Then I said—"Harry, I was wondering, well—is the copy of Donald I have the only one in existence . . . I mean, might it be possible, if there are some more . . . etc."

To which Harry replied in a tone of uncomprehending incredulity "but you said just now you have a copy." To which reply I, "yes but, I wonder, I mean, if there might be some more, well, you once said . . . etc." to which he said, "Oh we do have some more, but they're locked up."

SILENCE.
SILENCE.
SILENCE.

Then Harry rather patiently and painedly explained to me that all copies of *D and the* . . . had been sent back to the binder, about 1/3 to be destroyed most likely, some kept, and many to be reprinted and rebound since the binding was on crooked. (Actually, the binding on mine is a little crooked, and I suppose we have no kicks on A-W doing this right—but he told it to me as though of course I should have known. And anyway, why was I so importunate.)

Well, we talked about that a while longer; he told me he'll go to the book fair in Bologna in April, and ski afterwards with his daughter [. . .] who is studying Gaellic. He condescended then to say someday he might bring by another copy of Donald. I asked no further questions about when Donald would be born, when he would make a debut, when he would be confirmed, etc. I had been, it must be admitted, disarmed, and I fell like tapioca in a silo—there's no denying.

Then we hung up. Not a word, not one, about *Surprise for Donald*. Not one.

Harry did deign, though, to tell me they are working on advertising. They have a "girl" now. And they'll have nice little slips in the reviewers' copies, and will have a nicely designed box even in which to send out their rev copies. "You know, we even thought of having Ted Gorey do the boxes, but then there wasn't time," said Harry.

To which, I, "Yes, you know we did say something about that New Year's eve."

Harry, "Yes, and then in the Spring I'll be going to London and Bologna."

You don't want to hear more.

I don't want to write more.

I hope Henry Regnery, or Bushido Publishing Co., or Crowell Collier, or Kellogg's Cornflakes publishes all the other great things we are going to do. Harry is more pain than he's worth—much more—and as far as I'm concerned, all joking aside, I don't care if we chalk him off as far as the other books go. He's had more than a chance, and now he's not being simply Harryish, but a goddamn boor. End tirade which is to be taken literally.

Tomorrow I hope to get to answering your letter that does not require an answer.

P.S. Wonderful fantasy to be dreamed tonight:

April 7, 1969, Harry Stanton, browsing in Bologna Book Fair, coming upon
  Surprise for Donald
  Donald and the Umbrella
  Donald Has a Difficulty
  Snowflake
  Faithful Fish
  and
  3 Lionel Stories
published by Houghton Mifflin or Little, Brown or Harper
being displayed as the "most felicitous artist/author conspiracy of 1969."
Gold Medal Newdecott[114] *Award*

---

114. Neumeyer coinage combining Newbery Medal—given annually for the "most distinguished contribution to American literature for children"—and the Caldecott Medal—given annually for the "most distinguished American picture book."

19.i.69, Sunday

Dear Peter,

　　I must apologize again for that last dumb letter which never got around to answering yours, really; I think I must have been feeling shy, for no known reason. Anyway . . .

　　How poignant the penciled scrawl at the foot of your letter of a week ago: Mon, Tues — FLU. I trust it has all gone away by now. Say to yourself 'In my adamantine pure essence is knowledge of the void' (p. 31, Giuseppe Tucci's *The Theory and Practice of the Mandala*). Seriously, I hope you are better/well/whatever.

　　What dire things you recommend me to read from time to time. I did not know Herman Melville's *Bartleby* before but I do now. It blighted a <u>whole day</u>. A blacker work does not easily come to mind, but great, the more so because the minute you try and turn it into some sort of allegory or to figure out some symbolism for the whole thing, it resists you at once; it is just <u>there</u>. And I still can't see how he manages to make Bartleby, if not exactly lovable, completely unirritating, even when one is offered not the vestige of an explanation for any of his behaviour, though one constantly expects one, up to the very end, and even the tacked on bit about the dead letter office somehow works. If I feel strong enough I'll read the rest of the volume I bought, which has all the other short stories and BB [*Billy Budd*], which I'm not sure I ever read, but has always driven me up the wall anyway because it was everybody's favourite whatsit when I was at Harvard. I also bought *Pierre,* which I've always imagined to be the dottiest of all his works.

　　Vaguely apropos perhaps, a story which came to me one night on the way back from the ballet, the first part of it happening to me. Actually, I now think it would be best as a wordless animated cartoon lasting about three minutes maybe, in black and white of course. So.

　　An ordinary sober-looking middle-aged man is walking along a city street on a windy day. A large sheet of used brown paper or the like blows against his ankles; he disentangles his feet from it with some little difficulty and walks on. The paper begins to blow after him, unnoticed at first. Then he hears it crepitating or whatever and looks back. It never quite reaches him, but almost. He gets more and more nervous, and finally darts into a tall office building through the revolving door, and then looks back. The paper is waiting outside. He hesitates, then gets into the elevator and goes, say, to the fifth floor. He gets out, walks to the end of the corridor and looks out the window there. At first he sees nothing, but then the paper floats up from below, and hovers back and forth. He returns to the elevator, gets out at the eleventh floor, etc., etc., the same thing happening each time, until at last he reaches the top floor, the fortieth or somesuch, and climbs the narrow flight of stairs leading to the roof. The paper seems quite far away, above his head; he nevertheless dithers a bit, and then jumps off the roof. The paper begins a rather swift descent, and finally comes to rest on what is left of him in the street below.

Your mentioning Rilke and Oriental writers in the same sentence echoed thoughts of my own, and the other day in one of the bookshops where I buy Japanese stuff I came across a book entitled *Rilke in Japan* which turned out to be an extensive bibliography of Rilke translated into Japanese, so I guess they must feel it too.

As you have seen by now, Balthus catalogues tend to repeat themselves like Borges books in English, but there's usually something that isn't in any other one; you now have virtually everything that's been put out on him, apart from magazine articles here and there, which seems extraordinary, considering he is one of the great painters of our day, of which fact I have long been utterly convinced. I hope one day you will be able to see a fairly large show of his because when all is said and done, except for the *Wuthering Heights* drawings, the rest of his work, except for its strangeness, comes across so little even in colour reproductions; some of the paintings at least are as beautiful as any Vermeer or Georges de la Tour.

Were I someone else, I should try and convince a publisher to do a book on him by me and then get him to send me to Europe for ages and ages with all expenses paid to arrange for a catalogue raisonné and long sessions with Balthus himself, etc.

Do you know at all a German 18th century writer named Karl Philipp Moritz? He seems to have written *Journeys of a German in England in 1782* (a racy title if ever there was one) and an autobiographical novel called *Anton Reiser,* which I picked up; he was much interested in the education of children, among other things. I haven't started the book itself yet, only read the introduction.

I'm glad you're liking Kawabata, since I expect yet another one has arrived by this time. I trust the binding has reminded you of something. This is one of my spectacular displays of selflessness for which I am famous in some quarters; I now only hope that it will be rewarded by someone publishing a French or English translation of the book so I can read it too.

Speaking of the binding, it seems a pity that more countries, like this one for instance, cannot put out handsome little books like the Germans do. I also picked up two German translations of Lau Dse (as one spells him and *Tao Te Ching* becomes *Dau Dō Djing*) in beautiful little editions; these I can almost read because I have read the book so often in English. This brings my number of versions of same up to fifteen I believe it is, and I have come across two in French I must pick up. I still have a long way to go as the latest bibliography, which is already out of date, lists some forty-odd in English.

Are you having a nice wallow in Borges? Did I ask you how you felt about Samuel Beckett?

Thank you for putting me on to Liam Hudson's *Contrary Imaginations*. You will find/have found you won't have to try and get hold of it for me to read. I've just begun it, but so far it seems very sensible and witty; he sounds like you sometimes as a matter of fact.

I also liked the Abraham Maslow article very much, which had got buried under something, which is why I haven't mentioned reading it before because I hadn't, especially of course because of his Taoist attitude towards teaching children. Certainly he is much easier to read than most, but what a pity people like him can't dispense with jargon entirely. I suppose it is easier for his audience to absorb, as they all know what he is talking about even if he isn't expressing it really clearly because everybody has the same jargon tucked away in their heads for comparison so to speak. In some hazy way I began to think that all these academic types with their specialized vocabularies that they lean on so heavily should be made to read Gertrude Stein in things like *The Geographical History of America; or, The Relation of Human Nature to the Human Mind* . . . where if I have any recollection at all she was able to get across many unfamiliar ideas and ways of looking at things with great freshness and precision without ever using anything but the simplest vocabulary.

* * *

Am I to take it that the *Shorter Oxford* told you nothing else about Abraxas? In case not, he/it is a Gnostic ?deity with the head of a cock, a man's torso, and serpents for legs, and symbolizes wisdom. It's an iron seal set in a ring I got years ago from a marvelous man who looked like Sydney Greenstreet and whose name was Count S. Colonna Walewski. He had a dark little basement shop filled with mainly Tibetan antiquities and pornography in various forms (alas, I was apparently too young and innocent-looking to ever be shown any of it) to which definitely sinister types used to come for unknown purposes. I used to go there during my lunch hour when I was at Doubleday from time to time and we would have long amiable conversations about I forget what with no sign of impatience on his part—he was immobilized behind his desk—while, say, some criminal-appearing type who had slunk out as I went in, waited at the corner until I had left to return. [. . .] He died many years ago and the contents of his shop and various apartments which he rented as he needed another place to store things were sold at Gimbels I think it was. From time to time I come across strange esoteric books he wrote on things like Tantric Buddhism.

* * *

Perhaps you know this Chekhov bit already, in fact probably, but if not: when his wife Olga asked him about the meaning of life, he replied: 'It's exactly as if you were to ask me: "What is a carrot?" A carrot is a carrot, and that's all there is to know about it.'

22.i.69. Wednesday

Temporarily utterly swamped.
Long, un-newsworthy letter,
partly in typewriter, partly
in head, will follow.

Camille COROT. La Cervara.
1796-1875
6630.

LES ÉDITIONS NOMIS. PARIS. PRINTED IN

Mr Peter Neumeyer,
12 Powder House Road Ext.,
Medford, Mass.

02155.

Musée des Beaux-Arts, Zurich.

* * *

Thursday afternoon (apologies)

    I don't wonder you fell like tapioca in a silo (superb image; I see it as a sort of genre landscape by moonlight, the silo in the middle distance, trees, low hills, etc); I expect if he ever comes to about the way he has behaved to you, he will be more than sorry. I am not surprised, though somewhat shocked, I must admit, by his shall we call it insouciance? I have never felt, even when it was all in my favour, that my relationship with Harry was what I would call satisfactory, but I had the definite impression that you and he were really friends. Well. Idle speculation suggests that perhaps he had heard from Candida and was being annoyed, or more likely, that Harry cannot stand to be approached about anything, and that one must stand still or even better retreat so that he can do the approaching. I suppose eventually we will both get a satisfactory number of copies of Donald—if I don't, before too long I think I'll drop a note to Will and ask him for some—and after that <u>not</u> get in touch with Harry about anything, as indeed I have not for some time, never having bothered to answer that last letter. I hardly feel we have seen the last of him, and can only hope that by the time he chooses to notice us again we shall be able to say, O, well, So-and-so is bringing out a new Donald, or the like. I realize this must be a bit traumatic for you, him being (he being? yes) your first publisher, but take it from aging author, E.G., that it really hardly matters, one way or the other. Perhaps his private life is going even more eerily than usual [. . .].

The Fuseli drawings were quite beautiful as drawings and not at all offensive, though perhaps even my prudishness is beginning to be affected by the permissiveness of the age, if a trifle perverse—most featured several young ladies and one young man. They quite lacked the hysteria of his other work, perhaps because they lacked its ambiguity, since it was perfectly clear all that was going on, and there was even an air of gentility about them since everything must have been going on with a minimum of violence in order to keep the young ladies' elaborate coiffeurs from becoming disarranged, rather like thirties movies where no matter what, not a hair was ever out of place nor a lipstick smudged. It was only where one of his duenna figures stood guard and looked the other way that one got a little of the Fuseli frisson: I mean, why wasn't she watching, and so forth?

When you see a glove lying in the street do you think that, somewhere, someone has lost a hand? A shoe, a foot? (It does not, I think, work with hats.)

[. . .] Now I was thinking in terms of Donald perhaps buying some specially selected blocks of wood and carefully carving a small tree, each twig joint separately, and cunningly fitting them together, and then the larger limbs, and finally the trunk fitted together like a Chinese puzzle, the whole surface minutely carved to imitate bark and then stained with natural juices, and set out in the garden one night, to be called attention to as a mysterious arrival on the morning round of the flower beds. It is obvious that if you are ever carried off by the plague I can go on writing Donald stories and signing them with your name and only I will ever <u>know</u>, or don't you think so? (I hope you are not carried off by the plague or anything else, honestly.)

I'm sorry you told me about your activities in third grade.

[. . .] W. S. Merwin is only a name to me; is there no book of his poems? I have a faint notion there is, or I would not be so familiar with the name. [. . .]

Since my astrology classes do not begin until Feb. 10th, there is yet time for you and Helen to get the time of day of your births. It is interesting to note how many people cannot have their horoscopes done because they are reluctant to get in touch with their mothers. Really, I just noticed that the *Journal of Graphoanalysis* was mailed to you. Why? Are you a secret one? Did you send for it? What is going on? You are making me nervous. I am perusing the issue, however, with interest and alarm.

* * *

Entire contents, except for date and name and address, of a letter written on fuchsia-coloured paper: "Dear Mr Gorey, Your books fascinate me. Could I meet you? Sincerely." I look forward to your receiving messages of this sort before too long.

Don't you feel *The Querent and the Quesited* would make a rather grand title for <u>something</u>?

Which brings me to Hudson's *Contrary Imaginations.* My strongest feeling about it I can only express with a simile. I feel like I have watched someone who has been asked to cut a cheese sandwich in half, do so by slicing it horizontally through the cheese. I somehow manage both to completely agree with him and completely disagree with him. Somewhere there is something wrong with his division of converger/diverger I feel. I mean from one point of view I am the perfect extreme converger—his convergers on the uses of objects test are positively garrulous and overwrought compared to what I would be on it, and so forth, and this would have been equally true, or even more so, when I was the age for taking those tests. As it happens, the principle of (I think that should be principal, n'est-ce pas?) the school I went to lived in the same decaying mansion on the south side of Chicago as did a little group called, I think, the Human Engineering Laboratory which devised intelligence tests, so needless to remark, we got a new one of some sort about every week, sometimes oftener, and I was a perfect little whiz at all of them, because I have that kind of mind—I can do Double Crostics and things like that without even thinking, but it's a knack that develops with practice and has nothing whatever to do with intelligence—and furthermore I was terribly good at math and spatial relations and all that jazz, and so it would have been perfectly obvious that all this combined with my emotional makeup or lack of same, I should have gone into science according to Hudson, which I obviously didn't and never had any inclination to. Then, at least according to Hudson's criteria, I am also an extreme diverger, and a creative person with lots of originality and so forth and so on. I don't see how you can have it both ways. Because this somehow does not make me one of the allrounders either; I'm at the extreme ends and nowhere in the middle. I quite distrust the presumed difference of emotional bias in convergers and divergers; besides, according to his rather dismal implication you either have to treat people like things or else things like people, neither of which seems to be necessary even to us emotionally impoverished types; it does not seem to occur to him that you can treat things like things or people like people, and solve the problem(?) by just not treating them very much, if you see what I mean. The one thing I <u>can</u> put my finger on, where I think he is seriously misguided, is his confusion of imagination, or ingenuity, if you feel it denigrates imagination, with creativity. The two are most certainly not the same, and while they can exist in the same person, they certainly don't have to; you can be either without the other. A case in point is his saying that the zebra crossing drawing with the swimming three-tailed zebras was the most by implication creative of the responses seems to me to be taking mere ingenuity for creativeness (what we mean by it) and admittedly in a book he cannot convey the quality of a drawing, there is nowhere that he seems to realize this would have anything to do with creativity, and that an ordinary drawing as it were of an actual zebra crossing might very well have more quality than any of the meaningless, more or less, ingenuities on a verbal level. Also, those endless lists of things people thought up to do with barrels, paper clips, etc.,—the mind boggles, I couldn't have thought up any of them hardly, which means I have little or no imagination, which is true, but then if publishing a lot of books which many people greet with remarks like How did you ever think that up? makes one creative, which in his view it does, what then? I don't quite know what to think about his views on morbidity, repressed libidinous impulses, etc. Something seems undigested there too. What I should like to know—can you tell me at least a bit?—is just how important intelligence tests are in the educational scheme of things. I suppose it differs in different places and circumstances, but what I really mean is how seriously do they affect the life of a child in school and his development?

* * *

I discover there is no page 9 (in this letter). Rather, there is, but it has been misnumbered. So has this page. Shall I go on?

* * *

I'm running out of steam, and since there is little likelihood of this reaching you this week anyway, even if I went out into the rain and mailed it now, I'll stop and go on later. (Probably because the same thing has happened to the radiator for about the third time in the last two weeks, and my fingers are numb.)

Monday morning
 Abrupt termination of letter. The several hours after the ballet last night that had been earmarked for finishing this one up got lost discussing ballet (what else?) with other knowledgeable souls until after midnight in the pub across the street. Tsk.
 I now have to quickly rush out and see a friend with a dislocated shoulder (more of this in my next as is sometimes said) to his doctor.
 Your last letter in mailbox this morning. [. . .] Another package of nothing in particular is about to go into the mail. Sorry about that. Is it possible the Beatles invented this phrase? I do not recollect hearing it before one of them said it in one of their movies. Now this is the kind of research that would really mean something. I blither.
 Get well.

Sunday [January 19, 1969]

Dear Ted,

Seems like flu may (or may not) be beginning—so will get off quick line now just to say, Leonard Woolf's daily maxims brighten the mornings. The German/Japanese poems are appreciated—they are in German (one might have guessed as much), curiously thematic, Romantic, clinched with mots justes. But very good, very poignant—a Teutonic cross between Heine and Housman.

Quote of the month, from the Waley, p. 8 [see note below]:

"The translations in this book are chiefly intended to facilitate the study of the Japanese text . . . And since the classical language has an easy grammar and limited vocabulary, a few months should suffice for the mastering of it."

Particularly affecting to me in the Waley (I take it—I hope—you have a copy, too):

p. 19, top. no more can be said. no more has ever been said.

p. 86, top. one should make an anthology of all the ways that has been said in all languages. Everything I have ever written is a feeble attempt to come within hailing distance of the idea, to sneak up on it, to ambush it somehow so that some formulation may take me a step closer to saying it.

p. 90, top. Talk about working with the idea of Time! Figure just what is happening when in that poem. I don't know if it is meant as a puzzle in time, or says something Borgesian, or—well, in writing this I realize, obviously the two don't exclude each other, and so it does both.

***

Whatever is coming on is coming rapidly. Zack had it the last three days. So I must get to whatever needs to be done now. yrs.

Peter

[Note: The four brief passages quoted and referred to above are from Arthur Waley, *Japanese Poetry: The 'Uta'* (Clarendon Press, 1919), reprinted in 1965 by Percy Lund, Humphries & Company.

p. 19: How will you manage / To cross alone / The autumn mountain / Which was so hard to get across / Even when we went the two of us together?   —Princess Ōku (seventh century)

p. 86: Out of the dark, / Into a dark path / I now must enter: / Shine (on me) from afar, / Moon of the mountain fringe!   —Izumi no Shikibu (eleventh century)

p. 90: My pony's tracks / Being buried / Under the snow that has fallen since, / Those whom I have outstripped / Will be puzzled which way to go.   —Saigyō Hōshi (1118–1190)]

2.ii.69

I'm all right (this is only
sepia ink, not blood), but I'm
so distracted from?/by? drawing
that I just can't cope with
anything else for the present,
however long that is.

O the horror of it all.... (I
think this is a shade more poetic
than 'Oh, the.....etc.')

The Penguin Epic of Gilgamosh
is one of the great Dismal
Works.

Excuse handwriting.

Yr friend. E.G.

(Mumble...)

Mr Peter Neumeyer, 12 Powder House Road Ext., Medford, Mass. 02155

[mailed January 25, 1969]

[PN to EG]

[clipped from a newspaper's "Letters to the Editor," with the following circled in pen]

Sirs:
The United States has better artists than Picasso ever thought of being. Why don't you run a story on an artist I know who lives and paints in Key West, Fla. He is a good, wholesome father who minds his own business and takes good care of his children.

Walter H. Norman
Houston, Texas

[clipped from a newspaper or magazine, picture of dog; also this short piece]

Ketchup on Cottage Cheese?
"I really like a man who puts ketchup on his cottage cheese," said Friedl. Richard M. Nixon does it, and he's your President, beginning today.

[handwritten note]
"The average Oscar Mayer wiener is rotten."
Overheard Zack saying the above to nobody about 7AM today. No context.

Feb. 5, 1969

Dear Ted,
Dear analyst,
What do you make of this dream I had in the early hours?
My friend Larry Benson, a medievalist, was vacationing in the Berkshires, where he was talking with a crusty old New England doctor, who was mentioning the "summer visitor, the Hartford insurance man, Wallace Stevens." Benson says, "you probably don't realize it, but Wallace Stevens is one of your best poets writing in English."
"You mean he's like a swimmer?" asks the doctor.
(This is a pun, for in my <u>dream French</u>, "chasser" means "to swim," ergo: chasser—swimmer—Chaucer)
"Yes, chasser la femme," replies Benson.
And I wake up guffawing.

* * *

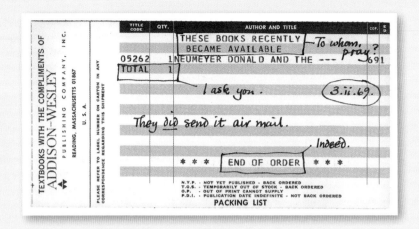

TITLE CODE	QTY.	AUTHOR AND TITLE	COP.	E D
		THESE BOOKS RECENTLY BECAME AVAILABLE	*To whom, pray?*	
05262	1	NEUMEYER DONALD AND THE ---	691	
TOTAL	1			

I ask you.   (*3.ii.69.*)

They did send it air mail.

Indeed.

* * *   END OF ORDER   * * *

N.Y.P. - NOT YET PUBLISHED - BACK ORDERED
T.O.S. - TEMPORARILY OUT OF STOCK - BACK ORDERED
O.P. - OUT OF PRINT CANNOT SUPPLY
P.D.I. - PUBLICATION DATE INDEFINITE - NOT BACK ORDERED
PACKING LIST

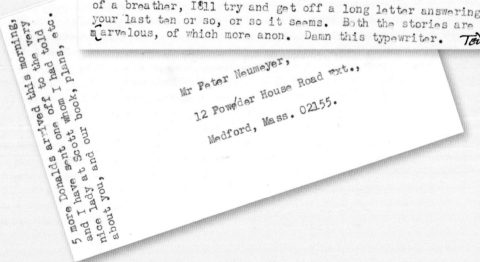

4.ii.69

Dear Peter,

Attempt at bald explanation. For hiatus, which you may not have felt. I have. Badly. I'm so far behind on my work that there seems no reasonable expectation of ever catching up. It is fortunate that reason so seldom obtains. No doubt things will change, or vanish, or something, or I might even get caught up. Anyway. Drawing going no worse than usual, but I find myself uncertain and doing the wrong sort and then having to re-do them, so work goes very slowly and precariously, and the only way I can cope is to keep myself in a semi-trance state about everything else. All of which fills me with negative emotions and so forth, and then I don't want to spew them out on anyone else, much less you. As soon as I get reasonably (that word again) far enough along with the Lear I'm doing to take a bit of a breather, I'll try and get off a long letter answering your last ten or so, or so it seems. Both the stories are marvelous, of which more anon. Damn this typewriter. Ted.

5 more Donalds arrived this morning, and I have sent one off to the very nice lady at Scott book, plans, etc. and our lady, and one whom I had told about you,

Mr Peter Neumeyer,
12 Powder House Road ext.,
Medford, Mass. 02155.

[mailed March 14, 1969]

[PN to EG]

* * *

Have been writing every morning for a while now 4 pages on the average of a very
peculiar novel, again rather obsessed with inside-out time. It's fictional autobiogr, true
in spirit, but not in particulars, and begins after death and works backwards. Hard
going, on a piecemeal schedule. The only thing fully pleasing me abt it is the possible
last sentence: "Unfortunately, this book has not yet been written, but it is demanding
to be written, and quite certainly it may be."
   I HOPE YOU ARE WELL! I HOPE THAT IF YOU WERE AILING YOU
WOULD CALL US. I HOPE YOU ARE WELL!

The Green Beads

The mother of Little Tancred sent him into the twilight to buy three pennies'
worth of tapioca with which to make their evening meal.

Before he had as yet not got even half-way, he saw a disturbed person whose sex
was unclear coming towards him while it waved its hands about.

Little Tancred started for the other side of the street, the three pennies falling
from his grasp in the middle, but the Disturbed Person was there before him.

'Is this a visionary child I see, or are you really Tiny Clorinda?' cried the
Disturbed Person, chewing on a string of green beads it wore around its neck.

'No,—for my name is Little Tancred. If it is of my infant sister you speak,
good sir,' he ventured politely 'she died last autumn from a disorder of the spine
brought on by a lack of nourishing food'.

'How it knocks my heart!' moaned the Disturbed Person, its teeth rending the string
asunder, the green beads flying in all directions and disappearing into the grimy
drifts of snow.

'I am the Baroness von Rettig,' she announced 'your grandmother' and so Little
Tancred led her back to where he lived.

In her astonishment at seeing her son in the company of a disturbed person on the
doorstep, Little Tancred's mother forgot to ask the whereabouts of the tapioca.

When she was told who the Disturbed Person was, she explained 'We thought you were
lost when the Moon of Valparaiso went down in the bay three years ago last April.

'Wilhelm, your only child,' she went on 'died of pneumonia contracted after helping
to man the breeches-buoy all night in vain; those of us who are left visit the
cemetery on the seventh of every month.

'But if you are not lying on the bottom of the sea,' she added 'can it be possible
that your emerald necklace is not there after all either?'.

'Grandmother, when I met her,' put in Little Tancred 'was chewing on some green
beads, but they broke and rolled away.'

It was now quite dark both indoors and out and so a lantern was lit, and all three
rushed into the street.

They hunted and hunted, but in the end found only one green bead, and that proved
to be a glass marble belonging to a more fortunate little boy named Hugo who lived
farther up the ~~street~~ *block*.

Friday Mar. 20

Dear Ted,

* * *

"The Green Beads," 'the disturbed person' and the sense of total loss is among the very best. [. . .]

* * *

And thank you too for *The Object-Lesson*. The inexplicable restitution of his lordship's artificial limb is marvelous, and is an example of the felicity of the unicorporeality of authorillustrator. It couldn't have come about otherwise, could it? Is it the Barnstable tower in the picture? Is one supposed to see what he sees a better view of after stepping backwards in the water? I sort of hope not, for it's a very good thing that we don't identify it. The general grayness of the whole book is indescribably sad/nostalgic. In this book you have a delicate balance, an overtone of mood, a sombreness, that to me makes it one of the most moving, putting it one step over those that are enormously amusing but less tenuous. It's a very beautiful book. Thank you.

Are you hungry? This is your time of writing stories of undernourishment. "Disturbed person whose sex was unclear" is masterly. In general, the daguerreotype prose in "The Green Beads" hits it off wonderfully. (I have to consciously work at not imitating you these days.)

It's not 9:30 AM yet this Friday morning. My brain is giving out. Let me only say, I have sat in a yurt and have been learning to make a leather bag.[115] Ask me and I shall tell you about it. See you within 24 days, I should think. Thank you for very many things. yours,

Peter

---

115. In 1969 William Coperthwaite (now of Machiasport, Maine) had settled at Harvard, having come from Alaska to undertake a doctoral program. In keeping with the mood of the time and the place, Coperthwaite decided that among his contributions to the community would be to build a yurt for himself to live in, and there to conduct a series of sessions in which congenial friends would discuss literary works while he instructed us in the construction of leather bags made of horsehide and filed-down soup bones. I still have my bag; it hangs next to me as I write. The leather has a scar that, Coperthwaite told me, had been caused by a fly larva implanted in the living horsehide.

[undated; presumably the week of March 24, 1969]

[EG to PN]

The March issue of *Harper's Bazaar* has three poems by Borges, one at least familiar (I only had a chance to glance briefly at the time) and a somewhat unnerving photograph of him and his wife (who she? I have never heard her existence mentioned, but perhaps since his mother can hardly <u>still</u> be alive, he married afterwards, if you are following me) by Diane Arbus, who is Howard Nemerov's sister and all of whose photographs are unnerving.

I just saw a three-minute movie they made of *The Doubtful Guest* for part of a Westinghouse TV program on animation; narrated by Cyril Ritchard and with a Haydn quartet taken from an old Edison cylindrical recording: rather fun, except of course for the <u>awful</u> drawings. I cringed.

'Yesterday the shade of the purple dame departed; and to-day the messenger of the green bird slowly comes.'

Ode, Li Shangyin

'You see all these cushions—every one of them has either purple or scarlet stuffing. There's happiness for you!'

'If you think it over properly, there is shipwreck everywhere.'

The Satyricon

A work [Petronius's *Satyricon*] I have decided goes on MY SMALL BUT SELECT (those aren't meant to be caps, my finger slipped) [list] of books whose reasons for survival totally escape me, thus joining *Don Quixote* and *The Vicar of Wakefield*.

I am glad to note the return of the psychotic heroine to the silver screen, rather younger than she was back in the forties, but just as lethal. I should have recommended *Pretty Poison* to you myself, but for some insulting reason I think of you as being terribly serious-minded and above trash. As a matter of fact I even found A.P. [Anthony Perkins] bearable in the film; my only complaint being that I think the people that made it thought they were saying something and tended therefore to be somewhat pretentious. Even more fun, and with no pretension at all is *The Big Bounce,* which is a much better movie than it seems to be on the surface, and even rather touching from time to time, and now with things the way they are they can end this sort of thing in the completely amoral way they always should have, and then last night I caught a new one called *Baby Love* where the girl is only fifteen, which is the strangest movie I have seen in some time; it reminded me of the blue movie described in *The Day of the Locust* and has a distinctly demonic quality which somehow manages to go far beyond the ostensible plot and even the characters. Apart from the Truffaut *Stolen Kisses* which I liked very much but which I think is being wildly overrated by everyone else but it is at least a serious film worth hiring baby-sitters etc to see, and *The Castle* which is also a good serious try, and the Orson Welles version of Isak Dinesen's "Immortal Story," do not be misled—everything else available is the purest junk, and you will do much better huddled in front of the telly.

Thursday evening (I forget when the rest of this was)

I hope it was only me being subjective on account of I was very hungry and because I am always prey to the direst apprehensions whenever I go from one place to another, but you did not somehow sound your most cheerful on the phone

Thursday again

I do not seem to have even finished the above sentence. However, you sounded better yesterday, or I thought you did, or something.

Wei Wu Wei on Jesus: 'He seemed to understand sparrows, but not fish; and his callousness where fig-trees were concerned was total.'

Things have got more fraught since the mail this morning, from which I discovered that two of the five films I most want to see in all the world are going to

be shown at the Museum of Modern Art on Thursday, April 3rd and Thursday, April 17th, both old (1918, 1919) serials by Louis Feuillade, *Tih Minh* which lasts seven hours and *Barrabas* which lasts eight, and since it is entirely possible I shall never have another chance to see them, despite the fact I have never before driven two hundred and fifty miles each way to see a movie there is nothing for it but to do so. Two of the remaining three are also serials by Feuillade, *Judex* and its sequel, and the fifth is a film by Henri-Georges Clouzot, *Les Espions,* which never made it here in the late '50s. His new one, *La Prisonnière* I'll catch Monday night in NY after my astrology class.

Anyhoo, if you were planning to stay here over night you could come down next Tuesday afternoon early and go back Wednesday, if that is possible, or if you only spend the day, you can still come Wednesday, if that is possible, because I won't be getting much done in any case between Tuesday and Thursday, when I shall have to get up at dawn to get to the museum by 1:00 in the afternoon. Or if Wednesday is for some reason unfeasible, anytime the middle of the following week will be okay since the next Feuillade is not until the week after that. I'm sure this all is fearfully clear, or not, as the case may be. If this all sounds a trifle demented, recollect that in the movie field it's the equivalent for me of a new volume of Borges, with the added complication that films have to be screened and are sometimes available to see but once in a lifetime. The only Feuillade I have seen hitherto has been several parts of *Fantômas* and all of *Les Vampires,* none of which I have ever quite gotten over yet. So . . .

[. . .] Do you feel this typewriter ribbon is on the verge of expiration? I do not think I can bear the thought, because I can never remember what kind to buy, and then when one has a new one, one has to remove the old one, and put the new one on properly . . .

I await rather impatiently the future-past mss. The 'before he had as yet etc' and another odd bit later on which I can't recollect were sudden inspirations as I was revising. (The typewriter ribbon has not miraculously revived; I only switched to the other band so to speak.) "The Green Beads" in any case is very much derived from you, a fact for which I can find no reason whatever for you to find complimentary, but then we all have to put up with our friends' vagaries, do we not?[116]

Good grief. I suppose I am hungry, I mean I feel hungry most of the time from dieting, but how too obvious for it to have turned up in my last two mss. It has never occurred to me that such obvious corollaries (I don't care for that spelling somehow, but don't know what another one would be) can creep into one's work; I shall have to be more careful, unless of course it is too late. No wonder I hate reading my past work, and now it will be doubly unpleasant.

---

116. *The Green Beads,* published in 1978 by Albondocani Press, is dedicated "For the Neumeyers."

I'd better get this to the mail so you will hopefully get it by Saturday, so you can call on Sunday if you want to come Tuesday, or come anyway even if you don't call, or something.

I enclose my ideas for anti-cigarette commercials for no apparent reason.

Wordless commercial II

One of Chpin's jollier valses is being played on the piano; a gentleman in evening dress with splendid whiskers and moustache sits on a small gilt chair smoking a cigarette. Art nouveau-like curlicues of smoke drift off to the right where in an urn on a stand there is a madly flourishing plant with huge elaborate leaves (if in colour they are a beautiful emerald green) and a lot of buds. As the smoke wreathes about the plant, its leaves turn gradually grey and limp, then shrivelled and black; the buds too turn black. The valse is suddenly stopped by the sound of a deep and ominous gong; the buds burst open, revealing little death's heads. The camera travels back along the smoke: the gentleman has also turned black, his corpse slumped in the chair.

Limerick commercial II

There was a young lady named Mae
Who smoked without stopping all day;
    As pack followed pack,
    Her lungs first turned black,
And eventually rotted away.

U.S. POSTAGE
5¢

Whunp?

Apologies: we never had the wine you brought &
(rather I had) in the icebox for dinner. (Faw
in marking Dorothy—Thursday)

Mr Peter Neumeyer.
12 Powder House Road Ext.,
Medford, Mass.
02155.

Look into *The Hampdenshire Wonder* by J. D. Beresford some time. 2. iv. 69.
Too exhausted to start a letter, but.... Hope your drive back was not
as unpleasant as it may have been, judging from the rain here. The
black panic that overtakes me when I'm left alone by the departure of
guests (the more valued the guest, the blacker the panic, so...) drove
me out for the mail (as a result of which something will be arriving in yours though it doesn't say how soon) and to Lorania's whore
I picked up, among other things, *The Green Child*. I'm not sure my
brain will be up to it this evening but I'll try it. Do you know
The Land of Green Ginger by Noel Langley? If not, I'll pass it
along after I've reread it, because I already have at least
one, & more probably two copies elsewhere. Hope you can
manage to get to *La Prisonnière*. I'll see it again Monday, no
____ Ti ___ write something about the one I saw _____fully.
Ted.

7. iv. 69, N.Y.

HUZZAH!
Donald is in the British Book Centre; they'll never stop
us now. Of course I told them to order it, but still.
Whether its anywhere else, I haven't had time to look.
I read it again without looking at the pictures. It
is a work of genius. Your brilliance is only exceeded by
your warmth, and vice versa (your warmth is only
exceeded by your brilliance). The bedraggled state of
this card is due to its having been for who knows
how long in my portefeuille (I never know which
is the vulgar one: wallet or billfold — both sound
it.)
Yrs, E.G.

Friday afternoon, 4.iv.69

Dear Peter,

I drove carefully both ways, your admonishment to do so in my figurative ear, and here I am back, at the typewriter, writing to you. One would like to think there was a connection, but can one be entirely sure? I think not. But then.

The clippings were at the post office when I got back. I'll return when I've read them. The clippings. What will be returned, not I. Eventually I probably will too, but that wasn't what I meant now. I did not mean either this flight of fancy. Is that what it is? It is peculiar. It is that.

This has been a week. Clouzot on Monday, you on Tuesday and Wednesday, and Feuillade on Thursday. It would have been too much, but: Too much is not enough (old Gorey aphorism you may or may not have heard) and so it wasn't that, but instead just splendidly enough.

There was a passage from some preface to one of the anthologies in the book on Japanese court poetry I meant to call your attention to before. Something to the effect that there must be a something which is above and beyond (I'm putting this badly as always) what the poem says and the words that say it if the poem is to be a good one; to be vulgar the whole is more than the sum of its parts as it were.

Then there is the vaguely Zen thing about before Zen trees are trees, mountains are mountains, etc. which I'm sure you're familiar with, and then how as you get into Zen trees are no longer trees, etc. but then when you have got satori or whatever, trees are again trees, etc. but somehow differently.

It occurs to me that perhaps these two ideas are the same thing, that the extra something in a good work that you find you cannot pin down to any part of it, is what indicates that the thing has passed from being merely it is through it is not (but something else understood) and finally reaching it is again.

(Parenthetically, I think this is why I have a sort of distaste for metaphor and simile because it leaves the thing in the second stage, and why the one simile I once had in something of mine—*The Beastly Baby* as it happens—I removed when I finally lettered the text.)

All of which is preamble to saying that *Tih Minh,* the Feuillade movie, is utterly indescribable, which is sort of too bad because it turned out to be the movie I most want you someday to see of all the movies I have ever seen.

Of anything I can think of it most reminds me of *Donald Helps,* and when I get to doing the drawings for it, they will be based on my memories of *Tih Minh.* Of my own work, it is most like *The Black Doll* for plot and literary content, and it looks most like *The Remembered Visit.*

Hierarchically speaking, if you follow, I would have been in abysses of despair at my incompetence to achieve anything at all within shouting through a giant megaphone distance of the film, had I not been so absolutely carried away by every second of same. And really, it was not of any noticeable consolation during the dinner break for someone I didn't know, though the friend of a friend, to rush up to me, and say it was just like watching my books. I mean if one were apprenticed to a tailor, it is hardly complimentary that people recognize your products as clothes rather than say pots and pans.

I must try and give you some faint fragments of *Tih Minh,* if nothing else. The plot itself is utterly simple. An explorer in Asia has brought back to his home in Nice a young half-caste girl (French father, Annamese mother) whom he intends to marry. He also has in his possession without knowing it, the secret of a vast treasure written on the flyleaf of a Hindu book. Three German spies, two men and a woman, are after the book, and really that is all. Almost at the beginning of the film they abduct Tih Minh, the girl, and give her a drug which causes her to lose both her memory and powers of speech. She is very beautiful and fragile-looking though very spunky later on when her memory comes back, but somehow the whole tone of the film is set when the explorer is sent a photograph of her after she has been abducted in which she is sitting forlornly by a table with a calendar on it with a very visible date, and across the corner of the photograph where you usually sign them is written 'Elle est vivante'; I know this does <u>not</u> convey why it all seems so incredibly poignant, but in context it does; later the photograph which has not been fixed or whatever you call it, fades or rather darkens and the image disappears completely.

The whole film takes place in Nice except for one brief flashback to the Orient, mostly in cube-shaped white villas surrounded by gardens filled with palms, spiky succulents, and incredible numbers of roses, great banks of them everywhere, sometimes walls twenty feet high of nothing but great white blooms, or the absolutely desolate mountain landscapes of rock and scrub outside Nice with the sea in the distance. Incredibly beautiful without ever calling attention to itself and adding to the dreamlike quality of the action which flows quite slowly, with great circumstantial reality and an unhurried allowance of even quite small things to be shown in their entirety, every now and again punctuated without warning by some absolutely dazzling bit of near-surrealism or outbreak of really terrifying physical violence (several people are beaten to death or nearly with rocks or ruthlessly strangled) or some really impossible bit of action but which only seems more real somehow because of its setting—the most brilliant sequence of the picture begins with Tih Minh deciding to hide unknown to her fiancé in a wicker hamper supposedly containing food, etc. for him and his friends to take along on their assault on the hideaway of the spies in the mountains; with the aid of his comic valet she is hoisted onto the top of one of those great high taxis and lashed to the roof, but unknown to them the cook is a confederate of the spies and notifies them of this so that as the taxi is hairpinning its way up the mountain, the hamper is seized by a hook as the taxi emerges from a tunnel and the hamper is hoisted a couple of hundred feet up to the top of the mountain; soon afterwards it breaks loose from the spies and hurtles halfway down the mountain, Tih Minh still inside, though she has in the meantime managed to shoot one of the spies in the arm, until it comes to rest in a tree over a precipice. Etc. Then there are bits like where two of the spies disguised as nuns get themselves admitted to the villa while all the men are away and succeed in kidnapping Tih Minh once more, or there is the part early in the film where the comic valet finds Tih Minh after she has lost her memory and can only lure her to safety by keeping her small black dog just out of her reach as he lures her onto a balcony, down a rather awesome drainpipe, through the garden, over a balustrade, down a lot of rocks and finally to ultimate escape in a dinghy. It all I fear sounds much more bizarre and foolish, which it never is, and what one ultimately comes away with are the really simple things which can't be described really at all—a shot of Tih Minh arranging roses in a vase, or just several of the characters walking down a little road in dappled sunlight, and the like.

So it was all more than worth it getting up at four in the morning and driving 250 miles for. Ideally, it would be better to have seen it in two sessions on successive days because one's attempt to concentrate on everything since one wonders if one will ever again have a chance to see it again is quite inordinately exhausting, not to mention what sitting all that time does to one's lower back and posterior. You suffer other ways than just being beautiful.

A thought from Anne Thackeray Ritchie:

But, after all, the whole secret of life is made up of the things one makes, and those one steals, and those one pays for.

Later

I finished Herbert Read's *The Green Child* over supper. I expect it will always stick in my mind, even haunt me rather, but while I find my admiration for it very great it is also at the same time not very warm. It is either, I think, because the book is so contained within itself, so pure that while I am not put off by it in the usual sense at the same time I can't say I exactly enter into it either; on the other hand, it may be that it is so exclusively masculine/active/positive/whatever in tone and concept, etc. that I am a- (as opposed to un-) sympathetic towards it temperamentally. It's like nothing else I can think of, especially in the extreme disparity between its three parts. And of course the simplicity of the style makes me absolutely green (pardon pun) with envy. Also the description of the crystals at the end really says all there is to be said about art and its relation to nature.

Speaking of which (and if you can figure out what I mean by that you are doing well indeed because I have not the least idea) your visit was very mysterious/very real. I use the slash, if that is what you call same, because I suspect it is the same thing. It was foremost a great pleasure to see you, but then ca va sans dire ["it goes without saying"]. On the other hand, everything else va sans dire too because I find our knowing each other becomes less definable, and then less again as things succeed themselves as we progress. I would say we _do_ progress. In an absolute rather than a relative direction perhaps?

You will be relieved to know it is time for me to go to bed. _More_ tomorrow, he threatened.

Tomorrow

Three books of possible interest culled from a Gotham Book Mart list:
The Narrow Act: Borges' Art of Allusion by Ronald Christ
The Cyclical Night: Irony in James Joyce and Jorge Luis Borges by L. A. Murillo
Thomas Mann's Doctor Faustus: The Sources and Structure of the Novel by Gunilla Bergsten.

No publishers given.

I hope my mind gets in sufficient repair one of these days to begin reading things like Doctor Faustus again; the prospects don't look exactly propitious, but then one never knows.

Beginningless time and the present moment are the same. There is no this and no that. To understand this truth is called complete and unexcelled Enlightenment.

Huang Po

Stepping into the public hall His Reverence said: Having many sorts of knowledge cannot compare with giving up _seeking_ for anything, which is the best of all things. Mind is not of several kinds and there is no Doctrine which can be put into words. As there is no more to be said, the assembly is dismissed!

P'ei Hsiu, reporting on Huang Po

I'm alternating this with a drawing I am getting nowhere in particular with for *Look,* which has to be delivered by Monday. I'm also working desultorily on *The Boggle Book* in my head, that's the one in case you have forgotten, which is going to have thirty drawings and thirty sentences of text, each on a loose card so the text can be read in any order, the drawings looked at ditto, so that reading one sentence in connection with one drawing, the possible versions of the book number 1 x 2 x 3 etc. through x 30, and that squared. It will all come in a box if anyone ever publishes it.

Fragment from a song called "Time" [Don Williams]:

At sunset I laugh,
Sunrise I cry,
At midnight I'm in between
And I'm wondering why

Poem by Hakuin Zenji:

Oh! let me hear again the echo of that snow,
    falling in the twilight
At that ancient Temple in the grove of Shinoda!

I trust you will disregard almost everything I said on Tuesday and Wednesday. Consider, where applicable, as Noises of Concern, and the rest as just Usual (I fear) Drivel.

At the moment I really must get back upstairs to that dumb drawing. (It is now 6:15 PM, damp twilight is rapidly turning to damp darkness, and . . . what? I have no idea.)

That drawing is making me potty. (It's eight o'clock now.)

Someday I think you ought to read *Snarleyyow; or, The Dog Fiend* by Captain Marryat.

Geoffrey Brereton on Charles Perrault, introduction to his Penguin translation:

. . . it appears likely that he meant his tales to be not so much moral in the
ethical sense as 'exemplary' or instructive. They taught children what the
world was like, bad and dangerous as well as good. To overcome the bad,
it was not always enough to be good oneself. One must also be wary and
clever. What more beneficial lesson could there be?

How true, but I fear the vicious but namby-pamby world in which we live, especially the part of it that passes on children's books, would be more horrified than anything else confronted with this idea.

Sunday night

Well, I finished the dumb drawings for *Look*. I hope they pay me lots of money because they are awful.

Afterwards I stared out the window for at least an hour thinking how I really should go out because it had turned into such a beautiful, if chilly, day, so I finally did, and drove to Scargo Hill, and climbed the tower, as did a great many other people while I was there, but it was quite elegiac all the same anyway. On the way back I was congratulating myself (<u>never</u> do <u>that</u>) that now I could get to work on one of the books I am supposed to be illustrating, more or less uninterruptedly, in the next few days. No sooner had I got through the door as it were than the phone rang and it was an unknown female admirer, quite young one assumes, calling from Boston, and she said she and her friends wanted to meet me, and so what on earth does one say, so I finally said they could come down next weekend for the purpose, and so she said she'd call on me Saturday morning, but perhaps she won't. It is unkind of me, but I hope this starts happening to you; I want to know how you'll cope.

I want to read "The Flower in the Bottle"[117] over several times more (and do send any further work on same), before saying anything more about it, but one thing did occur to me in passing, which is a distinction I've never quite made before. When I said I didn't care as much for the academic jokes as much as other parts of it, I think it was because one's reaction to them can only be: 'Isn't the author clever?' whereas the baking sequence at the present end of the MS makes one think: 'Isn't it clever?' It's not exactly a question of self-consciousness, but the reason I think I find some authors forever unreadable is because they are always forcing you to think of them rather than their works. Now that it comes to mind, I think this is one of the reasons I find Salinger so unbearable. Holden Caulfield doesn't really exist at all, nor do the Glass family; it's all just J.D. admiring his sensibilities in a lot of mirrors.

* * *

I think I'll trot to the P.O. with this, and then read my astrology book. I'm becoming consumed with curiosity about what the mails will be bringing you and bringing me; two people have told me the results are really quite uncanny.[118]

Feeling the need for some creative self-indulgence, I may bring *Donald and the Splinter* (what is the name of it? I can't remember) along, the dummy that is, and get your final thoughts on it and the text, when I come up . . .

Ted.

---

117. The novel I had begun writing, in which time flows backward.
118. The results of the astrological charts EG had sent for.

Sat., April 5, 1969 [this letter and the next two mailed together in one envelope]

Dear Ted,

Thank you for your postcard, for your wishing me a speedy and safe trip home, both of which it was, rain notwithstanding, though driving even an hour and a half made me think again that you are tempting fate excessively with the amount of driving—elegant driving though it may be—that you do. So, be careful. Drive as though the <u>others</u> are mad.

You undoubtedly know that Carla Stevens[119] wrote me a very nice letter, saying she wanted both "The Moustache" and "The Faithful Fish." That's wonderful—and again, I have you to thank. A change she wanted on "The Faithful Fish" is absolutely right, and very easily made. Her dissatisfaction with the moustache story is very much more difficult to accommodate. You'll see from a copy of my letter to her which I'll eventually make what is involved. I hope it'll all turn out somehow.

Of course, first thing, we went to see *La Prisonnière,* and the only complaint I have is that you're not here to talk about it. It was of course incredible—in all ways— from the pictures to the acting to the story to the problem—and one does walk out stunned by it. One matter seems to me a real crux to understanding the film: When at the end on the rooftop Stan says to the husband that he (the husband) is as limited, as fragmented, as cut off in his understanding of women, and entirely too, is Stan there speaking only for and as Stan? Or is Stan speaking for Clouzot (i.e. saying something we are to take as a 'world-view' for the writer)?? Perhaps knowing so much more about Clouzot, and by now having seen the film perhaps several times, you have thoughts about this. It makes a world of difference.

By the way, the ending—her in the hospital, and thinking still of Stan—that was fine. No complaint at all. At the same time, had it all ended ten or fifteen minutes earlier, don't you think no harm would have been done—though perhaps no improvement either? I anyway didn't need the twist, and thought it added nothing essential to the anatomization of one raw nerve fiber under a million power microscope, which was what I thought the film was.

Anyway—it is an enormous film. It deserves to be in a gallery as a major opus in the genre for our time—boy does that sound like tissue thunder—but you know what I mean. No, I don't know *The Tale of the Land of Green Ginger* [by Noel Langley; illustrated by Edward Ardizzone]. And I will get the J. D. Beresford.

Have the wine when you do a wonderful illustration with a lighthouse and an aunt and a hare and spectacles.

I'll go on with this in a day or so when new things have happened. The leather bag progresses.

---

119. At that time Carla was an editor at Young Scott Books.

March 29, Saturday [misdated, as EG observed; see bottom of page 210]

Dear Ted,

Do you know Harold Altman? We went to the "Boston Printmakers" exhibit at the MFA, and there—calling from across two rooms—was an amazing picture, very much a Gorey picture, and absolutely fantastic and remarkable. I would doubt it's a purposeful imitation of you—just probably a kindred soul. And the picture, the lithograph, of ten mysterious and hard-to-see figures, sort of crosses between meaty Gorey children and Henry Moore-s in shape, were standing in ominous places in a very very green park. As I say—stunning. But unfortunately $125.

I just saw for the first time *The King Who Saved Himself from Being Saved*. Your drawings are so benign! The verses are, however, awfully uneven, aren't they. [. . .] The story is fine, and with very little effort, I can't but think John Ciardi could have smoothed it enormously.

You should have been here. We've just anatomized a whole chicken, which we are now boiling, and will glue the bones of together again tomorrow to make a museum skeleton. Aahh, the joys of parenthood.

April 9 (Wednesday)

Nothing noteworthy since my writing of April 5—except the arrival, thank you, of the clippings [. . .]. Thank you. Oh yes—and a girl, a nice girl, breaking down in complete and utter and bordering on suicidal hysterics in my office last night, and her boyfriend coming later to "explain," and my feeling quite out of my depth and not knowing what to say other than muttering "come come now," and "won't you sit down please," and "can you think of an assignment that would please you more," etc etc etc. After sixteen years' teaching, one would think I ought to be able to see such things coming, and forestall them. But I didn't. And I keep wondering, how would Professor So and So have handled the matter? Or would it ever have happened in his office? Such excitement happens about once in three years to me, and is unsettling every time. (And tangent to that matter—as good teaching advice as I've ever read is Jacques Barzun's warning that teachers should keep in mind that in every class of fifty there's going to be at least one who is deranged, or who is taking down every word, convinced you are a Jesuit or a Communist or something.) I wonder how psychiatrists learn to preserve themselves from utter and complete spiritual depletion, living all day every day the crises of others?

Enough—to work. Toynbee says to write every day. I'm trying to write a story that won't come. Seven pages completely false start—and I know what it ought to be. Thanks for *Green Ginger,* which I can get to when I've done today's duty stint. yrs, Peter

[EG to PN] Tuesday afternoon, 8.iv.69

You all right? I don't know why I (especially) ask. I trust your visit was not harder on your neck than if you hadn't made it.

You did not care for or could not even finish *The Lost Traveller*? I think it was one of the two, which mildly surprises me. That's mildly. I quite took to it; I like the way he writes, and the first and last parts, the desert and the hunt for the auk, really quite marvelous. I never particularly am convinced by pseudo-Kafka or whatever parables about totalitarianism and whatnot so the section in the city I liked less, but again I thought the physical things: the buildings, the furnishings of the houses, etc. quite haunting. I was impressed by the set-piece description of his funeral (if you got that far) and, since I suppose you must have looked at the ending in any case, the actual fate of the last Great Auk is one of the great (sorry) anecdotes on the subject of what is the matter with man's relationship or lack of same to the rest of the natural world. However, surrealism or whatever is one of the least predictable things as to whether other people will like. There's a sentence for you.

Anyhoo, thank you very much for putting me onto it; unless I hear to the contrary, I assume you don't want it back.

I found in the mail when I got back this afternoon a letter from Tufts inviting me to participate in a symposium on "The Relation between Fantasy and Reality in Children's Literature" on May 12th to be moderated by John Ciardi; a fleeting temptation to accept was naturally occasioned by possibly seeing you then and also by its being an opportunity to shoot my mouth off on a subject I feel strongly, but in spite of all, I think not. Somewhere along the line I decided never again to utter (except books) in public; I'd rather not do it in private either, but that is too much to expect.

Crumbs. I discovered in class last night that what you [are] and what I am getting in the mail takes three weeks or more to arrive, so we've at least two more to wait. Why it should take so long (you will see what I mean), none of us can figure out.

It is boredom makes the world go round, sometimes anyway. In this case, I've decided to start work on *Donald Has a Difficulty;* when it will get done is another question entirely; we shall have to see. I had various minor inspirations looking over the dummy and your letter of 9 December annoys me just as much as it did then; however, I am simply ignoring it, in a nice, accommodating way of course. Actually, as one says, if I get anything done on it, I'll bring it with me if our tentative date of the 19th (roughly) is still on, and still on when the day rolls around. I feel my wisest course is to simply ignore your protestations about the story's fancied (by you) weakness; besides, I think I succeeded afterwards in talking you out of it/them/ whatever long ago over the phone. As to what Donald looks like, he can only look like what he looks like already: ancient, Semitic, etc. (Ironic sentence)

Early or rather earlier in the day I was feeling madly euphoric with the absolutely splendid futility of <u>everything</u>, but now I am depressed, and want to have a good cry. Perhaps I am hungry. I shall have my supper.

Wednesday evening

Well, the cover for *D has a D* is half-done, and more will get done tonight. I <u>should</u> be doing other things. I spent the morning cleaning kitchen cupboards and so forth and so on, and now there are more ants than ever. Very mysterious. I have put ant cups about in places where the cats can't get to them, though presumably the ants can. I am really more and more tolerant to all insect life, as life goes on, but I think I'd better get the ants out of here before I leave, and keep my fingers crossed that they will stay away until the rest of the family gets here, probably in June. They panic easily, even at a ladybug for instance. And I am always having to save earwigs from them when they come in on flowers or foliage for bouquets.

I do not suppose you are trapped on one of the upper floors of University Hall.[120] Who would have thought it of Harvard? Though now that I do think of it, didn't they keep immuring people recruiting from places that manufactured war materiel last year? Or something of the sort.

I do not think my tiny mind is ever going to be able to master the intricacies of astrology, but I guess I'll persevere. For a time at least. Not being able to remember anything for three minutes is no help either.

I saw *La Prisonnière* again Monday night; I must admit a second time made me feel quite, quite sick. I don't think it really matters to one's appreciation of the film, but a great deal of its wit and its references are to other films of the past few years, sometimes to one specific one, but more often to the kinds of films that have been fashionable and critically over-scrutinized so to speak.

I fear I'm going to be driven before the week is over to seeing *West Side Story* (a work I have avoided assiduously ever since I saw the opening night of the musical on Broadway, due to a curious but dull set of circumstances) at the drive-in.

It's back to Donald until it (my back) gives out, and then another tussle with astrology. How exciting it all is!

Wednesday (no, Thursday, now that I consider)

Your letter found in the mailbox a few minutes ago was a relief, as I was beginning to worry that perhaps you were not well. Though when at the foot of the first page it said: I'll go on with this in a day or so, etc. and when page 2 was headed March 29th I began to wonder about one of us.

---

120. It was the era of student protest. Professors were indeed trapped in their buildings, though I was not.

The cover for *Donald Has a Difficulty* is done, and looks rather elegant to me for the moment. I am of two minds, or rather my fractional one is in two pieces, as to whether to show you any of it until it's all done or not, a confused statement if ever there was one, and my letters consist mostly of nothing else. Well, we shall see.

How nice about Carla taking <u>both</u> stories though I am hardly surprised. I just sent her back a couple of contracts, which is why I was in the post office so of course I hadn't had your letter yet. I did mention in my covering note that I hoped it would be possible for me to design the book if the illustrator didn't, and also made noises of inquiry about who she had in mind. Anyway, sucks boo, as they say to Harry Stanton. I'm not certain, but I may have been cut by the girlfriend in the post office a day or two ago, while we were opening our separate boxes if indeed that's who it was, because I was resolutely concentrating on the combination in an ostentatious manner. Do send me her comments on the two stories, or whatever is involved at any rate. (Carla's.)

My aunt Isabel, whom you met briefly last summer, got back from Europe yesterday, calling me from the bus station in Hyannis (she had missed the train to Boston from NY) to come and rescue her. Poor dear, she got a sinister infection while in Zurich of the sort that caused her to lose the hearing in one ear some forty-odd years ago, and while she seemed all right last night, this morning had a relapse and was understandably rather in a panic at the prospect of losing the hearing in her other ear; it turns out there is precisely one ear specialist on the Cape and one is rather dubious about him, so she is toying with the idea of fleeing to Philadelphia where her brother (the owner of this house) is, and getting treatment there, so things are rather a hooha at the moment. She's calling the family tonight to see what they say.

La Prisonnière. Clouzot is or was here in the US for its opening, and I have heard at third and fourth hand various things he was supposed to have said in radio and TV interviews, one of which was that the movie was strongly autobiographical, whatever that could possibly mean, the character of Stan I suppose, though I don't really believe it.

Anyway, my feeling about the film, the main one that is, is that it is about banality in its largest possible sense and how it is the chief characteristic of life and art today. Everything in the film, the décor, the art, the people, the dialogue, the situations, everything is banal in the extreme, and this is what to me makes it so absolutely horrifying. I can't even believe that Stan is really a sadist, but only, if not exactly pretending, at least driving himself into pushing it far beyond his natural bent; the triangle couldn't be more banal, and everything that happens in the affair between Stan and Josée. Even her suicide attempt and the way it's presented in the film is a dim little rehash of *Anna Karenina:* the train ride at the beginning, the accident later on, and then the actual crash at the end, where everything is shown in terms of just another bit of modish modern sculpture. In short I feel that everything that's said is meant also to be as cliché-ridden as possible, not that it makes it possibly less true, but I don't think you can pin Clouzot down to any particular bits of it. He is, I have always felt, one of the most fearfully intelligent people who has ever made films, and his sardonic, to say the least, views on everything, always have to be considered, even when he most seems to be saying something himself; it may just be another twist, as it were. As for example Josée's delirium at the end, which at first I thought was singularly misplaced and let's be brutal tacky for Clouzot to have put in until I realized that of course this was one of the chief points of it: parody of all the movies that have done this (specific references to all sorts of films here: Ingmar Bergman's *Persona* to name the first that comes to mind) and at the same time quite ghastly and pathetic because this is just the sort of delirium a girl like Josée would have. Incidentally it only occurred to me from your letter that the hospital ending is I think necessary because now for the first time, more dead than alive, she really is a physical prisoner, totally immobilized in all that plaster and those slings, and green cords, after all the silliness of chains and whatnot beforehand. To get back to the dialogue, I think perhaps when Josée says that when you're in love nothing is dirty and when you're not everything is, is a favourite Clouzot idea—he says much the same thing at the end of *Manon,* which he made after the war and which was an updated contemporary version where they fled to Israel rather than America, and which sort of said all there was to be said for the corruption of the immediately post-war world; after both Manon and Des Grieux have spent the entire movie in the most shoddy, despicable fashion with her betraying him at every possible turn and so forth, she says as she is dying, "We were better than the others because we loved more than the others," and one is forced to accept this.

The two moments of *La Prisonnière* which may very well have not registered with you at all because they are both so peripheral are one at the beginning where they drive away from the apartment, the car is reflected in a pond, or river or something, and some unseen person tugs at a fishing line, and the camera goes up the line to the bridge the car is now crossing over: heaven knows what it means, but it is very obviously there for something, and the second time around gave me a real chill. I suppose it is a first indication of being hooked, as simple as that, but it is all in the elegance of the photography just as a tiny transition shot. The second thing is the last scene on the roof where the building across the way begins to proliferate in a totally surrealist way more and more red awnings as the scene progresses. The first time there are only perhaps five to be seen, and then more and more until the whole building virtually is covered with them. Also there are two men on the roof of the building opposite, hardly noticeable, but who keep pointing over and over again to the foreground fight. It makes no rational sense, but somehow the awnings give me a feeling that the whole natural world is breaking open in some monstrous and inexplicable way.

I expect I may very well totter off to it again on Monday. There is a lot of it I still do not quite see how it fits, and past experience tells me that there is nothing in the film that wasn't carefully calculated. Another great comment I think is her job of sitting watching all those dreadful interviews with put-upon ladies which are somehow much more real than what is actually happening in the film until the very end. The whole thing of art and life (as the scene in the apartment where the sexual preliminaries behind the frosted glass looks exactly like one of the constructions in the gallery; the coloured ropes on the boats again like some crazy construction, and even more disturbing I felt, the paint being dumped in the water as if the whole natural world would end up contaminated by dreary humanity and its works). I could go on for hours. But it is supper time.

Have you not got the letter with the flight from the sunset on the envelope? Not that it needs answering as I recall, but you mention everything else but not that.

There was to have been more of this, I've forgot now just what, but then I realized if I do not get it to the mail this evening, you will definitely not get it before you go to SB [Stony Brook]. (Good luck house-hunting.) So you have been spared.

P.S. There is a new country and western song about a girl from the wrong side of the tracks, but it is called "A Rose Is a Rose Is a Rose." I expect Gertrude would have approved, really, don't you?

Thursday, April 10

Dear Ted,

Yesterday, after I had sealed the little notes from various days to you, your letter arrived, and today your "huzzah" card announcing Donald's first communion at the British Book Center. Well, huzzah (said limply), I guess. Spurred by your card, I phoned the Phillips and Harvard Coop bookstores to inquire, and neither had ever heard of our child. So.

I protest your overstatement of the contribution of the text. I myself recognize a pleasing felicity in several phrases—the kind of thing that was a danger of becoming an artificial application rather than a natural growth, which is why Donalds must now take a long rest. But you and I know that your illustrations are not only superb, but that perhaps 84% of the things that people find to laugh about in the book (surveying, the imagined beast) are wholly your invention. Except for the fact that they are heartfelt, we ought probably not take up our time with Alphonse/Gastonianism.[121] Except that, as I say, I mean it.

By the way, I thought afterwards, typically for you the genius and the human depth in your marriage manual illustration is hidden japaneseaically and unobtrusively in the tiniest space—in the eyes, the four little dots, man and wife's eyes looking at each other with lord knows what, fear, love, stage fright, apprehension, probing, heaven knows. But those little eyes shifted shyly or surreptitiously toward each other are so typical of you/your work.

Two days ago I made a false start on a very good story idea given me by my leather-bag-making teacher while we all were playing sardine—a variant on hide-and-seek—in the woods. But it was very poorly written, and I knew so well what it would read like if it were good. Today I begin another version.

As for the "Flower in the Bottle," I feel a little sheepish having given that self-indulgent stuff to you. You're going to politely protest that that's not what you meant/wanted etc., but nonetheless, I'm dropping that project because I have enough trust in your instinctive response or lack of response to be clued to when something is worth doing. Anyway, had I no critical acumen at all, that would be one thing, but I have enough of it to at least recognize the truth of your reaction and to see its point. Dropping that is very small loss. My life is too atomized to do it now anyway, or to do anything of that length.

Monday we go to Stony Brook to house hunt. Thursday I'm intending to phone you. I'll try Barnstable first, in case you're there. If you're not, I'll phone yr N.Y.

---

121. Alphonse and Gaston were two comic strip characters in 1901 who were always deferentially bowing to each other: "After you, Alphonse," "No, after *you*, Gaston," etc.

answering service and leave a message. If we're back very early (unlikely) Friday is fine; otherwise, I expect, if still suitable with you, we see you Saturday. What a pleasure. (We, by the way, will be staying at the Port Jefferson Motel in Port Jefferson, L.I. Very nice student couple will be here with the children, and we'll phone home every day or two to check.)

You must have gotten a lecture or symposium or whatever invitation from Tufts by now. My or our part in that is as follows. Perhaps the only nice people we know in Medford are at Tufts, and they of course know all about the Donald book. They're also instrumental in setting up affairs like this one at Tufts. They asked me, and (they're very nice friends) I said yes. They asked me about you, and knowing that you can be very reticent, but unwilling similarly to conclude that you might not want to see John Ciardi again, or come up for kicks, I said the only thing sensible, I think. I said: "ask him." Though I knew it all was brewing when I saw you last, I knew I could write this explanation more easily than try to explain it. So there. Do as you like. Know, at the same time, that we would use insidious means to see you after we haven't for some time.

The neck has its regressive and its progressive days. Curious business.

Tell me, did your covey or bevy of female admirers arrive from Boston? Oh to have watched. One pictures in one's mind's eye . . .

Your description of *Tih Minh* is incredible. The film, you may protest, was even more so. But I suspect that in your onandonandonandon description of it, with each of the on and on's being worthy of a story or a picture, gives as good a transliteration from film to words as may be possible. Whether the present writer could sit still the length of it is open to question, but it sounds absolutely marvelous, like *The Count of Monte Cristo* or something in movies, albeit different of course, but the same kind of "getting lost in the volumes and volumes of it" being possible. Thank you for as they vilely say, "sharing" it with me.

Melipety, our cat, is pregnant.

I doubt that I will assist at the delivery.

I am glad we shall be talking about the Splinter of Donald. (A writer and an illustrator talking about a splinter of Donald might, in itself, make—perhaps posthumously—a nice Fantod sequel to *Donald and the Splinter*. "Shall I," said the artist, "depict Donald suffering his splinter in the shin or in the calf?")

I'll show you the letter to Carla Stevens, if you want to see it, when you're here. I had forgotten to make a second carbon of it.

Do <u>you</u> think California will disappear?

I will read *The Black Doll* and *The Remembered Visit* tonight again. Jonathan Kozol and friends of his, and the bag maker [William Coperthwaite], and others are coming for who knows what sort of educational something tonight. What they will get is turkey and rice in green peppers. More cannot be promised.

I went downstairs to look for Herbert Read's *The Green Child,* but can't find it. It's time to move if only to straighten out the bookcases. But I wanted to reply to your thoughts, and so wanted to look at it again. Because I don't remember it that well, except I had thoughts about Jesuits and Education while reading it, and I had curious recollections of other books ending in crystallization and encapsulation—Madeleine L'Engle's *A Wrinkle in Time;* W. H. Hudson's *Crystal Age;* Hesse's *Magister Ludi,* and I can't recall now what else.

Yes—predictably at about the same time you were typing the names of the three books I should note, I was writing my secretary to order the same three. The book on Faustus, I read consequently last week, or rather, thumbed through. Widener had it only in German. It's one of those one ought to know exists in case one needs it.

We are deep into a new political quarrel, and the superintendent of schools [of Medford] has sent me a letter telling me in effect the great pleasure with which he contemplates my imminent departure.[122] Helen is on the phone at the moment playing fifth ward or whatever to a Negro community representative at the moment, and so suddenly this letter has become fragmented and is now about finished and to live for five hours in a tight mailbox and then find itself pushed with 431 similarly shaped things into a dirty gray bag and then go by car to Cape Cod where new adventures await it before and after air and sunlight will [rest of letter missing]

[also mailed to EG on April 10]

I had never dreamed how gross the responses of our friends (I'm sure not yours) would be to *Donald and the . . . .* I have heard so often now "Oh it was such a surprise. All the while I was expecting a butterfly." Such an idea obviously never never occurred to me.

There are two types of people in the world, those who . . .

---

122. As president of the Medford Education Council, I had been active and vociferous in school and political matters in the city.

* * *

I dropped cards to Carla and Candida about the latter acting as your agent; I trust you still feel this is OK; I certainly did my best to convince you. I also asked Harry to send me 25 copies of *Donald* for strategic giving.

(Quotation: 'I was always searching out dismal places and sitting there as if I was dead.'   Hakuin Zenji)

Donald Has a Difficulty is going to look different than I thought it was going to. Isn't that a remark calculated to make the heart go pitty-pat? I have a new diae (idea)—(Either my wrists are crossed or else my thumbs are on the outside edges of my hands.)—for the string drawing which I think is funny, authentic, elegant, and mysterious. The battle I think is going to be Japanese weapons, and possibly the pots in the market. Don't panic, you'll love them all, or if you don't, I'll change them to the sound of grinding teeth. Mine.

Thought about the Clouzot: I suspect that in some way I haven't figured out—and if anywhere he does speak in his own voice it is here—the business of the words rien and etre in various famous authors' handwriting on the slides may be the key to the film, and Stan's remark that they wrote the same word but didn't mean the same thing (by the fact of the extreme physical difference in the way the words looked). I can't get further with this, but it echoes, sort of, other things in his previous films.

Five-ish

Apropos of nothing at all, except that I started to read yet another book with one, I feel compelled to categorically state that there is one thing that could irrevocably destroy our friendship and that is if you ever decide to attach a coy dedication to anything. I do not much care for reasons attached to them, however austere (and that includes Mr Eliot dedicating to Mr Pound) but the arch variety cause me to wish to murder the author in a nasty manner. Well, so much for that teeny outburst.

Your letter came this afternoon, so all my worries about my letter are at rest. It flitted through (through being the important word) my head that you might have had something to do with the Tufts invitation, but anyhow, it is probably better I didn't know because then I probably wouldn't have declined it, and I think I was right to. You (especially) would never think it, but I really don't enjoy hearing myself talk. Apart from that it would of course be great fun, and I seldom see John [Ciardi] so that would have been pleasant too, but by the time one is 44, one should really stop doing idiot and unsuitable things, and that's what it would be for me.

Your note on yellow paper I slightly don't understand. I mean it did occur to you that it [*Donald and the . . .*] was a parody of the butterfly story, I take it, but I gather what you mean is that people seriously expected it to turn into a butterfly as the denouement? I wonder if there is a difference between our friends. I would say offhand that my friends would not expect anything as it were, and simply read it; on the other hand my friends seldom say anything more than things like 'I loved your new book.' Period.

Anent, always a classy term, your remarks about my illustrations for *Donald* could not be more erroneous. Just because things aren't specifically mentioned in a text does not mean they are not there just the same, if not more so. Your remarks would apply to something like the Muriel Spark where I practically made the whole thing up in a way because there was nothing in the text, but *Donald* was an entirely different thing, and I never felt that I was doing anything but drawing on your imagination and not mine, and this was after all before we had even met so it is not a question of anything but what was there in your text from the beginning. So enough of this sentimental slop.

My mind is really not functioning well enough to write intelligently on the rest of your letter and several unanswered bits of the previous one. I finished two more drawings for *D has a D* today: the title page and string (would you mind dreadfully if it were in the singular as it is all one piece?) and I'm depleted, and besides you won't get this until the end of next week anyway when you get back. I have a dreadful feeling that I am going to find myself driving to Chatham tonight to see the one movie on the Cape I haven't seen which is, alas, *Therese and Isabelle,* probably dubbed, and in any case I am not exactly entranced by seeing two thirtyish actresses pretending to be Sapphic schoolgirls. Oh well, anything will be better than *West Side Story* which I saw at the drive-in last night. Surely the most meretricious film of the past decade if not much longer. I loathed it on the stage, but had never realized before just quite how tacky it was in every respect. Ugh . . .

I am pleased to know at long last how to spell Melipety, unless of course this is one of your endearing misspellings.

I'd <u>like</u> to think California will disappear, though I have nothing against it personally, but I fear nothing so amusing for the rest of us is going to happen in this dreary world.

* * *

Do you know the Green Knowe books of L. M. Boston? Or did I ask you this before? I'll bring one to leave with you next week.

Also you might look up *The Boy and the River, The Fox in the Island* (I think) and there's one other whose name I can't remember by Henri Bosco. Are you an admirer of Alain-Fournier's *The Wanderer* or not?

Therese and Isabelle was of such an ineptitude that it became downright creepy, though most of the audience found it good for a giggle. It had some good photography and a sinister and florid score by Georges Auric that occasionally convinced one something was going on and even making sense. It was not however, and the ladies were not even particularly well preserved for being in their thirties. What anyone was thinking of apart from making a salacious heap of money I cannot conceive.

Saturday morning

I must remove this from the typewriter because I have an idea for a story I got yesterday and which materialized further as I drove back from putting my aunt down at 128 so she could catch the train to Philadelphia. I just got back, 11:15, and am wondering whether my female admirer called while I was out. Whether it would/will be fun or not if she and her friends materialize—I do hope they all aren't female, which I do not mean in the depraved way it obviously sounds—I could do without them as I want to work on *Donald,* and perhaps take some pictures—I finally got to the point of buying a couple of rolls of film and putting one in the camera, but have so far not pulled myself together sufficiently to go out and start snapping at the spring.

The new story idea has Donald in it; I hope you will forgive me. Only at the end. Donald I mean.

George MacBeth: 'And I sense the flow
Of death like honey to make all things whole.'

First draft of story done. It is about how Donald got the pet that appears in *D has a D.* I'll no doubt have a sufficiently finished version for you to read by the time this gets to the mail. All I can say is I am becoming a believer in possession in the occult sense: you have written this, not me; whether or not you like it has nothing to do with it. Needless to remark, it is very strange. I feel quite faint.[123] I must go in the living room and soothe my nerves with the current jigsaw puzzle. A pity we can't both get perpetual Guggenheims or the like so that we could sit and scribble endlessly.

I'm glad I don't like killing things. This is occasioned by looking out the window and seeing our resident covey of quails zipping madly about the side yard.

---

123. "The Last Stoej-gnpf"; see next page. Reading this more than forty years later, I feel faint too.

The Last Stoej-gnpf: or, Donald Acquires a Pet

The time for the yearly Stone Walk of the Stoej-gnpfs had come
around once again.

The ceremonial paths were tidied up and whitened;

the trove of Suitable Stones was unearthed and carefully washed.

On the third day of the walk the stoej-gnpf who was carrying the
least Suitable Stone (**though small, it was exceptionally heavy**)
took a nap to rid himself of a dull headache.

When he awoke towards sunset he was surprised to see no other
stoej-gnpf in view.

He returned the stone to the top of his head and made as quick a
circuit of the paths as possible, but came upon no one.

He put down the stone again, and went to look everywhere else.

There was no one behind the Trees;

there was no one on the Heights;

there was no one in the Hollow.

All the stones had vanished too; the stoej-gnpf sadly pushed the
least Suitable one into the trove-hole.

He then went xxxx to the river where he found a raft just as the
sun went down.

All night he floated down the ever-curving river, but heard nothing.

At dawn the raft came ashore on the opposite side from that which he
had set out.

He walked across fields until he came to the back of a house.

He stood by the steps and coughed several times in a deprecatory manner.

Donald, who was at breakfast in the kitchen, came out the door and
saw him. 'Would you like a pancake with current jelly and powdered
sugar on it?' he asked. 'There is another one on my plate.'

The stoej-gnpf nodded, so Donald went and got the pancake, and that
is how the stoej-gnpf became his pet.

11 April 1969—12 April 1969

1:50

Story done ["The Last Stoej-gnpf: or, Donald Acquires a Pet"]. Enclosed. On white paper. Envelope self-explanatory. One trusts. I feel quite giddy.

No female admirers have called; presumably they are not coming, at least today, and tomorrow I am cooking dinner for a retired spinster schoolteacher of my acquaintance, so they better not turn up then.

Perhaps I will go and buy a book at Parnassus [Book Store]. More anon.

Sunday morning

I was wakened this morning at six by horror and violence going on in the attic, which revealed itself to be Kansuke[124] in mad pursuit of a starling that had for reasons best known to itself flown in through the one window that was open at the top all of two inches. I managed to shut a snarling, clawing Kansuke in the main part of the attic. Fortunately for both of us ultimately the starling was paralyzed with fear and took refuge in the corner of one of the bookcases so I was able to pick him up without fuss and get him out the window with no damage done presumably as he flew away, to recover his equanimity one hopes. I staggered back to bed shaking all over for about five minutes while Kansuke desperately searched all over the place; after about fifteen minutes he decided that whatever had happened, he was not going to get his bird back so he crawled back under the covers and went to sleep. Nature indeed.

I went to see *Yellow Submarine* last night for the second time; I do like the songs and I wanted to see if it was as dreary really as I had thought it the first time. It was. All ingenuity and no imagination and no sense of pace at all. Also its dear little message of Love was somehow contradicted by the inhuman and faintly unpleasant appearance of everything. A pity, really, as I do adore the Beatles, but then they did allow the thing out, as little as they had to do with it personally, and of course all the dear little teenagers around me who were also seeing it for more than the first time thought it was 'real cool'.

One of the ladies who works in Parnassus and I got talking about movies yesterday, and she said that in the old days of silents (she is rather my senior) she read much faster than anyone else so the subtitles always lasted much too long for her, and she'd close her eyes and think get on with it for Heaven's sake, and she says now she has the same feeling every time she goes to a movie, that the point has been made long before the scene ends, and there one is bored over and over as this situation keeps repeating itself. How true. It all has to do with banality again, or partly at least, I think.

Look at: *A Few Flies and I: Haiku by Issa,* Pantheon. Whether you will find it in the poetry or children's books is a toss-up. It's mostly the Blyth translations, but I was

---

124. Kansuke was one of EG's cats.

wondering what you thought of the format and illustrations. There's also a quote from Thoreau as an epigraph which you should perhaps not read until the fishing season is over for another year, he remarked ambiguously.

Wednesday afternoon

I suppose if this is to get to you by Saturday, I'd better call a halt shortly and take it to the post box.

I trust you are finding a house, or perhaps even have already, as I write this. The weather seems the sort useful for this no doubt rather horrid occupation, though I expect you won't know whether the roof leaks in consequence until you have moved in. Aren't I cheerful? Actually in theory buying a house sounds like fun, but I don't think I'd care for it. However, you're more robust.

Various thoughts refuse to organize themselves sufficiently for putting down on paper, among them some on "The Flower in the Bottle" and your idea of what my reaction to it was, which it wasn't. Anyway, perhaps Saturday, if it is still convenient for me to come—convenient for you I mean; I can see it might well not be, in which case I hope you will say so when you leave message. It also depends on what I'm thinking at the very moment whether I bring what I've done on *D Has a D;* I teeter in my attitude about showing it only partly.

Thump.

Mr Peter Neumeyer,
12 Powder House Road Ext.,
Medford, Mass.

02155.

Sunday night, 20.iv.69 [excerpt]

[EG to PN]

The funny bits from today's *Times* enclosed.

I've been running around all day cleaning, and stuffing everything I can think of into first the washing machine and then the dryer. I have now had to cease because I have done something terrible to the side of my neck. And my entire right arm now that I stop to consider. Into my fingers. What fun. Pay no attention <u>ever</u> to me when I mention your neck.

The thought of New York (I have got to get away from it permanently I think more and more) makes me feel very murky.

* * *

[. . .] NY paralyzes my mind I have decided, which is why the thought of it prevents me from explaining the end of paragraph 2, but possibly you know what I mean.

There is an <u>extremely</u> <u>sinister</u> white spot on one of the kitchen windows; whether it is the thing itself or only its track (like a snail) cannot be determined. I blither.

Back to the struggle of making the house presentable. Probably only to myself on my return, as I talked to my aunt this morning and she did not seem sanguine as to when my uncle will deign to come to the Cape for the summer; he is one of those who won't tell anybody what his plans are until the last possible moment.

Mr Peter Neumeyer,
12 Powder House Road Ext,
Medford, Mass.
02155.

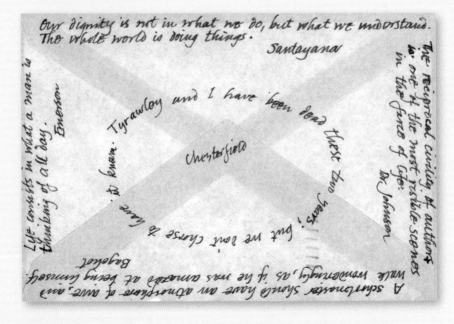

Our dignity is not in what we do, but what we understand.
The whole world is doing things.
Santayana

The reciprocal civility of authors
is one of the most risible scenes
in the farce of life.
Dr Johnson

Life consists in what a man is
thinking of all day.
Emerson

Tyrawley and I have been dead these two
years; but we don't choose to have
it known.
Chesterfield

A statesman should have an atmosphere of quiet, and
walk remembering, as if he was amazed at being turned up.
Bagehot

April 23, 1969

Dear Ted,

Thank you for the cat letter. How is your neck? I hope well by now. From
the symptom you describe it is rather easy to imagine, more or less, what may be
involved, when you figure that between your cervical vertebrae nerves run out
and down your shoulder and into your arms, all the way to your fingers. So there's
nothing mysterious anyway, and let's hope you twisted or turned so as to temporarily
pinch or something one of those. I do hope it is all well now.

Did you get the incredible and weird "book," presumably by Harry Stanton, that
I got in the mail yesterday, the one beginning "But then one day Donald grew up"? It
is the strangest thing I've ever seen. What, what, what do you make of it? Do explain
it please. And if you haven't got it, for some reason, I shall phone you and read it to
you, or send you my copy. [. . .]

* * *

yours,
Peter

I almost forgot to say, the Horoscope—thank you—was indeed in a pile of mail I
had not opened yet when you were here. [. . .] I have read it once rather quickly, and
will read it very carefully later this afternoon and tomorrow morning again, and—if
you are interested (as I would be for yours!)—send it to you. In some cases, I can say
already, it is remarkable, in others not, and in still others I haven't decided whether
the statement is one that could be made of any number of people, or whether there
is in fact something spookily close to home. In any case, again, again, thank you for
this very strange thing.

* * *

I like to read Edward Gorey stories, and it is with misgivings that I write Neumeyer
phrases into a Gorey story. The opinion of the lady from *Publishers Weekly*
notwithstanding, N does not write G stories (any more, it is superfluous to say,
than G writes N stories). We know that. There is some pleasure in occasionally
paraphrasing some phrases in this ["The Last Stoej-gnpf"], as long as it is not taken as
being an 'improvement' of a Gorey felicity as it stands. So then—if I were trying to
say some things here—they might look like[125]

----

125. I sent EG a revised version of "The Last Stoej-gnpf," now missing.

[EG to PN] Saturday morning, 26.iv.69

* * *

The winter issue of *Partisan Review* has appeared; it does not have me in it, but it does have an interview with Borges by someone named Richard Burgin, which is apparently from a book of interviews with Borges that is coming out sometime or other. *The Narrow Act,* incidentally, the Borges book we have been waiting for, is not out yet according to the Gotham Book Mart.[126]

The twenty-five copies of *Donald* I asked Harry to have sent to me came, and so I am sending them out to various and sundry, among which several children's book editors of my acquaintance; who knows? The only famous person I can think of to send it to is Edmund Wilson.

That thing from Harry I seem to have seen in rough form ages ago, but why he is sending it out . . . the mind reels. His effusion on you and me I also found somewhat unnerving. One could not say any of it was precisely untrue, but the effect was so relentlessly icky-poo that had I read it about anyone else I would have thought, Dear God, those people must be the absolute end. As to the review from PW [*Publishers Weekly*], I suppose from a practical point of view a good imperceptive review is better than a bad imperceptive review, but otherwise.

The world however seems inexplicable in practically any direction you'd care to mention. When I returned the car to the Kinney people, I was horridly apprehensive about how much more I was going to have to pay on account of all the excess mileage I had piled up to the tune of several, say five, thousand miles or about $250, so when the young lady after a prolonged session with the adding machine came back and pointed to a figure of some $70 odd dollars, I breathed a sigh of relief and said: 'Oh, I expected I owed you much more,' she looked at me and said: 'We owe it to you,' so I said, 'But what about all the extra mileage?' and she said 'Never question a lady' so thanking her profusely and blithering away, I took my $70 refund and departed. So Kinney got about half of what they should have, and I am still wondering.

What with the ballet, I've only managed to get to one movie since I've been back: *Teorema,* which is obviously the big enigma movie of the season. I don't particularly recommend it: it is terribly simple minded, as the director/author obviously feels that just making an allegory is somehow superior to other forms, and that therefore you don't have to do anything else about it, so to speak. Furthermore, it shows a certain lack of sense I think to use the explicit sexual act as a metaphor for a religious

---

126. Ronald J. Christ, *The Narrow Act: Borges' Art of Allusion,* preface by Jorge Luis Borges (New York University Press, 1969).

(for lack of a better word) experience in a film, however well it works in mystical literature; it doesn't really work very well when the young God figure in the person of Terence Stamp pops maid, mother, and daughter into bed one after the other with all the perfunctoriness of someone opening packages of cereal, but when he does the same thing to son and father, it all becomes rather giggly I fear. There is some pretty photography in a sparse sort of way, lots of shots of wind blowing volcanic dust across a lugubrious and featureless landscape, and they play the Mozart *Requiem* on the sound track a lot, but . . .

I've spent several hours looking through children's book departments in a quest for an illustrator for you; oh dear. Competence everywhere, and no real quality or sense of illustration except literal renditions of the text. I came to the sad conclusion that except for Ardizzone and Sendak, I am about the best around. A sad commentary on the state of things if ever there was one. I recollected afterwards (seeing you) that John S. Goodall, whom Carla mentioned as a possibility, did the *Paddy Pork* book, the wordless pig story I showed you last summer when you were down. I don't know how you'd feel about Ardizzone or whether he was available, but at the moment I feel the best thoughts for [*The Faithful Fish*] are him or Erik Blegvad. After going through several hundred children's books one can get very depressed.

Thank you for your version of "The Last Stoej-gnpf"; I was afraid you wouldn't come through with it. (You become more mysterious—to me, at least—rather than less.) Rereading them several months from now one can better decide how much the two versions differ, and whether it would be interesting to do both texts as you suggested. I'm working on *D Has a D* in the interstices so to speak. I'd like to get it finished and into the hands of my printer before I take off for the Cape the middle of June; provided no unseen sales (unforeseen) take place, I guess I said I wanted to do it along with a French story and another twiddly bit Status is going to publish for Fantod. Apropos of nothing at all have you taken a copy of *Donald and the* . . . to Gordon Cairnie? You also might think of how many copies of *Donald Has a D* you'd like, and I'll have that many extra of it printed up. Needless to remark, though I don't quite see how, I'll of course show you all the drawings before we go into production so you can have a fit.

* * *

You seem to have reacted to your horoscope as I did to mine. I'd love to see it some time, but not for a while, as I want to try my hand at yours as soon as I know a bit more, and obviously once I'd read the Time Pattern thing, I'd not got it out of my head sufficiently to operate independently. If you want, I'll send mine along for your perusal when I have a batch of things accumulated.

I must to work, the weekend's being an especial problem what with four ballet performances to contend with.

I do like Sendak, especially *Mr Rabbit* (an otherwise absolutely <u>vile</u> book); his own writing I am ambivalent toward.

Symeon Shimin is too much, and downright creepy of late—see something or other about something going on in the desert where everything is blue and orange, positively nightmarish; there are incidentally a great many people of this sort beginning to be around too. He draws beautifully, but I find it all somewhat oppressive.

I've never really looked at Robert McCloskey, but I have a sense of cartoon, for some reason. I shall. [. . .] And so forth and so on. (I am rather frazzled, and as various of the other illustrators you mention are obviously not possibilities for the *Fish,* I won't natter on at this point.)

I spoke to Carla Tuesday; I think you will be getting contracts to sign from Candida before too long, as things seem to be about to be put into the works. We had a fairly longish chat about illustrators, and she agreed about the difficulty of finding quality ones who aren't strange like myself. If you follow me; we did talk about this on the phone, yes? Or is it? as my astrology teacher always says.

Carla I think would like to find someone in this country to do the *Fish* book—Blegvad, Ardizzone, etc being in England—but we still haven't come up with Mr/ Miss Right so far. I had one thought of an absolutely cartoony nature, except he isn't really, who might at first horrify you, but then he might grow on you, or might not. He has lots of fun and vitality. His name is Quentin Blake, and somewhere I have a couple of books illustrated by him, but probably won't be able to find them, and all I can suggest is that he has illustrated a book of riddles or the like by Ennis Rees, and also something called something like *My Nephew the Hippopotamus* [it was *My Son-in-Law the Hippopotamus*] by someone with a name like Ezo. Aren't I a big help?[127]

Anyhoo, I expect it will all work itself out, and someone absolutely splendid will be thought of, and you will all make pots of money.

A day or two ago Harper and Row sent me a most peculiar MS, not for children, to see if I wanted to illustrate it. It was about some mousechildren who eventually turned into human children named Peter and Alison, and since the book was dedicated to Peter and Alison, it seemed reasonable to assume that this was a little fable concocted by said children and put into very literary form indeed by doting father, whom I had never heard of. Anyway, it went on for about thirty pages, and struck me as absolutely pointless, and then I got very depressed because I thought how many people think my work is absolutely pointless, and oh dear, and so forth.

---

127. What a prize it would have been to have gotten Quentin Blake in 1969!

Do <u>not</u> go to see *Isadora;* it is Perfectly Awful and Vanessa Redgrave is as fascinating and incandescent as a cold baked bean, but <u>do</u> read, or at least give a good try—she does not <u>really</u> get going until page 75, though it is all interesting—to *My Life* which I'll send you; the real Isadora has entered my pantheon to stand beside Isabelle Eberhardt, Ono no Komachi, [inserted in pen:] *Mrs Inchbald, Amanda Ross, Violent Pageant,* etc.[128] It is an extraordinary book in all sorts of ways.

D Has a D progresses slowly; I have a new idea for the string drawing, which I think is better. I am working like mad, which has put me into a sort of continuing stupor, so that I keep myself half-thinking of work whatever else I am doing at the time, like watching ballet, so that I won't slip out of the habit, and if I don't faint dead away from exhaustion and troubled sleep—I get all wound up, and have the most gharstly dreams—I may actually sooner or later finish up some of these dreary illustration jobs (<u>not</u> *Donald*) hanging over me. We shall see. I think I'd better get this into the mail, feeble and fragmented as it is.

E. H. Gombrich's *Art and Illusion* is absolutely enthralling, but perhaps visual problems are not as enthralling to you as to me, but take a look. He writes delightfully, and there are nice anecdotes such as at an Academy meeting a Constable was brought in while Constable was there, and someone else said 'Take that nasty green thing away.'

---

128. EG was referring to the novelist and prolific critic Violet Lee Paget, who often wrote under the name Vernon Lee.

5.v.69

[EG to PN]

Here it is, horrid old Monday morning. Tidy-up time, and all that dreary jazz.

Bit of description overheard some days ago on the street, the speaker being approximately the same colour as you and I: 'It's about sex and white women . . .'

And does it mean anything that someone is advertising in *The Antiquarian Bookseller* for a copy of a work of mine entitled *The Harlem Child* (sic, *The Hapless Child*)? Someone else is looking for a copy of my 'pornographic novel'.

The Mad Room, a distant remake of *Ladies in Retirement,* turned out a disappointment despite good reviews—mainly because everyone has lost all sense of genre these days and thrust in all sorts of irrelevancies—but there were several delightful shots of a large, shaggy, and utterly lovable dog padding about with a severed hand in its mouth.

I saw Carla at the ballet yesterday afternoon, and she said a contract is on its way to you. We are having lunch next week sometime to tackle seriously the illustrating problem.

I find that absolutely nothing is due according to my horoscope until sometime in June so the package that is piling up will contain it.

I wish my mind would stop thinking up books—a remark I may be sorry for in later years when I haven't thought of anything for over a decade—but it won't and I'm in the throes of a little item about a witch inspired by the woodcut on the cover of the new book about same in Salem; it is about done, so I suppose a copy will get enclosed with this by the time it's ready for the mails.

I managed, but just, to pick up the Borges *Encounter.* There was a bit in the interview about two other people that perfectly described, if did not explain, how I felt about the stoej-gnpf story.

Whence came the news from Addison-Wesley? Cheer up. Donald will be worth his weight in gold/platinum/rubies on the rare book market, and that within a month or two I should think at the rate things progress.

I must go and cope with things like cashing a check, retrieving my Water Pik (sp?) from the clutches of the Turnpike Appliance people who repair such things. &c., &c.

The children's book section of the *Times* yesterday, needless to remark, had no ad for A-W nor mention of any of their publications in the reviews. On the other hand, everything they <u>did</u> mention, ad- and editorial-wise, sounded perfectly dreary, and I couldn't find one title I wanted to even go and look at.

Afternoon

I don't know why it comes to mind now, but did I ever mention the absolutely incredibly macaronic conversation I overheard some time ago between two middle-aged ladies in a Zum-Zum? They were chatting away about nothing in particular in English, French, German, and a fourth Middle European tongue I couldn't identify; they never stayed in one language for more than a sentence, and that infrequently; most of their sentences were in two or three languages, and sometimes four. For a while I thought there was something the matter with my ears. I still don't quite see how they managed it.

* * *

Tuesday

My only thought for the day:
Being organized is even more boring than being disorganized.

Wednesday

Thoughts for today:

O dass wir unsere Ururahnen wären.
Ein Klümpchen Schleim in einem warmen Moor.   —Gottfried Benn

Man becomes what he is.   —Ernest Toller

(Culled from *The Writer in Extremis: Expressionism in Twentieth-Century German Literature* by Walter H. Sokel, McGraw-Hill paperback. Rather fascinating if you don't already know it, but they (Expressionists) certainly weren't much of a one for a giggle, were they?)

My own variation of the above, which I'm about to work into something. (I'd hate to have it go to waste.)

O if I could only choose,
I'd be a bit of primal ooze.[129]

For two days now there has been virtually no mail for anybody in the building. What can it mean? The total breakdown of the post office obviously. Perhaps I'd better mail this <u>now</u>, and start another later.

---

129. Here is my literal translation of the German: "Oh that we could only be our own ancestors, / a clump of slime in a warm swamp." EG's translation seems to me superb—and he hardly knew German.

May 14, 1969 [excerpt]

Dear Ted,

All news from here is minute. The Tufts thing was—well, chicken thighs stuffed with almonds. Ciardi did not show up. The people at the dinner were (or worked at being) nice. Then to a crowded, very crowded lecture hall, and a panel. Maxine Kumin [. . .], who is both bright and nice, was ok. A fellow named Tannin was obstreperous and obnoxious and a salesman for his products. Emberley pulled the to me enormously offensive (and frequently employed) "I'm only an artist (who is hugely gifted) and I'll leave the theorizing to the professors" ploy, which won the co-eds' hearts. The Reys [Hans and Margret, creators of the *Curious George* books] did their usual set-piece nicely, successfully, charmingly. etc. etc. Helen had called Addison-Wesley again and, to her surprise, got Harry, and asked if they wouldn't get some books to Tufts for the occasion. Notwithstanding Helen's having talked to their new girl Friday last week, Harry hadn't heard of the Tufts affair. Slothfully and apologetically he moved, and the girl showed up that evening with a copy of *Donald* (as other publishers did with theirs too). She is UNIMPRESSIVE. Has a strange bone under her thumb's thigh which one feels when shaking hands with her. She is from Somerville.

Yesterday, en-route to Gordon Cairnie with *Donald,* I met Harry in H. [Harvard] Square. He had what looked like a movie carrying case over his shoulder, with international transportation stickers hanging from it. He was looking in a bank window. We talked sporadically (I've been writing letters for 4 hours today, and this is the last, so this will go haltingly and read inanely, which you are by now used to and will perhaps forgive—no?). I told him I was just going to G.C. to present him with a *Donald,* and Harry of course said how he knew G.C. well, etc. etc., which made me want to ask why the hell he didn't . . . etc. But I didn't. I went to G.C., who for the 5th time did not recognize me, but was then touchingly and rather silently moved by the book, by your remembrance of him, who wanted to know who the hell was Addison-Wesley, and had me write it and its address in his ledger so he could order some *Donalds,* and who then dimly and more and more strongly recalled Harry Stanton, whom 20 years ago he had given a ride to Cape Cod to, and who then got out his photo album, and blew his nose, and was kind to people who dropped in, and so forth, for about half an hour. So, that was a nice thing.

Did you get the "fan letters" from the second grade class from Addison-Wesley? Some nice spellings.

Stanton did say something not very coherent, but nonetheless grand, about doing a retrospective exhibit on Edward Gorey, on which he would be helped by Kurt Vonnegut. Has Harry told you? Don't ask me more, I don't know. I thought it was to be an art show, but then Harry talked like he wanted to get *Life* or the *Saturday Evening Post* or somebody to do a special issue. I don't know. It sounds glorious. Tell me about it, if you know about it.

I got a nice letter from Carla. She says she likes the moustache story even more now than before—and then she suggests what I see as rather huge reworkings of it. I don't know. I don't know. I'm not sure what she wants, or whether I can supply it. You'll have seen her by now. And if you want I'll send you a copy of my answer to her, of which by accident I made only one copy, so would have to have back.

Mr Peter Neumeyer,
12 Powder House Road Ext,
Medford, Mass. 02155.

yet another infant carried off — how sad.
(The altitude is in process of turning it
blue with cold. It has reached the lavender
stage apparently.)

Mr Peter Neumeyer,
12 Powder House Road Ext.,
Medford, Mass. 02155.

I wrote to EG that Helen had found his envelope illustration of the blue infant sad.
We soon received another, wherein the baby triumphs.

Mr Peter Neumeyer,
12 Powder House Road Ext.,
Medford, Mass. 02155

THE MUSEUM OF MODERN ART
11 West 53 Street, New York 19, N.Y.

Post Card

Amusements and the Arts
Unauthorized "Fiddler" to be
staged by students. Page 16
New d'Amboise work has un-
expected premiere. Page 16
Edward Gorey work becomes
an opera.   Page 16

Printed in Western Germany

Mr Peter Neumeyer,

12 Powder House Road Ext.,

Medford, Mass.

          02155.

Pablo PICASSO: Baboon and Young. 1951. Bronze,
21" high. The Museum of Modern Art, Mrs. Simon
Guggenheim Fund.

June 24, 1969

Dear Ted,

* * *

[. . .] We have five (5) Siamese kittens that are about to have been weaned.
They are about to leave their mother. Four are males. One is a female. They turn
somersaults and play that they are in the jungle. We are going to advertise them at the
end of this week—but we would first like you to have one if you want one. Do you
want one—honestly? [. . .] We would love to think you had one—it would be a good
feeling—but only if you think you can and want to increase your family. [. . .]

Got a short note from Harry Stanton "Do keep sending us stories. We would like
to have another story as good as Donald, which we think is a winner!" I responded
with what Helen calls a stinging acid reply—I don't know if it's all that—saying I
thought we had reached an understanding about stories he had of mine, and that I
doubted I could satisfy him with anything I wrote, but if he really thought different,
I'm here and the stories are here.

We are euphoric to be here. I probably told you, a little beach at end of our street,
and one minute by car the university's superb large one.

* * *

yrs,
Peter

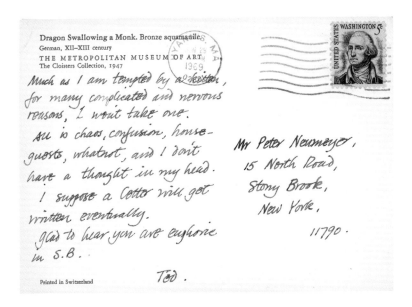

Dragon Swallowing a Monk. Bronze aquamanile,
German, XII–XIII century
THE METROPOLITAN MUSEUM OF ART,
The Cloisters Collection, 1947

Printed in Switzerland

Much as I am tempted by a kitten,
for many complicated and nervous
reasons, I wont take one.
All is chaos, confusion, house-
guests, whatnot, and I dont
have a thought in my head.
I suppose a letter will get
written eventually.
Glad to hear you are euphoric
in S.B.

Ted.

Mr Peter Newmeyer,
15 North Road,
Stony Brook,
New York.

11790.

July 2, 1969

Dear Ted,

A very brief and hasty note, first to thank you for *The Dong [with a Luminous Nose]* and *The Iron Tonic,* on both of which I'll write you longer later. The ingenuity of the monocular inserts, making the pictures have a movement and dimension kindred to film is most ingenious. [. . .]

* * *

I'm sorry you are harried, harassed, and seemingly more distracted than you want to be. I hope your summer settles down to where you have the time and peace to do what you must do.

* * *

Reading an author new to me—Franz Grillparzer—a sentimental and charming German Romantic, who evidently greatly appealed to Kafka, and who is, it seems to me, without my having read what is officially said about him, a precursor of Hesse's *Knulp.*

* * *

I've got to get to work. I've typed so little that this letter is full of mistakes, but I wanted to wish you encouragements in whatever hurdles you seem to be gnawing (!) at this summer.

yours,
Peter

22. vii.69

I have been overcome by the utter tedium of it all (mostly the stupid book I am doing stupid drawings for).

August 18, 1969

Dear Ted,

This is a sort of business letter. First, however—

If you are not writing because I have in some manner offended you, let me say it was entirely inadvertent, I apologize, and I wish you would tell me. If, on the other hand, it is merely that you are in fact unprecedentedly busy, I ask only that you forgive this intrusion.

* * *

[. . .] Various letters and a call from Harry arrived here today, and regarding those, this letter.

1. His Disneyland Donald: I suppose we sit and wait.[130]

2. He wants Donald digging the hole. [. . .] I told Harry I had 2 better ones—the umbrella, and Miss Jane's attic. If he took either of those, I'd be pleased (if you wanted to do them too, of course). But short of that—I feel actually sufficiently distant from Donald digging the hole that I'd re-do it along Harry's lines without soulhurt. [. . .]

My question to you: Harry wants it for Spring 1970. If I re-wrote right now, would you want to work on it (presumably for then) too?

* * *

Do, however:

1. Tell me if I have hurt your feelings, and how I may make amends.

2. Reassure me if/that you are well.

3. not work so hard that you lose perspective. [. . .]

yours,
Peter

---

130. Stanton had written to me about a massive syndicated production he had in mind for EG and me but had said I should write my future stories with his sort of endings.

22.viii.69

[EG to PN]

Unless some of the humidity has dried out of the typewriter, there are going to be a lot of doppelgangerish letters in this.

Of course you haven't offended me, unless of course you have done something positively awful that I haven't found [out] about yet. I feel more and more guilty every day about not writing, and think about it constantly, incessantly, uninterruptedly, etc., but I've been in my usual state of paralysis and non-communication. Not non-communication with you, but just non-communication with the world. Let us just say it has been rather a blah summer in some ways and leave it go at that. I don't mean to sound sinister, just bored. I've gotten some work done, but I'm still way behind, and I have to keep trying to keep my tiny but scattered wits pulled together, and this can only be done by not thinking, which of late has been not difficult. Things improve slowly I guess.

Re Harry. He's called twice, and sent me a copy of the letter he sent you, or one of them at least. I have not seen him, nor do I really expect to. Not thinking, see above, I have not thought about Harry and his various bits of blather. Disneyland Donald, who knows? Something might come of it, something might not; I'm not

even going to sit and wait, so it may all come like a glorious sunset after a day of cloudy gloom. As for Donald digging, the story was finished long ago as far as I'm concerned—in fact I recall a whole story board as it were for the drawings, though it's not here but in NY. Anyway, in passing, Harry's intimations about my sophisticating/corrupting/perverting influence or whatever does not endear himself or his ideas to me. I wouldn't write or rewrite another word for him—he's already had too many perfectly splendid mss as is, without any revision whatever—contract dangled in front of me, or not, which incidentally your message I think did get through as he mentioned the dirty word. I'm being incoherent and snotty, more the latter than I thought I meant to be.

People like Harry depress me terribly. If he wants to publish another book by us, all he has to do is say so and start putting it in the works as it were. So far this new flurry of interest still leaves us far from where we were this time last year when he definitely accepted a second one, and we both know what came of that.

In a way however, it is all up to you, or almost all, what you want to do. As far as drawings are concerned, I am still so far behind and so apprehensive that I won't even tentatively guess even to you when I could get to them. Oh dear.

Re Candida, all I can say [is] this has all been very unlike her, I don't understand it, but won't interfere further as I already seem to have created a nice muddle.

This dreary little letter doesn't strike me as coping at all. I'll call you on the 27th.

Glup.

Sept. 23 [1969]

Dear Ted,

First, thank you for the Borges study. I began it last night. Obviously (even without the man's confession) it was a thesis—but, nice to consider, its scope is broader than the preface promises, and far from limiting itself to a study of Anglo-American references in Borges (and falsely thereby calling itself a comparative literature study), it dives deep, ties Borges in with what I presume to be accurate lines to Berkeley,[131] etc. It is a stutteringly written but rich and instructive book. [. . .]

With us there's too much new in our lives to begin to put it into a letter. We still hope you'll chuck it all some weekend—or Thursday—and join us. The family is in good shape; [. . .] our boat is in the water and we use it much. Stony Brook—the university and the ambit—are as warm, as friendly, as rich and happy-making as Cambridge and environs were to me (I see now) really quite hateful. [. . .] Anyway, as I say, more friends here in six weeks than in six years at Harvard. A lovable Eeyore of a department chairman [. . .]. A family doctor with whom the first visit was rather abortive medically since he was just reading Klaus Wagenbach's book on Kafka (exists in German only) and wanted to talk about that instead. Even our more-or-less neighbors, many of whom run to being airline pilots, except for being beyond the pale politically, swamp us with cocktail parties of a savoirviverishness which one is hard put to look cool with. We dig for clams, spear eels (that's not for you!), the flounder will be in soon. . . . as I say, too much for one letter.

* * *

I'm teaching the usual course for teachers. And for my 12 tutees, we're reading Piri Thomas *Down These Mean Streets* [. . .], Eldridge Cleaver *Soul on Ice* (straight, honest, unembellished, unrhetorical till the pseudo psychological madness at the end), John Stuart Mill's *Autobiography* (plotted and schemed for effect), p/haps St. Augustine as an honest foil to Cleaver. Then *Tristram Shandy,* fictional autobiogr. At the same time, Percy Lubbock's *Craft of Fiction* and Wayne Booth's *Rhetoric of Fiction.* Obviously the object, my object, is to get them to see the crafting, the conscious adjusting and fidgeting, that goes into writing. They'll re-cast their own autobiographical starts into different tenses, voices, moods, etc. too.

Why do I drivel on? I don't know. To establish contact, as Mr. Thant[132] would say. And on that unexpandable note, I shall remain

Peter

---

131. Bishop George Berkeley, an important eighteenth-century philosopher.
132. U Thant, secretary-general of the United Nations, 1961–1971.

[handwritten note, EG to PN]

I don't mind eels
except at meals
and the way they feels.   [Ogden Nash]

28.ix.69

[EG to PN]

I'm glad you all like Stony Brook.

I'm glum and newsless. I've done nothing but draw (bad pictures for other people's books), read trash, and see every awful movie the distributors deign to send to the Cape [. . .]. It has been a forgettable summer.

A couple of weeks ago I caught my first glimpse of Harry, fortunately in time, and I fled our general store before he saw me (I hope).

I threw away the A-W catalog when tidying up, so don't know, because I can't remember, what that illustrator's work is like.

The ballet season may be delayed or cancelled because of trouble with the orchestra, and if this is the case, I've not decided whether to stay on here or return to New York the third week in November as planned, not that it matters.

I finished the drawings for *Donald Has a Difficulty.* They are certainly insipid, which is what I had in mind, but whether they are brilliantly so, I don't know. I hope so. I'll look at them again in a couple of weeks possibly.

Flup.

Last interior illustration for *Donald Has a Difficulty.*

13. x. 69

A.W's Coss is someone else's gain—
I wonder whose? I find it a relief
to know I shan't have to cope
with H.S. again.

Since my previous suggestions
about what to do with your work
have been fairly disastrous, I
won't, at least for the moment,
make any more.

I've just started the Irene
Iddesleigh drawings this morning,
and am wondering what direction
they will take and where they
will end up, which I'll eventually
discover I suppose, as I keep at
them.

I had a mad idea on Japanese
poetry yesterday, but I very much
doubt if I have the ability to
do anything with it.

Alas.
Letter

One of EG's Irene Iddesleigh drawings.
He completed seven, but they were
never published as a book.

27.x.69

[EG to PN]

It is nicer if a publisher wants to publish a book than if he doesn't, though not very much; otherwise it has always seemed to me a subject wholly lacking in interest.

If you <u>were</u> writing the way you were to go with my drawings, I think it was a mistake, but then I doubt if you were really . . .

I am in one of my more extreme Japanese phases, and have given up thinking, acting, and having opinions.

. . .

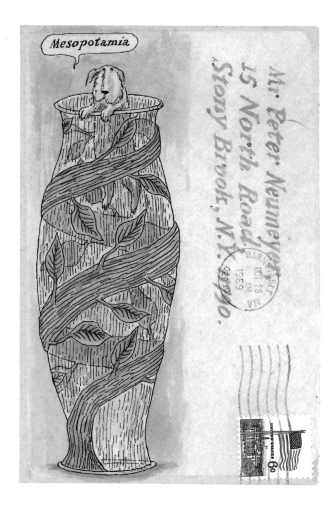

Persons who have seen the
damage caused by the fallen
ceiling say it is fortunate it
happened when no one was in
the building as it would have
endangered anyone in the room
at the time it occurred.

116626

UNITED STATES WASHINGTON 5¢

BARNSTABLE, MA
JUL 20
AM
1970
06630

POST CARD

Address

NEUMEYER,
15 NORTH RD,
STONY BROOK,
NEW YORK.
11790.

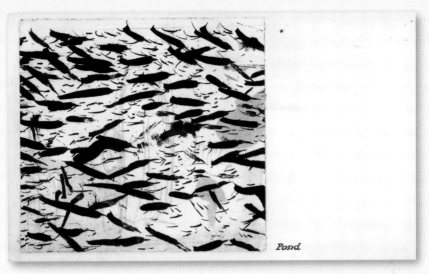

EG had used this piece of paper as an ink scratch pad; later he pasted it onto a postcard, titled it *Pond,* and sent it to me.

The illustrated label from an anchovy can!

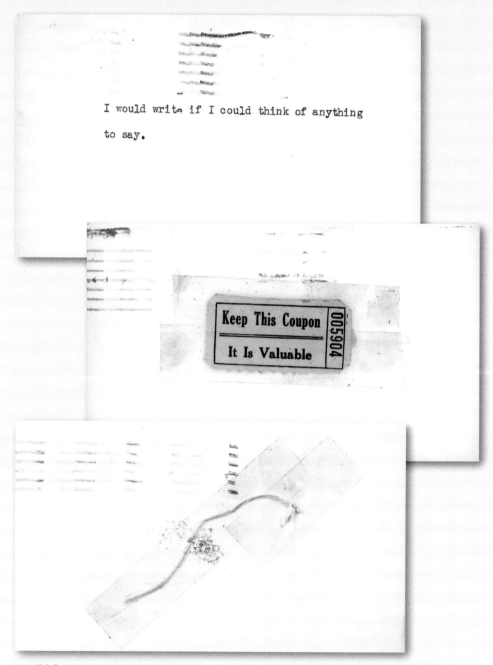

I would write if I could think of anything
to say.

Keep This Coupon
It Is Valuable
005904

Still life with string and splinter.

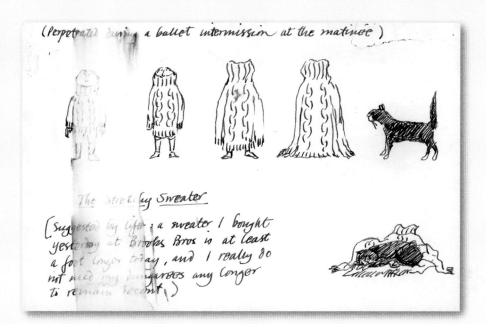

(Perpetrated during a ballet intermission at the matinée)

The Stretchy Sweater

(Suggested by life: a sweater I bought
yesterday at Brooks Bros is at least
a foot longer today, and I really do
not need my dungarees any longer
to remain decent.)

Just after you fall asleep, your toes cross,
and just before you wake up, they return to
their normal arrangement. Even your family
doctor cannot say why.

Short sheets make the bed
Cook Conger.

Song title

The nursery windows
  Wide open to the air,
But the faces of the children,
  They are no longer there!

Epilogue

The last extant note from the Gorey-Neumeyer correspondence is a short one from me to Ted dated September 20, 1971. It begins, "Doldrums from here to there, a poxy Muse, eight yipping puppies with their parents next door," and ends, "Do you know Christmas Humphreys? Worth reading."

PHOTOGRAPH BY PETER NEUMEYER

Index